9/20/11
#109.95

THE RISE OF THE ISLAMIC MOVEMENT IN SUDAN (1945-1989)

THE RISE OF THE ISLAMIC MOVEMENT IN SUDAN (1945-1989)

Mustafa A. Abdelwahid

With a Foreword by
Jill Crystal

The Edwin Mellen Press
Lewiston•Queenston•Lampeter

Library of Congress Cataloging-in-Publication Data

Abdelwahid, Mustafa A.
  The rise of the Islamic movement in Sudan, 1945-1989 / Mustafa A. Abdelwahid with
a foreword by Jill Crystal.
        p. cm.
  Includes bibliographical references and index.
  ISBN-13: 978-0-7734-5031-8 (alk. paper)
  ISBN-10: 0-7734-5031-9 (alk. paper)
  1. Islam and politics--Sudan--History--20th century. 2. Islam and state--Sudan--
History--20th century. 3. Sudan--Politics and government--20th century. 4. Sudan--
History--20th century. I. Title.
  BP64.S8A24 2008
  320.5'570962409045--dc22
                            2008027999

hors série.

A CIP catalog record for this book is available from the British Library.

Front cover painting by Sudanese artist Khalid Hamid Yousif

The Edwin Mellen Press   The Edwin Mellen Press
Box 450   Box 67
Lewiston, New York   Queenston, Ontario
USA 14092-0450   CANADA L0S 1L0

The Edwin Mellen Press, Ltd.
Lampeter, Ceredigion, Wales
UNITED KINGDOM SA48 8LT

Printed in the United States of America

This book is dedicated to my parents, wife, and children. Without their patience, support, understanding, and most of all love, the completion of this book would not have been possible.

Table of Contents

Foreword by Professor Jill Crystal i
Acknowledgments.. iv

CHAPTER 1
Introduction to Political Islam and Literature Review 1
- Introduction 1
- Organization of the Book...11
- Literature Review..13
  - Introduction 13
  - Islam and Politics..13
  - What is political Islam? 14
  - The Socio-economic and Political School 19
  - The Cultural-religious School...25
  - The Islamic Movement in Sudan: A Literature Review 30

CHAPTER II
Methodology 41
- Introduction...41
- The Modernization Explanations 42
- The Socio-economic and Political Explanations 45
- The Gramscian Approach 47
- Toward an Alternative Approach 48

CHAPTER III
Sudan: Historical Background 57
- Introduction 57
- The Islamic States 57
- The Funj Sultanate (1504-1820) 57
- The Fur Sultanates (1596-1879 and 1899-1916) 59
- Turco-Egyptian Rule (1821-1885) 60
- The Mahadia State (1885-1898) 62
- Anglo-Egyptian Condominium (1898-1955)..................................63

CHAPTER IV

The Leading Ideologues of Contemporary Political Islam 67
- Historical Background 67
- Organized Islamic Movements 71
- Hasan al-Banna 71
- Abul A'la al-Mawdudi 74
- Sayyid Qutb 76

CHAPTER V

The Islamic Movement in Sudan 1945-1989....................................81
- Introduction..81
- The Early Years (1945-1954) 82
- The Formative Years (1955-1963) 88
- The Islamic Charter Front (ICF) (1964-1968)............................93
- The Movement and Nemeri (1969-1976) 97
- The Expansion Years (1977-1984) 100
- The National Islamic Front (NIF) (1985-1989)..........................105

CHAPTER VI

Factors that Influenced the Rise of the Islamic Movement in Sudan 111
- Introduction..111
- Al-Turabi's Intellectual Contributions.......................................114
- Women 133
- Students..148
- Islamic Financial Institutions...160
- Organizational Structure 170
- Military 175
- Trade Unions and Labor Movement..186

CHAPTER VII

Conclusion 193

Bibliography 199

Index..226

Foreword

When a coup led by Sudan's Islamic movement overturned the leadership of that country in 1989, I was in my first years of teaching general courses on the Middle East. My knowledge of the Sudan was largely shaped by those who viewed it through an Egyptian lens. This picture of the Sudan, as a variation on an Egyptian theme, however, offered little insight into the movement that had emerged there. Mustafa Abdelwahid's book tells us why. It examines the Islamic movement in the Sudan, a topic on which very little is written in English, on its own terms, from the inside out, giving us a nuanced understanding of both the intellectual bases and the internal workings of the movement. This book reminds us that Islamic movements anywhere, from Uzbekistan to Palestine to the Sudan, including even those with transnational aspirations, are best understood within the framework of their national context. Thus readers interested in Islamic movements anywhere in the world should find this book fascinating.

Dr. Abdelwahid focuses on two aspects of this movement. The first is ideology: an analysis of Hassan al-Turabi's ideas. As in Egypt, the Sudan's Muslim Brotherhood emerged to fill the gap created by, first, the end of colonialism and then the defeat of Arab nationalism. But the two movements moved in different directions as al-Turabi developed a set of arguments that allowed him to move away from the centralized recruitment model of Egypt and to develop a large, diverse, inclusive base. One of the most interesting ideas that Abdelwahid explores in this regard is al-Turabi's development of *ibtilah*– experiencing life as a perpetual challenge posed by God to test one's faith.

Through *ibtilah*, al-Turabi reconciles rather than rejects society's contemporary challenges. Abdelwahid also explores al-Turabi's treatment of *ijmaa* (consensus) which he reinterprets as the consensus of the community rather than, as historically interpreted, the consensus of religious scholars. This view, along with al-Turabi's treatment of *ijtihad* (interpretation of Islamic jurisprudence), and *tajdid* (renewal) allowed a more comfortable reconciliation of Islamist and democratic ideas and even cultural expression in music and art. These views were consistent with a more general democratic inclusiveness in the movement that allowed it to recruit widely.

The second aspect of the movement that Dr. Abdelwahid explores is its organizational genius. Dr. Abdelwahid analyzes the way the internal dynamics of the movement -- its organizational structure and recruitment strategies -- explain why people turned to this Islamist movement rather than, say, to the historically dominant religious sects and their political parties (the Umma and Democratic Unionist Party). He chronicles the rise of the movement as a political force and demonstrates how the movement managed to transform itself from a small elitist group into a massive political organization.

Hassan al-Turabi has emerged in the late 1960s as the Movement's ideologue, took a different path than Hassan al-Banna (founder of Egypt's Muslim Brotherhood); and Sayyid Qutb the main ideologue of the Egyptian Brotherhood at that time. Rather than building a movement from the top down, beginning with a vanguard, separated from society and its ills and based on the prophetic paradigm of the *umma*, the first Islamic community, as it was advocated by Qutb, al-Turabi advocated building a movement from deep within society, welcoming initiatives as well as acolytes and a diverse set of supporters that included students, the military, women (especially educated women), Sufis and trade unionists. When he faced challenges with the latter group, he forged a broader coalition by co-opting Communist Party issues.

Al-Turabi also built for the future by having party activists serve tours of duty as middle and high school teachers, recruiting students who would then go on to join the ranks of the Movement when they enter higher education institutions. He encouraged followers to join the military, and in particular the intelligence services tasked with screening applicants to the military. In this and other ways Turabi succeeded where most Islamist groups failed, in building a strong, diverse organization that could not be easily penetrated by the state security apparatus.

Dr. Abdelwahid is particularly well-situated to tell this story. This book is a step on a journey that began in the Sudan, and took him from there to the Soviet Union and on to the American South, where the book began as a dissertation, picking up degrees (Law, Information Science, and PhD) along the way. The book ends in 1989 but the story continues. Since I still have classes to teach, I can only hope the journey continues as well. I await the sequel.

Professor Jill Crystal, Ph.D. Program Director
Political Science Department -Auburn, University
Auburn, Alabama USA

Acknowledgments

I would like to express my gratitude to Professor Jill Crystal, my advisor for her constant support, patience, and encouragement throughout my graduate studies. This study could not have been written without her. Special thanks also to Professor James Nathan, Lee Farrow, Linda Dennard, and Anne Permaloff, for their invaluable feedback and advice.

There are numerous academic colleagues who helped along the way. They include: Professor William Crowther at University of North Carolina at Greensboro, his monitoring guided me through my educational journey in the United States. Special thanks to Carolyn Clark from Auburn Avenue Research Library on African American Culture and History (AARL) in Atlanta, Georgia, for her continuous assistance in editing this dissertation and to Akilah Nosakhere, Manager of the Reference Division at (AARL) for her support and for providing the needed time, resources, and space to complete this study.

I am also deeply indebted to my family in the Sudan: my parents for their unconditional love and support, especially my mother for encouraging my academic journey from Sudan to the former Soviet Union then to the United States and for supplying all necessary Arabic materials from the Sudan and Egypt. Finally, I wish to express my appreciation to my small family, my wife, Nagla and my children, Osman, Azza, and Reem, whose tremendous love and caring at every stage of my research, cannot be overstated.

CHAPTER I

Introduction to Political Islam and Literature Review

Introduction

In the early morning of June 30, 1989, the residents of Khartoum woke up to the sound of tanks roaring into the capital's streets. A few hours later the central radio station --the only one in the country-- began to broadcast military marches. Soon Brigadier Omer Ahmed al-Bashier started to broadcast his first proclamation which explained the reason behind his military coup. He cited a long list of grievances concerning the deterioration of security in the country especially in the south and the west. In the south, as a result of military pressure from the Sudanese People's Liberation Army (SPLA) the Sudanese army was forced to retreat and evacuate from several major cities. For the first time since the beginning of the second civil war in Sudan in 1983, southern rebels were able to capture some of the major cities in the south such as Toreit and Kajo-Kaji and to surround Juba, the capital of the south. In the west, Darfur had become a theatre for the ongoing civil war in Chad and the Libyan/Chad conflict over the Aozou Strip. In Khartoum, the high level of corruption, and abuse of power by upper echelon government officials had became the norm of government operation.

The military coup was bloodless and peaceful and at the beginning many people were supportive of the move. Although Sadiq al-Mahdi was the democratically-elected Prime Minister, his rule had divided and destabilized the country and Sudan had been in a state of intense political turmoil since he assumed his role as the country's Prime Minister in 1986. In February 1989 al-Mahdi refused to accept the peace agreement with the rebels, brokered by his rival Mohammed Osman al-Mirghani, the leader of the Democratic Unionist Party (DUP). Only after the army's ultimatum, massive rallies and protests from trade unions and professional associations in Khartoum did al-Mahdi accept the negotiated peace agreement and the formulation of a national unity government, which included representatives of all political parties with the exception of the National Islamic Front (NIF) which reiterated its former position to oppose any move –even if temporary- to freeze or abolish the September 1983 "Islamic" Laws.

The leaders of the coup presented themselves first as a group of independent officers with no ties to any political ideology or party.[1] The only political party to declare the NIF involvement in this coup was the Sudanese Communist Party (SCP). In a leaflet addressed to the Sudanese people published on the second day of the coup, the leadership of the SCP declared that the June 1989 coup was orchestrated by the (NIF) and its military wing in the army. The following months proved the SCP was right. Step by step the NIF cadres became more visible in new political organs created by the military junta and NIF members were tapped for all leading civil and military positions in the country. Months later, the largest purge in the country's history among civil servants, military, and police forces began. Tens of thousands of people lost their jobs because of their political allegiance and were replaced by the NIF cadres and sympathizers. The long-planned NIF program of Islamization had begun.

The Islamic nature of the coup in Sudan took many western diplomats in Sudan by surprise, as many of them first assumed the coup officers were loyalists of the former president Nemeri.[2] Neighboring countries were also taken by surprise, for example, the Egyptian government which was among the first countries to recognize and support the new military regime in Sudan, found itself in an unprecedented position. For decades the main goal of Egyptian foreign policy was to maintain a friendly political regime in Sudan, thus securing its

---

[1] Kamal Osman Salih. "The Sudan, 1985-1989: The Fading Democracy." *The Journal of Modern African Studies* 28, no. 2 (1990): 199-224.

[2] Alan Cowell. "Military Coup in Sudan Ousts Civilian Regime" *The New York Times. Late Edition (East Coast)* July 1, 1989.

southern borders. Having an 'Islamic' regime at its southern border would enhance the Islamists position in Egypt which constitute the main opposition groups to the Egyptian regime.

The Islamists rise to power also came as a surprise for many western political observers and academicians with interest in Sudanese politics. Influenced by the Egyptian Brotherhood's experience and history, the majority of these observers and academicians looked to the Islamic Movement in Sudan as a movement with limited influence among students and professionals and without wide support among the Sudanese people who traditionally gave their political allegiance to the other two Islamic parties: al-Umma party led by al-Sadiq al-Mahdi, and the Democratic Unionist Party (DUP) led by Mohammed Osman al-Mirghani.

Despite its unique and unprecedented political rise to power, the Sudanese Islamic Movement and its role among Islamists in the region have not been recognized by western Middle Eastern specialists. This failure resulted in few published materials that cover Islamists in Sudan. The absence of western literature on the Islamic Movement in Sudan could be attributed to two main factors. First, unlike Egypt, Sudan is not directly involved in the Arab-Israeli conflict and is not considered of strategic importance for the United States and European countries. The second factor is the general approach that Middle Eastern specialists take in studying Islamic movements in the region. The majority of these specialists look to other Islamic movements in the region including the Islamic Movement in Sudan as an extension of the Muslim Brotherhood in Egypt. By trying to generalize the specific experience of the Egyptian Brotherhood with regard to other Islamic movements, these specialists clearly underestimated and overlooked the historical uniqueness of each Islamic movement in the region.

The place of Islam and politics in Sudanese society has immense importance not just in academic terms but in everyday affairs. And, despite the numerous studies focusing on contemporary Muslim politics, there is a perennial need to take a balanced perspective on the general role of Islam in political development and social change not only in Sudan but also in other Muslim societies.[3] As Shahin (1997) observed "with few exceptions, most studies of Islamic political movements have expressed either sympathy towards or hostility against the rising influence of Islamic movements in the political affairs."[4] This book parts ways with previous analyses by examining the Islamic Movement in Sudan without assuming a position in this ideological debate. This is a purely academic attempt to place the Movement in Sudan in its historical context and view it as an essential part of the culture and political environment within which it has evolved.[5]

The study attempts to fill the existing gap between social movement theories and Islamic movements or Islamic activism. The findings suggest that the rising influence of the Movement can best be understood when the aforementioned factors are studied as complementary explanatory tools. By doing so, the activism of the Movement in Sudan is analyzed as dynamic in the sense that every element that affects mobilization is conducted in relation to other elements. This relational analysis is adapted from the contributions of Dough McAdam, Sidney Tarrow, Charles Tilly and other social movement theorists.[6]

The findings of this study represent a radical departure from traditional views that dominated the literature on Islamic movements. These traditional views fall short of providing clear explanations of the rising influence of Islamic movements in the Islamic world. This failure could be attributed to several factors: First, the influence of Orientalist school of thinkers led by scholars such

---

[3] Emad Eldin Shahin. *Political Ascent: Contemporary Islamic Movements in North Africa.* Boulder, Colo.: Westview Press, 1997.

[4] Ibid.,1.

[5] Ibid.,1.

[6] Sidney Tarrow. *Power in Movement: Social Movements and Contentious Politics.* 2nd ed. Cambridge: UK: Cambridge University Press, 1998. Charles Tilly. *Social Movements, 1768 - 2004.* Boulder, CO Paradigm Publishers 2004. Marco Giugni, Doug McAdam & Charles Tilly, ed. *How Social Movements Matter.* Minneapolis, MN: University of Minnesota Press, 1999.

as Bernard Lewis,[7] and other post-Cold War influential theorists such as Samuel Huntington who see the emergence of Islamic movements as a reaction against the political, moral and technological incursions of the West into Muslim societies. The Orientalists and post-Cold War thinkers also viewed Islamic movements as movements that are emerging in single and monolithic trends across the Muslim world, representing a politico-religious "civilization" that would ultimately come into direct confrontation with the West.[8]

Second, the "society in crisis" approach still dominates most of the literature on Islamic movements. Representatives of this approach are divided between two major groups: the modernization group and the socio-economic group. The first of these groups tries to explain the rise of Islamic movements in Islamic countries as traditional reaction to the impact of Western modernization on Muslim traditions, culture, social structure, and value systems. This group of writers heavily emphasizes external cultural and ideological factors as major reasons behind the phenomenon of political Islam or the rising influence of Islamic movements in the Islamic world. The second group overemphasizes the socio-economic factors of Muslim societies as the major reason behind the unprecedented rise of these movements. Islamic movements, according to representatives of this group, represent the political ideology of certain social classes that used Islam and Islamic slogans and symbols to reach power.

Third, unlike Middle Eastern and Islamic studies specialists from the Islamic world, Western specialists with interest in the Islamic movements tend to be influenced by the early writings about the Muslim Brotherhood in Egypt which is the largest and most studied Islamic movement in the West. By concentrating

---

[7] Bernard Lewis. *The Crisis of Islam: Holy War and Unholy Terror*. New York, NY: Modern Library 2003. "Islam and Liberal Democracy." *Atlantic (0276-9077)* 271, no. 2 (1993): 89. *Islam and the West*. New York, NY: Oxford University Press, 1993. *The Political Language of Islam*. Chicago, IL: University Of Chicago Press 1990. "The Roots of Muslim Rage." *The Atlantic Monthly* 266, no. 3 (1990): 47-60. *What Went Wrong? The Clash between Islam and Modernity in the Middle East*. New York: HarperCollins Publisher, 2002.

[8] Samuel P. Huntington. *The Clash of Civilizations: Remaking of World Order*. New York: Simon & Schuster, 1997.

on the writings of the Egyptian Brotherhood such as al-Banna and Qutb, these specialists tend to ignore the unique characteristics of each movement in the Islamic world. Intellectual contributions of other Islamic thinkers such as Malik Ibn Nabi and Mohammed Arkoun (Algeria), Hasan al-Turabi (Sudan), Rashid al-Ghannoushi (Tunisia), Yusuf al-Qaradawi (Egypt) tend to be ignored, despite the fact that their contributions could provide more detailed information about the ideological base of contemporary Islamic movements and the unique characteristics of each nation's movement.

This study focuses on examining the factors that contributed to the unprecedented rising of the Islamic Movement in Sudan in the period from 1945 to 1989. It argues the rise of the Movement came about the time when the post-independence governments in Sudan failed to transform the country's political independence into economic independence and to build a prosperous society. The rise of the Movement also came at a time when other adopted ideologies such as Communism, Arab Socialism, and Arab Nationalism had failed to respond adequately to the post-independence challenges that faced many of the countries in the region, including Sudan. This failure led to the creation of a vacuum of alternative ideas which could counter the Islamists' ideology.

A major factor that contributed to the unprecedented rise of the Movement in Sudan was the intellectual contributions of its leader Hasan al-Turabi. Al-Turabi's renewal ideology on *ijtihad* (interpretation of Islamic jurisprudence), *ijmaa* (consensus), *shura* (consultation), art and music, women and their role in society played a major role in presenting the Movement as a modern progressive Islamic movement among the Sudanese educated class. His pragmatic approach to politics and his rejection of the "isolationist" approach of the main Muslim Brotherhood thinkers such as Sayyid Qutb resulted in expanding the Movement's support base. His views on the importance of creating an open organizational structure, and his innovative recruitment strategies among students, women, trade union members, military personnel, coupled with the establishment of powerful financial institutions, and excellent cadres of communication specialists, all facilitated the Movement's unprecedented rise to power in Sudan.

The findings of this study provide a clear example of how Islamic movements are not a homogeneous group but rather heterogeneous groups that vary in ideology, political tactics, and worldviews. The Sudanese Islamic Movement in this study is a clear illustration of such uniqueness and variances. While the intellectual contributions of early Egyptian Brotherhood leaders such as al-Banna played a major role in shaping the Movement's discourse in Sudan in its early years, still the contributions of the Movement's Sudanese thinkers such as al-Turabi constituted the decisive factor in directing Movement work and ideology in the last four decades. For example, in Sudan, the Movement's position toward the role of women in society, secular regimes, non-Muslim groups in Islamic countries, and the usage of *ijtihad* differ greatly from the positions of the Islamic movements in Egypt, Syria, Palestine, and Lebanon.

These findings also indicate that the rise of the Islamic Movement in Sudan was not an aggressive reassertion of religious traditionalism or reactionsim but an essential part of the rise of modern mass political and social movements in Sudan, which later transformed themselves to effective and influential political parties such as the Sudanese Communist Party (SCP) and the Arab Nationalists Movement, which later became the Sudanese Baath Party. The rise of the Islamic Movement in Sudan in its early days represented a growing self-consciousness among Muslim Sudanese intellectuals and the educated elite who had been alienated by the dominant influence of the two traditional parties in the country, al-Umma and the Democratic Unionist Party (DUP), and by rising influence of the Communism ideology among the Sudanese educated class.

The pillar of the Movement's growth was not the appeal of religious traditionalism. This is evidenced by the predominantly well-educated character of the Movement in addition to its failure to win a significant following among Sudanese at traditional religious education institutions whose members gave their allegiance to the two traditional religious sects in the country, al-Khatmiyya and al-Ansar and subsequently to their political organizations -- al-Umma and the DUP. Instead the appeal of the Movement leaders was linked to their ability to distance themselves from the image of 'traditional' Islamic reactionsim, which was the hallmark of the Islamic establishment at that time.

The writings of al-Turabi played a major role in distancing the Movement not only from the traditional religious establishment in Sudan, but also from other Islamic movements in the region, particularly the Muslim Brotherhood in Egypt, whose intellectual contributions provided the guidelines for other Islamic movements in the region. A very significant component of al-Turabi's renewal project was his shift from the uncompromising and rejectionist attitude of al-Mawdudi and Qutb to political and ideological pragmatism. The main thesis of al-Mawdudi and Qutb was the Islamic movement should abstract from society and then confront it from outside as a moral ideal. Al-Turabi, on the other hand, advocates the building of a powerful movement within the system capable of advocating for Islam and ultimately establishing the Islamic state.

Al-Turabi's renewal ideas on *ijmaa* and *ijtihad* were in a sense also a reaffirmation of the ancient Sufi teachings, which emphasize the spirit of Islam, as opposed to its letter, with its confidence in the ability of mankind to genuinely enrich the original message by individual endeavors. Al-Turabi's greatest achievement is his ability to hover on the borderline between numerous antagonistic positions. He sits comfortably astride modernity and tradition, pragmatism and idealism, calculation and faith.[9] The main problem of al-Turabi's renewal project is the existence of a wide gap between high theory and mundane practice which his Movement was unable to fill. As one observer notes:

> Al-Turabi, like comparable reformers, works at the level of philosophy. His main concern was to achieve a theoretical grounding for what he sees as essential reforms. But he is at the same time a consummate tactician, and the Movement as a whole is practically-oriented. In many instances it

---

[9] Abdelwahab El-Affendi. *Turabi's Revolution: Islam and Power in Sudan.* . London: UK: Grey Seal Books, 1991.

moves first to implement policies which it deems expedient and starts the search for justification later. This led to a situation where theory did not blossom in practice, but actually grew out of it. [10]

During the 1960s, and after the return of al-Turabi from France and his election as the Movement General Observer, the Movement started to gradually change its elite-centered nature. Al-Turabi's pragmatic approach to issues surrounding the Movement recruitment strategies, its relations with other political parties, and the International Organization of the Muslim Brotherhood helped in revolutionizing Movement activities not only among its traditional base, which is the educated class, but also among Sufi groups, women, trade union members, and workers. During this time in its history, the Movement was mainly concerned with the rising influence of the SCP and concentrated its activities on trying to limit and then eradicate that influence. During this period the Movement functioned as a pressure group designed to influence the two traditional parties to adopt an 'Islamic' constitution and to outlaw the SCP, presumably because of its 'anti-religion' ideology.

Following the National Reconciliation Accord (NRA) of 1977, the Movement started an ambitious plan to expand its base among different groups of Sudanese society. Benefitting from its relatively peaceful relationship with Nemeri's military regime, the Movement built a network of financial institutions, non-profit health and education organizations, and youth and women's organizations that greatly enhanced Movement presence among the Sudanese people. Attention to the development of human resources was fundamental to Movement growth. The establishment of Islamic banks and other Islamic businesses allowed Movement leadership to create full-times cadres who toured the country spreading Movement ideology and teachings.

---

[10] Abdelwahab A. M. Osman. "The Political and Ideological Development of the Muslim Brotherhood in Sudan 1945-1989."PhD Dissertation, University of Reading: UK 1989, 412.

The Movement also dominated trade unions, professional associations, and student unions. This domination became clear in the 1986 election when the Movement won 23 seats in the Graduate Constituencies (out of 28). The gains in the Graduate Constituencies included all the 21 seats allocated for the Northern regions, plus two from the South, and 28 seats in the geographical constituencies (out of 236). This made the Movement the third largest party following al-Umma (100 seats) and the DUP (63 seats). The Movement's leaders interpreted their strong performance in the 1986 election, which occurred mainly among the educated and within urban areas, as a clear mandate and support for their program by the Sudanese educated elite.[11]

The success of the Islamic Movement in Sudan in the 1986 election, the sweeping success of the Islamic Salvation Front (FIS) in the 1991 Algerian election, and more recently, the success of the Muslim Brotherhood in Egypt during the 2005 election, the sweeping victory of Hamas during the 2006 election and the Justice and Development (AK) Party in Turkey's 2007 election are clear demonstrations of the need for more innovative approaches in the study of Islamic movements in the Islamic world. More important as noted by Brynjar (1998):

> Scholars should devote more attention to the process in which Islamists absorb and integrate modern principles and ideas within their ideological framework instead of analyzing Islamism within the paradigms which counterpoises Islamism with so–called "Western values" (whatever they may be). This process of the adoption of modern ideas cannot be studied merely by textual analysis of isolated ideological tracts. More attention should be given to the political practice, organization and activities of Islamist movements. [12]

Finally, many of the declared objectives of Islamic movements: solidarity or unity of the Muslim nation, economic, political, and cultural independence, control over natural resources, and resolution of the issue of Palestine, have put these movements on a collision course with the West. The apparent contradiction

---

[11] Ibid., 305.
[12] Lia Brynjar. *The Society of the Muslim Brothers in Egypt: The Rise of an Islamic Mass Movement 1928-1942.* Dryden, NY: Ithaca Press, 1998, 287.

between these objectives and Western interests in the region often clouds Western intellectual and political perception of and response to these movements. As a result, Islamic movements are increasingly, and needlessly, being seen as major threats and imminent dangers to the West. The two cultures are obviously different, as products of two unique historical experiences, but this ought to be recognized in terms of diversity and not enmity. The differences are over policies and interests and not essentially ideological.[13]

As a result, this study, while taking into account the limited ideological influences of the Egyptian Brotherhood thinkers on the Movement in Sudan, still focuses on the ideological contributions of the Islamists in Sudan and the features of their movement, their relationship with secular governments in Sudan, their position toward women, students, military personnel, trade unions, professional associations, and others and on their ability to build financial institutions as major determinants of their unprecedented rise to power in Sudan.

Organization of the book

The book is divided into seven chapters. Chapter One gives a general introduction to the phenomenon of political Islam with some emphasis in Sudan, It also details the organization of the study and provides a literature review for materials published on the subject of political Islam in general and the Islamic Movement in Sudan. Chapter Two discusses the theoretical framework for the study. Chapter Three provides a historical survey of Sudan and how Islam entered the country. Chapter Four discusses the modern Islamic reform movements and the intellectual and historical background including the writings of Hasan al-Banna (1906–1949), Abul A'la al-Mawdudi (1903-1979), and Sayyid Qutb (1906-1966). Chapter Five examines the historical development of the Islamic Movement in Sudan from 1946 to 1989, its ideology and organization. Chapter

---

[13] John L. Esposito & James Piscatori. "Democratization and Islam." *Middle East Journal* 45, no. 3 (1991): 427-440.

Six discusses the rise of the Islamic Movement in Sudan. A conclusion of the study is given in a brief conclusion in chapter Seven.

Literature Review

Introduction

This chapter gives a brief description of the literature published in Arabic and English on Islamic political movements, in general, and on the Islamic Movement in Sudan in particular. The chapter is divided into three parts. The first part discusses terminological difficulties that researchers encounter when discussing the role of Islam in politics. The second part gives a brief introduction to political Islam, its history, emergence and development, and how both Western and Middle Eastern scholars look at this phenomenon. The third part provides brief descriptions and analysis on the limited amount of literature published, in Arabic and English, about the Islamic Movement in Sudan. Given the previously mentioned limited Sudanese and Western sources on the subject of the Islamic Movement in Sudan, I will review studies that attempt to explain the phenomenon of political Islam elsewhere and apply them to the context.

Islam and Politics

In the last four decades an increasing interest in the phenomenon of Islamic Fundamentalism or political Islam has emerged among both Western and Middle Eastern scholars. The phenomenon refers to the noticeably growing influence of Islamic movements in the Islamic world. Despite the differences in their names and immediate programs, these movements invariably call for a greater role of Islam in the legal, political, social, economic, and public life of Islamic countries. These growing tendencies toward the establishment of an "Islamic State" and the wide support that these Islamic movements are gaining, have confronted scholars and politicians alike with a complicated set of questions as to the nature of this phenomenon and the reasons for its emergence, its impact on the political stability of the Islamic world, and its relation to the West.

Thus, political Islam has become a major topic of scholarship in international relations particularly in the realm of Middle Eastern politics. This began with the military coup of Zia-Alhaq in Pakistan in 1977, but, more important with the Islamic Revolution in Iran in 1979. Other early incidents that brought political Islam to the agenda included the 1954 assassination of the Egyptian Prime Minister Naqrashi Pasha, who disbanded the Society of Muslim Brotherhood, and the retaliatory assassination of Hassan al-Banna, the Brotherhood's supreme leader by the Egyptian Secret Police in February 1949; the conflicts between former Egyptian president Nasser and the Muslim Brotherhood in Egypt in 1954 and 1966 that resulted in the hanging of Sayyid Qutb and five other Muslim Brotherhood leaders; seizure of the Grand Mosque in Mecca in 1979; the assassination of President Anwar Sadat in Egypt in 1981; bloody battles of 1982 between the Muslim Brotherhood and the Syrian government in the city of Hama, Syria; and the Islamists' successful military coup in Sudan in 1989.

What is political Islam?

Various definitions of political Islam exist. According to Fuller (2003) adherents of political Islam believe that "Islam as a body of faith has something important to say about how politics and society should be ordered in the contemporary Muslim world and implemented in some fashion."[14] Noah Feldman, Professor of Law, who was appointed in 2003 by the Coalition Provisional Authority as chief U.S. advisor to Iraq for the writing of the country's new constitution, defines political Islam as "a comprehensive political, spiritual and personal world-view defined in opposition to all that is non-Islamic."[15] Olivier Roy, a French scholar, prefers a narrower definition; for him "political Islam is the attempt to create an Islamic state."[16]

A more analytically useful definition is provided by the political scientist Guilian Denoeux, who writes of Islamism as:

> "A form of instrumentalization of Islam by individuals, groups and organizations that pursue political objectives. It provides political

---

[14] Graham Fuller. *The Future of Political Islam*. New York: Palgrave, 2003, xi-xii.
[15] "The Gods That Failed." *Economist* 368, no. 8341 (2003): 5-6.
[16] Ibid., 5-6.

responses to today's societal challenges by imagining a future, the foundations for which rest on re-appropriated, reinvented concepts borrowed from the Islamic tradition."[17]

Because of the challenge presented by problem of multiple definitions, many authors dispense with a definition altogether, leaving the reader to infer the meanings of political Islam. This is also reflected in the common practice of "prefixing" Islam to create a bewildering conceptual plurality, which, to name but a few, includes *radical* Islam, *militant* Islam, *extremist* Islam and *fundamentalist* Islam. This diversity points both to the many aspects believed to characterize political Islam, as well as to the problem of finding an appropriate term.

Proponents of Islam itself often use the following expressions: *al-ba'th al-islami* (Islamic resurrection), *al-sahwah al-islamiyyah* (Islamic awakening). *Ihya 'al-din* (religious revival), *al-usuliyyah al-islamiyyah* (Islamic fundamentalism), *al-harakah al-islamia* (Islamic movement), *al-tayyar al-islami* (Islamic current), and *al-ittijah al-islami* (Islamic tendency).[18] The Islamic resurgence is both complex and multifaceted, and the variety of concepts illustrates the difficulty of coming to terms with this diversity. As pointed out by Dessouki, the Islamic resurgence is "not a monolithic phenomenon but, rather, socially and historically conditioned."[19] Nevertheless, all of the concepts and terms mentioned above describe the Islamic resurgence in one way or another. It is thus difficult to find a common definition of Islamic resurgence, but Dessouki offers a good description when he writes that Islamic resurgence "refers to the increasing prominence and politicization of Islamic ideologies and symbols in Muslim societies and in the public life of Muslims individuals."[20]

In general, it is very difficult to find a clear and agreed-upon definition of what Islamic fundamentalism or political Islam means. This is especially true with

---

[17] Guilain Denoeux. "The Forgotten Swamp: Navigating Political Islam." *Middle East Policy* 9, no. 2 (2002): 61.

[18] Hrair R. Dekmejian. *Islam in Revolution: Fundamentalism in the Arab World.* Syracuse, NY: Syracuse University Press, 1985, 4.

[19] Ali E. Dessouki. ed. *Islamic Resurgence in the Arab World*: Praeger Publishers, 1982, 14.

[20] Ibid.,4.

the term Islamic fundamentalism. The ambiguity surrounding the term is directly related to the loose and interchangeable character employed by various writers and the concept of "Islamic Revival Movements." In this regard, many scholars that employ the term either ignore providing definition on the assumption that the meaning is self-evident or too subtle to spell out.[21] A good example of those scholars who attempted to define Islamic fundamentalism along previous lines is Ann Lambton in her chapter "The Clash of Civilizations: Authority, Legitimacy and Perfectibility." According to Lambton, religious fundamentalism, in general and Islamic fundamentalism, in particular, consists of belief that:

> Religious fundamentalism, whether Jewish, Christian, or Islamic, consists of an assertion that the received sacred text consists of a set of eternal living truths. It has therefore, an in-built guarantee of infallibility. It is an ideology of the books as the all sufficient guide in every condition and circumstance of life in whatever century and whatever purpose. It neglects transcendence and open-endedness and avoids the need for a creative interpretation of the faith. It sees God in the light of its own concepts. Having made up its mind what the faith should be, isolated texts are then used as proof texts, often in support of particular cause. [22]

Such belief is usually associated with the fundamentalists' view of themselves as the authentic expressions of their respective tradition; they usually claim to be true Muslims or Christians. While these characteristics are definitely true and shared among fundamentalists of all religions, they are not essential or sufficient, alone, to define the phenomenon of political Islam or the Islamic revival, because these characteristics also exist among secular political groups and movements such as Marxism or Fascism.

In origin, the term fundamentalism, as many scholars have argued, was largely an extension of the term "Christian Fundamentalism," which emerged to

---

[21] For example see: Lawrence, Bruce "Islamic Fundamentalist Movements." In *The Islamic Impulse*, edited by Barbara Stowasser. London: UK: Croom Helm, 1987.

[22] Ann Lambton. "The Clash of Civilizations: Authority, Legitimacy and Perfectibility." In *Islamic Fundamentalism*, edited by M Burrell. London: UK: Royal Asiatic Society of Great Britain and Ireland, 1988, 33.

describe a particular American Protestant movement.[23] According to Ibrahim (1999), "Ideas of the movement had evolved around five points, specifically authority of the scripture described in terms of the "inerrancy, "infallibility" or "plenary inspiration."[24] Ibrahim further notices

> ... it has been argued that the most important element in the definition of Christian fundamentalism, the "inerrancy" of scripture, is utterly irrelevant to Muslim religion. All Muslims invariably view The Quran as "inerrant." To them the Quran is the direct and verbatim Word of God in a way that is not normally claimed for the Christian Scripture. [25]

On the other hand, there are no words exist that are equivalent to the English word "fundamentalism" in the Arabic language or its meaning. The nearest Arabic word to the English is *"Usuliyyia, Usully adj"* which means one who is faithful to the rudiments of his religion. Within this meaning obviously, no Muslim would mind being described as a "fundamentalist," faithful to the rudiments of Islam.

In all cases, Islamic political movement members neither called themselves "fundamentalists," nor were they called so by the mainstream Muslim population. The "fundamentalists" generally view themselves as true Muslims and refer to themselves as *Islamiyoun* "Islamists" or *Nashiteen islamyyeen* "Muslim activists," while their opponents label them *Mutatarfeen* (extremists) or *Mutshaddedeen* (fanatics). Interestingly, Hasan al-Turabi the leader of the Islamic Movement in Sudan, expressed a similar critique, stating:

> Actually the term has no correspondent in the Islamic language or in Arabic in particular. The term is used to describe a Christian phenomenon here [in the U.S.A.] after the war, a tendency of being literally attached to scripture. In Islamic context this movement, the closest analogy to the phenomenon that we are describing is perhaps the Renaissance in Europe, whole intellectual renewal which ultimately seeks to translate into social

---

[23] Abdullahi Ali Ibrahim. "A Theology of Modernity: Hasan Al-Turabi and Islamic Renewal in Sudan" *Africa Today* 46, no. 3/4 (1999): 195.

[24] Ibid., 195.

[25] Ibid., 195.

reform, active social reform, as opposed to dormancy, the dogmatism of the traditional societies which have become decadent. [26]

In general, political Islam is a part of broad intellectual, cultural, social, and political movements throughout the Islamic world. The movements are often referred to as Islamic Resurgence or Islamic Revival, and political Islam is only one component of the greater resurgence and revival of Islamic ideas, practices, and rhetoric. The terms "Islamic movement" and "Islamists" are applied throughout this book for several reasons. First, they are the most commonly used terms by the Islamists in the Islamic world to describe themselves and their political activities. In addition, they are the most commonly used terms by Middle Eastern and Islamic scholars from the Islamic world.[27] Second, from a linguistic point of view, the word 'Islamist' is different from the word 'Muslim.' Islamists refers to Muslims who believe that Islam is not only a religion but also a political system, while the word Muslim simply means anyone who is a Muslim regardless of his/her views about the role of Islam in society.

The rise of Islamic movements in the Islamic world, in general, and in the Middle East, in particular, has led to widespread debate in the West regarding the causes, values and goals of these movements. Two general schools of thought have emerged on the subject: the socio-economic and political school and the cultural-religious school.

---

[26] Committee on Foreign Affairs. *Islamic Fundamentalism in Africa and Implications for U.S. Policy*, 102nd Congress, 2nd Session, May 20 1992, 8.

[27] For example, see: Ibrahim Abu-Rabi. "Arabism, Islamism, and the Future of Arab World." *Arab Studies Quarterly* 22, no. 1 (2000): 91, Mohammed Ayoob. "Political Islam: Image and Reality." *World Policy Journal* 21, no. 3 (2004): 1-14, Nazih N. Ayubi, "The Political Revival of Islam: The Case of Egypt." *International Journal of Middle East Studies* 12, no. 4 (1980): 481-99. Roksana Bahramitash,. "Myths and Realities of the Impact of Political Islam on Women: Female Employment in Indonesia and Iran." *Development in Practice* 14, no. 4 (2004): 508-20. Asef Bayat. "Revolution without Movement, Movement without Revolution: Comparing Islamic Activism in Iran and Egypt." *Comparative Studies in Society and History* 40, no. 1 (1998): 136-69. Leon Carl Brown. "The Islamic Reformist Movement in North Africa." *The Journal of Modern African Studies* 2, no. 1 (1964): 55-63.

The Socio-economic and Political Schools

The socio-economic political schools view the emergence of Islamic movements as a result of a complex series of factors with both internal and external origins. These factors include; the ideological vacuum in the Arab world that was a consequence of the Arab defeat in the 1967 War, and the resulting collapse of Nasser's "Arab Nationalist" ideology, the failure of post-independence governments in the Middle East to achieve economic prosperity, the undemocratic nature of political regimes that exist in most of the Islamic countries, the secularization of Muslim societies, and the alienation of Islam from public life. Proponents of this school do not view Islam as a threat, but rather as the resurgence of a desire by the populace in Muslim countries to bring Islam back to the forefront of political and social life of their countries.[28]

The highest quality and the most authoritative works on the subject in this school have been produced by John Esposito. The depth of his coverage and his clear understanding of the subject, coupled with his detailed accounts surrounding the emergence of these movements around the Islamic world are impressive. His books *The Islamic Threat: Myth or Reality? Islam and Politics* and *Islam in Transition: Muslim Perspectives, Islam: The Straight Path*, plus numerous articles on political Islam are of outstanding quality.[29] The strength of Esposito's writings about political Islam is that he explains the phenomena and events from the viewpoint of Muslims and Islamists themselves. Also, his accounts of political Islam tend to cover a wide range of geographical areas and include all the centers

---

[28] John L. Esposito. *The Islamic Threat: Myth or Reality?* New York: Oxford University Press, 1992.

[29] For example, see: John L. Esposito. *The Islamic Threat: Myth or Reality?* New York: Oxford University Press, 1992. *Political Islam: Revolution, Radicalism, or Reform?* Boulder, Colo.: Lynne Rienner Publishers, 1997. "Sudan's Islamic Experiment." *The Muslim World* 76, no. 3-4 (1986): 181-202. *Voices of Resurgent Islam*. New York: Oxford University Press, 1983. John L. Esposito & Yvonne Y. Haddad, *Islam, Gender, and Social Change*. Oxford: Oxford University Press, 1997. John L. Esposito & James Piscatori. "Democratization and Islam." *Middle East Journal* 45, no. 3 (1991). Esposito John L. Esposito & John Obert Voll. *Makers of Contemporary Islam*. New York: Oxford University Press, 2001.

of political Islam activities such as Egypt, Sudan, Pakistan, Iran, and, lately, Asian countries such as Indonesia and Malaysia.

Esposito's writings also cover issues such as women and political Islamic groups, Islamic Laws, and ideology with a great deal of neutrality. His book with Yvonne Haddad titled *Islam, Gender, and Social Change* is clear illustration of such work. Esposito and Haddad shed light on the impact of the Islamic resurgence on gender issues in Iran, Egypt, Jordan, and other Islamic countries. They reveal the wide variety that exists among Muslim societies and believers, and the complexity of the issues under consideration. They show that new developments are happening for women across the Islamic world, and how these developments being initiated, in many cases, by women themselves. The book as a whole militates against the stereotype of Muslim women as repressed, passive, and without initiative, while acknowledging the very real obstacles to women's initiatives and ambitions in most of these societies.[30]

Hrair Dekmejian has written several works on the Islamic movements in the Middle East, such as *Islam in Revolution: Fundamentalism in the Arab World* (1985) and *Egypt under Nassir: A Study in Political Dynamics* (1971). In these books he looks at the history, socio-psychological roots, ideology and practice, motives and goals of Islamic fundamentalist movements in the Arab world. The disadvantage of Dekmejian's writings is that they cover the Arab world only;[31] the same problem exists in Dessouki's writings, such as *Islamic Resurgence in the Arab World* (1982).[32]

Another excellent account of the subject of fundamentalism was written by James Piscatori. In this edited book *Accounting for Fundamentalisms: The*

---

[30] John L. Esposito & Yvonne Y. Haddad. *Islam, Gender, and Social Change.* New York: Oxford University Press, 1997.

[31] See Hrair R. Dekmejin. *Egypt under Nasir: A Study in Political Dynamics.* New York: State University of New York Press, 1971. *Islam in Revolution: Fundamentalism in the Arab World.* Syracuse, NY: Syracuse University Press, 1985.

[32] Ali E. Dessouki, ed. *Islamic Resurgence in the Arab World.* New York: Praeger Publishers, 1982.

Dynamic Character of Movements, Piscatori and other contributors surveyed fundamentalist movements in Christianity, Judaism, Islam, Hinduism, Sikhism, and Buddhism. Contributors to the anthology describe the organization of these movements, leadership and recruiting techniques, and ways in which their ideological programs and organizational structures shift over time in response to changing political and social environments.[33]

John Voll and Esposito also edited one of the most interesting and informative books in the field. In their book, *Makers of Contemporary Islam*, the authors explored the development of contemporary Islamic movements and thoughts through the biographies of nine major activist intellectuals who represent a wide range of Muslim societies such as Rashid al-Ghannoushi (Tunisia), Hasan al-Turabi (Sudan), Anwar Ibrahim (Malaysia), Abdurrahman Wahid (Indonesia) and other prominent Islamic thinkers and activists. These thinkers contributed to some of the most significant intellectual developments in the Muslim world during the 1980s and 1990s--the period during which Islamic movements became a major force in Muslim societies and international affairs. They helped to organize and lead movements of Islamic renewal and provided the conceptual foundations for the programs advocated by those movements.[34]

Olivier Roy a senior researcher at the French Center for Scientific Research is another prominent representative of the socio-economic school. His views on Islamic Movements depart radically from those prevalent among the cultural-religious scholars. Rather than depicting Islamic movements as a clash between world-views or civilizations, he considers the activities of Islamic movements to be mostly a typical secular anti-imperialist movement, using religious motives as a cover. He compared contemporary Islamic radicals with leftist radical groups of the 1970s, such as the Red Brigade in Italy and the Baader-Meinhof group in Germany. "The violence that we see now has little to do

---

[33] James Piscatori. *Accounting for Fundamentalisms: The Dynamic Character of Movements.* Chicago: University Of Chicago Press, 2004.

[34] John L. Esposito & John Obert Voll. *Makers of Contemporary Islam.* New York: Oxford University Press, 2001.

with Islam, it is nationalism," Roy said. "These guys are fighting American imperialism, they are not fighting Christianity."[35]

Another French scholar who tackles the issue of political Islam is Gilles Kepel, a professor at Paris's Institute for Political Studies. In his book *Jihad: The Trail of Political Islam* (2003), Kepel traces the rise of the contemporary Islamist movement from its origins in the mid-20th century through its later appearance in countries such as Malaysia, Algeria and Turkey, as well as in Western Europe. Its apogee, he argues cogently, was the 1979 revolution in Iran that brought about the defeat of the Shah and the rise of a fundamentalist Islamic regime. But while ideologies that fused Islam with political power gained adherents throughout the world in the ensuing 20 years, says Kepel, in no other country were Islamists able to seize and hold power for more than a few years, a factor that he attributes to the ideology's inability to attract both the middle class and the poor.

Kepel's approach is not without weaknesses. In many places around the globe, fundamentalist political Islam has transformed society and politics, even if Islamists have not been able to attain political rule. For example, prior to 1989 in Sudan, the Islamic Movement influenced Nemeri regime in adapting Islamic course and later, the largest political parties in the country to adapt political and economic programs that guaranteed a larger role for Islam in public life. This is also true in Egypt; as a result of the rising influence of the Islamists in the 1970s and 1980s, the Egyptian government started to give more attention to Islam by increasing the funds for Islamic education and institutions, and increasing the visibility of Islamic symbols and programs in its state-controlled radio, television and newspapers.

Another major problem with Kepel's arguments about the declining influence of political Islam is that he does not clearly differentiate between the three major political groups: *Salafiyya*, Muslim brotherhood, and Jihadist groups. While it is true that the influence of *Salafiyya* and Jihadists groups is in decline,

---

[35] Olivier Roy. "Radical Islam: A Middle East Phenomenon or a Consequence of the Globalization of Islam?" *Press Freedom in Afghanistan.* New York, NY. Open Society Institute, 2003.

the influence of the Muslim Brotherhood and other mainstream Islamic political parties and organizations is increasing. The latest election results in Egypt and Turkey, for example, are clear indicators of the rising influence of mainstream Islamists.[36]

Fawaz Gerges, author of *The Far Enemy: Why Jihad Went Global* (2005), did extensive research on Jihadist movements and their emergence in the early 1970s as a reaction to Nasser's authoritarian regime in Egypt. His discussion highlights the prominent role that Qutb's writings played in formulating the ideological base for these movements. Gerges points out those Jihadists always saw the near enemy--particularly the secular Egyptian regime--as their main foe. Secular Muslim rulers stood in the way of their goal of establishing an Islamic government based upon *Shari'a*, or Islamic law. To this end, *al-Jama'a al-Islamiya* (Islamic Group), one of the largest Jihadist organizations in the world, and *Tanzim al-Jihad* (Islamic Jihad), led by Ayman al-Zawahiri the current Al Qaeda number two, collaborated on the 1981 assassination of Egyptian president Anwar al-Sadat. "The overwhelming majority of Jihadists have been religious nationalists whose fundamental goal was to effect change in their own society" argued Gerges.

In general, Gerges book presents a clear picture of the Jihadists' world for western readers, and clearly explains the relations between Al Qaeda and other Islamic Jihadist groups. Gerges also seems to agree with Kepel's arguments about the declining role of Jihadist groups. He writes, "Al Qaeda striking out at the United States was not the pinnacle of the Jihadist movements as some might imagine. Rather, it was an act of desperation that aimed to save the sinking ship by precipitating a (clash of civilizations) with the West that would bring the *ummah* or world-wide Muslim community into the battle on the Jihadists' side."[37]

---

[36] Gilles Kepel. *Jihad: The Trail of Political Islam.* Translated by Anthony F. Roberts. New Edition. Cambridge, MA: Belknap Press, 2003.

[37] Fawaz Gerges. *The Far Enemy: Why Jihad Went Global.* New York: Cambridge University Press, 2005, 157.

Representatives of these schools of thoughts call for giving Muslims the opportunity to freely choose their governments and to create political and economic institutions that reflect their Islamic identity -- a reality that the West is not yet ready to accept. They also argue that while culturally constructed Western structures such as total separation of religion and state, western model of democracy, and government institutions are effective in the West, they are not the best model for other regions. According to representatives of the socio-economic and political schools of thought, colonialism destroyed the traditional state, cultural and social structures in Islamic countries. Political Islam is the natural resistance to the artificial structures left behind by colonialism and perpetuated by authoritarian rulers. As a result, Islamists are embroiled in internal and external struggles; internal struggles against the imposed institutions and ideologies, and external struggles against Western intervention in internal political, economic and military affairs.

Representatives of the socio-economic and political schools of thought further argued that extreme Islamist movements are a result of political issues and not of religion. Opposition groups have become increasingly radical as Muslim populations are being oppressed in Bosnia, Chechnya, and in the Palestinian territories. Muslims who normally oppose the use of violence, see these violations as the work of the West and as a justification for retaliation.[38] They insist that these urgent political issues must be addressed in a constructive manner in order to provide stability and reverse the rapid trend of radicalism. As reviewed, representatives of this school of thought such as, Esposito,[39] Piscatori,[40] Voll,[41]

---

[38] Maysam al-Faruqi. "Engaging Political Islam." *Policy Briefs*, no. 11/14/2006. Available at: http://www.mideasti.org/articles/doc588.html. Accessed 01/21/2007.

[39] For example, see following by John L. Esposito: *Political Islam: Revolution, Radicalism, or Reform?* Boulder, Colo.: Lynne Rienner Publishers, 1997. "Sudan's Islamic Experiment." *The Muslim World* 76, no. 3-4 (1986): 181-202. *Voices of Resurgent Islam.* New York: Oxford, 1983. *Islam, Gender, and Social Change.* Oxford: Oxford University Press, 1997. *Makers of Contemporary Islam.* New York: Oxford University Press, 2001.

[40] For example the works James Piscatori: *Accounting for Fundamentalisms: The Dynamic Character of Movements.* Chicago: University Of Chicago Press, 2004. *Islam in the Political*

Arjomand,[42] Dessouki,[43] and Dekmejian,[44] have produced superb and excellent accounts of the political Islam phenomenon.

The Cultural-religious School

The second school of thought, the Cultural-religious school, views the rise of Islamic movements with both alarm and trepidation. Adherents to this school include Bernard Lewis, Samuel Huntington, Daniel Pipes, Judith Miller, and Peter Rodman. Representatives of this school look upon the emergence of Islamic movements as movements that arose as a reaction against political, moral and technological incursions of the West into Muslim societies. They also view Islamic movements as movements emerging in single and monolithic trends across the Muslim world, representing a politico-religious "civilization" that would ultimately come into direct confrontation with the West.[45] Representatives of this school of thought tend to compare political Islam with western-style concepts and simply conclude that political Islam is the opposite of democracy, personal freedom, equality, human rights, and liberalism.[46] Others have said that while the west is based on secular materialism, scientific reason, and lacks moral philosophy, Islam is based on faith, patience, pace, and equilibrium.[47] For them, Islam is militant and a confrontation with the West is unavoidable.

Process Cambridge: Cambridge University Press, 1983. *Muslim Politics* New Edition ed: Princeton University Press, 2004.

[41] John O. Voll. "The British, the 'Ulama', and Popular Islam in the Early Anglo-Egyptian Sudan." *International Journal of Middle East Studies* 2, no. 3 (1971): 212-18.

[42] Said A. Arjomand. *The Political Dimensions of Religion.* New York State University Press, NY,1993. *The Shadow of God and the Hidden Imam: Religion, Political Order, and Societal Change in Shi'ite Iran from the Beginning to 1890.* Chicago: University of Chicago Press, 1987. *The Turban for the Crown: The Islamic Revolution in Iran.* New Edition. Oxford: Oxford University Press, 1989.

[43] Ali E. Dessouki, ed. *Islamic Resurgence in the Arab World:* Praeger Publishers 1982.

[44] Hrair R. Dekmejian. *Egypt under Nassir: A Study in Political Dynamics.* New York: State University of New York Press, 1971. *Islam in Revolution: Fundamentalism in the Arab World.* Syracuse, NY: Syracuse University Press, 1985.

[45] Samuel P. Huntington. *The Clash of Civilizations: Remaking of World Order.* New York: Simon & Schuster, 1997.

[46] Ray Takeyh. "The Lineaments of Islamic Democracy." *World Policy Journal* 18, no. 4 (2001): 59.

[47] Ahmed S. Moussalli. *Moderate and Radical Islamic Fundamentalism.* Jacksonville, Florida: University of Florida Press, 1999, 71-72.

A major figure in the cultural-religious school of thought is Bernard Lewis who produced numerous books and articles on the subjects of Islam, Arab, and Middle Eastern cultures.[48] Lewis's main argument about Islam asserts it to be a religion that can not be changed and thus will remain antagonistic to western values and cultures. Lewis also touches upon similar themes, such as the historical legacy of slavery, the miserable situation of minority rights in Muslim societies, obstacles that stand in the way of women's participation in public life, and the lack of separation of religion and state that further alienates the Muslim world from the secular and democratic forms of governance that originated in Western Europe.[49] In addition, Lewis tends to depict democracy, secularism, civil society, and economic development, i.e. capitalism (the major features of the Western world), as opposed to the values of Islamic societies. Lewis also sees the revival of Islam as the outcome of centuries of suffering and humiliation of Muslims at the hands of the West, which was reinforced by the non-separation of religion and state within Islamic culture.[50]

Lewis's Orientalism projects and arguments about Islam and Arabs are criticized by many Middle Eastern scholars, especially Edward Said who writes:

> [Lewis's work] purports to be liberal objective scholarship but is in reality very close to being propaganda against his subject material." Lewis's work is "aggressively ideological." He has dedicated his entire career, spanning more than five decades, to a "project to debunk, to whittle down, and to discredit the Arabs and Islam ----The core of Lewis's ideology about Islam is that it never changes, and his whole mission is to inform conservative segments of the Jewish reading public, and anyone else who cares to listen, that any political, historical, and scholarly account of Muslims must begin and end with the fact that Muslims are Muslims.[51]

---

[48] For example his most recent works include: Bernard Lewis. *The Crisis of Islam: Holy War and Unholy Terror*. New York: Modern Library 2003. "Islam and Liberal Democracy." *Atlantic (0276-9077)* 271, no. 2 (1993): 89. *The Political Language of Islam*. Chicago, IL: University of Chicago Press 1990. "The Roots of Muslim Rage." *The Atlantic Monthly* 266, no. 3 (1990): 47-60. *What Went Wrong? The Clash between Islam and Modernity in the Middle East*. New York: HarperCollins Publisher, 2002.

[49] Bernard Lewis. *The Crisis of Islam: Holy War and Unholy Terror*. New York,: Modern Library, 2003.

[50] Bernard Lewis. *Islam and the West*. New York: Oxford University Press, 1993.

[51] Edward W. Said. *Orientalism*. New York: Vintage, 1979, 316.

Another major representative of this school is Samuel Huntington. In his 1993 article, which was published in *Foreign Affairs* and later iterated in his book *The Clash of Civilizations: Remaking of World Order*, Huntington argues that the next conflict in the world will be drawn along the line of civilization. He writes:

> It is my hypothesis that the fundamental source of conflict in this new world will not be primarily ideological or primarily economic. The great divisions among humankind and the dominating source of conflict will be cultural. Nation states will remain the most powerful actors in world affairs, but the principal conflicts of global politics will occur between nations and groups of different civilizations. The clash of civilizations will dominate global politics. The fault lines between civilizations will be the battle lines of the future. [52]

Huntington further describes Islamic culture as being essentially militaristic: e.g., the Quran orders violence against non-Muslims in numerous places; its young, unemployed, and overcrowded population is ready to resort to violence; the inseparable nature of the state and religion in Islamic political philosophy promotes intolerance towards the non-religious forms of life; and there is the lack of a developed civil society and economy in Muslim lands. [53] Huntington's thesis about the clash of civilizations sparked an unprecedented debate about the nature of the post-Cold War era among academicians and politicians. His work received blessings from some of the Western political establishment and has, of late, become a touchstone for contemporary theorizing about the post-Cold War world. The problem with Huntington's argument is that it overstates the homogeneity of the Islamic world and the Arab world, and errs to the extent to which he appears to suggest that so-called 'Islamic fundamentalism' represents the sole authentic expression of Islam.

Representatives of the cultural-religious school of thought were heavily criticized by many scholars in the field such as Emad Eldin Shahin. In his book *Political Ascent: Contemporary Islamic Movements in North Africa*, Shahin

---

[52] Samuel P. Huntington. "The Clash of Civilization?" *Foreign Affairs* 72, no. 3 (1993): 22.
[53] Ibid.,32.

writes "political Islam is increasingly, and needlessly, being seen as a major threat to the West."[54] Such views make the conflict with the West imminent and unavoidable, according to Shahin. The heaviest critique for the cultural-religious school of thought came from scholars such as Emad Eldin Shahin and Edward Said. Shahin argues the two cultures are obviously different, as a product of different historical experiences, but this ought to be recognized in terms of diversity and not enmity.[55] His point is that different traditions and experiences do not necessarily lead to conflict. Therefore, to avoid conflicts, one has to study and understand the phenomenon of political Islam in its historical, political, religious, and social context.

Said, on the other hand, argues that one of the great obstacles in clearly understanding and objectively examining the phenomenon of political Islam is the influence of representatives of the old "Oriental" school of thought. In his book *Orientalism,* Said explains the destructive role that representatives of this school played in shaping the picture of the Arabs and Muslims in the West, Said argues:

> Orientalism can be found in current Western depictions of "Arab" cultures. The depictions of "the Arab" as irrational, menacing, untrustworthy, anti-Western, dishonest, and--perhaps most importantly-- prototypical, are ideas into which Orientalist scholarship has evolved These notions are trusted as foundations for both ideologies and policies developed by the Occident …The system now culminates into the very institutions of the state. To write about the Arab Oriental world, therefore, is to write with the authority of a nation, and not with the affirmation of a strident ideology but with the unquestioning certainty of absolute   truth backed by absolute force …One would find this kind of procedure less objectionable as political propaganda--which is what it is, of course--were it not accompanied by sermons on the objectivity, the fairness, the impartiality of a real historian, the implication always being that Muslims and Arabs cannot be objective but that Orientalists. . .writing about Muslims are, by definition, by training, by the mere fact of their Westernness. This is the culmination of Orientalism as a dogma that not only degrades its subject matter but also blinds its practitioners.[56]

---

[54] Emad Eldin Shahin. *Political Ascent: Contemporary Islamic Movements in North Africa.* Boulder, Colorado: Westview Press, 1997, 3.

[55] Ibid.,3.

[56] Edward W. Said. *Orientalism.* New York: Vintage, 1979.

Said's second work *Covering Islam* was influential in highlighting the
distortion of Islam in Western media.[57] In this book Said looks at how American
popular media has used and perpetuated a narrow and unfavorable image of
Islamic peoples, and how this has prevented understanding while providing a
fictitious common enemy for the diverse American populace.[58] He lashes out at
self-proclaimed Middle Eastern 'experts" among academics and journalists, such
as Barry Rubin, Samuel Huntington, Martin Kramer, Daniel Pipes, Judith Miller,
and Steven Emerson, who try to advance their arguments about "the Islamic
threat" to the West.[59] The job of these self-proclaimed 'experts' according to Said
"is to make sure that the 'threat' is kept before our eyes, the better to excoriate
Islam for terror, despotism and violence, while assuring themselves profitable
consultancies, frequent TV appearances and book contracts. The Islamic threat is
made to seem disproportionately fearsome, lending support to the thesis (which is
an interesting parallel to anti-Semitic paranoia) that there is a worldwide
conspiracy behind every explosion.[60] Said further criticizes representatives of this
school as lacking the needed knowledge and basic linguistic training on the
region's history, traditions, and languages. He writes:

> It would be impossible to be taken seriously as a reporter or expert on
> Russia, France, Germany or Latin America, perhaps even China or Japan,
> without knowing the requisite languages, but for "Islam," linguistic
> knowledge is unnecessary since what one is dealing with is considered to
> be a psychological deformation, not a "real" culture or religion.[61]

The latest wave of literature about political Islam came immediately after
September 11, 2001 when the world became deluged with books on the
relationship between Islam and the West and Islam and terrorism. Suddenly it was

---

[57] Edward W. Said. *Covering Islam: How the Media and the Experts Determine How We See the Rest of the World.* Revised edition: Vintage: New York, 1996.
[58] Ibid.
[59] Edward W. Said. "A Devil Theory of Islam." *New York Times*, no. 08/12/1996 (1996). Available from http://www.thenation.com/doc/19960812/said Accessed 02/01/2007.
[60] Ibid.
[61] Ibid.

felt by writers, opinion-makers, columnists, journalists, researchers and academicians that people in Western countries wanted to know and read about Islam and what Muslim people think. I mention academicians last because a great deal of what was written had a sensationalist aspect, seeing Islam as a war-mongering religion. Examples of works that distorted Islam as the "religion of the sword" are Wright's *Sacred Rage: The Crusade of Modern Islam* and *Sacred Rage: The Wrath of Militant Islam* (2001).[62] Daniel Pipes's writings are another example that clearly distorted Islam and Muslims. His books such as *In the Path of God: Islam and Political Power* and *The Long Shadow: Culture and Politics in the Middle East* are clear demonstration of such distortion.[63] These writings do not explain the nature of the phenomenon and all that readers can get from these writings is a sense of militant Islam on the move. The impression given is one of equating Islamic political movements with violence.

The Islamic Movement in Sudan: A Literature Review

A large body of writings has emerged in the past four decades to explain the phenomenon of political Islam and to address the questions it has raised. Yet, strangely none of the writings has attempted to study the phenomenon of political Islam in Sudan. This is in spite of the special importance of the Sudanese Islamic Movement in Sudanese political life and the recognized leading role of the Sudanese Islamic Movement and its leader, Hassan al-Turabi, among similar movements, not only in the Middle Eastern region but also in other parts of the Islamic world.

The limited literature about the Islamic Movement in Sudan is due to two major reasons. The first reason, which is external, is the political insignificance of

---

[62] Ahmad S. Moussalli. *Moderate and Radical Islamic Fundamentalism.* Jacksonville, FL: University of Florida Press, 1999.

[63] Some of Daniel Pipes works include: *In the Path of God: Islam and Political Power.* New edition ed. Edison, NJ: Transaction Publishers, 2002. *The Long Shadow: Culture and Politics in the Middle East* Edison, NJ: Transaction Publishers 1999. *Militant Islam Reaches America* New York: W. W. Norton & Company 2003. *Miniatures: Views of Islamic and Middle Eastern Politics.* Edison, NJ: Transaction Publishers 2003."The Muslims Are Coming! The Muslims Are Coming!" *National Review* 42, no. 22 (1990): 28-31.

Sudan in the region. Sudan, unlike other Middle Eastern countries, is not a major player in the politics of the region, particularly in the Arab-Israeli conflict. The major bulk of the literature about Islamic movements in the region is written about the movements in countries that are involved directly or indirectly in the Arab-Israeli conflict, such as Egypt, Jordan, Syria, Iran, and other oil-producing countries, such as the Gulf countries. The second reason is internal; there is a lack of information about the Islamic Movement in Sudan due to the secrecy that surrounds its activities. Like many other Islamic movements in the region, the Islamic Movement in Sudan during the period from 1945 to 1989 functioned under great secrecy.

Unlike other social and political movements in developed democracies, the Islamic Movement in Sudan functioned under a constant threat of prosecution from the military regimes that ruled Sudan for a period of more than 23 years since the country's independence in 1956. Even during the short periods of democracies (1954-1958, 1964-1969, and 1985-1989), political parties in Sudan -- especially the ideological ones (such as the Islamic movement and the Sudanese Communist Party) -- were forced to function on two levels, underground and in public. In the case of the Islamic Movement, the underground level usually consisted of the core of the organization and its second-in-command political leadership. The public level usually included its well-known political leadership.

All that has so far been written in Arabic about the Islamic Movement in Sudan was the work of the Islamists in Sudan or their supporters.[64] The leading Sudanese historian, Ahmed Hasan Makki, who is also a member of the Movement's *Shura* Council, published a two-volume set that detailed the history of the Movement in Sudan. The first book *Harakat Al-Ikhwan Al-Muslimin Fi Al-Sudan* 1944 -1969 (The Movement of the Muslim Brotherhood in Sudan 1944-

---

[64] For example see the Hasan al-Turabi: *Al-Harakah Al-Islamiyah Fi Al-Sudan*, (Afaq Al-Ghad 8). Kuwait: Dar al-Qalam, 1988, *Al-Harakah Al-Islamiyah Fi Al-Sudan: Al-Tatawwur Wa-Al-Kasb Wa-Al-Manhaj*. Cairo: Egypt: al-Qari al-`Arabi, 1991, "Islamic Fundamentalism in the Sunni and Shia Worlds." Abdelwahab El-Affendi. *Turabi's Revolution: Islam and Power in Sudan*. London: UK: Grey Seal Books, 1991.

1969) details the history of the Movement from 1944 to 1969. According to Makki, "the Muslim Brotherhood in Sudan was established in Sudan as a direct answer to challenges that faced the Sudanese society as a result of the rapid growth of Marxism in Sudan especially among the elite and the working class."[65] Makki also argued that the ideology of the Muslim Brotherhood was spread in Sudan through two main groups. The first groups were Egyptian soldiers and civilians who were members of the Muslim Brotherhood organization in Egypt, and who were sent to work in Sudan during the Anglo-Egyptian co-dominium rule of Sudan (1899-1955). The other groups were the Sudanese students who were sent to study in Egypt.[66]

It was the first group that dominated the Movement leadership and activities during the early years of the Movement in Sudan (until the early 1960s), after independence, the second group super ceded the first group as a result of the rapid growth in the numbers of Sudanese students in Egypt, and the dominant role in the Movement leadership shifted dramatically in favor of the second group. The second volume of Makki's is a book titled *Harakat Al-Ikhwan Al-Muslimin Fi Al-Sudan, 1969 -1989* (The Movement of the Muslim Brotherhood in Sudan 1969-1985). In this book Makki talks in detail about the internal structure of the organization, its recruitment and strategies, and its relation with Nemeri's military regime (1969-1985).[67] Makki's work is the only published work that sheds light on the early history of the Movement, but he relies almost exclusively on personal interviews with the Movement's founders and leaders rather than on documentary evidence.

Another major work about the Islamic Movement in Sudan was published by its leader Hasan al-Turabi in 1988 titled *Al-Harakah Al-Islamiyah Fi Al-Sudan*

---

[65] Hasan Makki Muhammad Ahmad. *Harakat Al-Ikhwan Al-Muslimin Fi Al-Sudan, 1944-1969.* Silsilat Al-Kurrasat Ghayr Al-Dawriyah; Raqm 16. Khartoum - Sudan: Ma'had al-Dirasat al-Afriqiyah wa-al-Asiyawiyah, Jami'at al-Khartum, 1982, 25.

[66] Ibid.,16.

[67] Hasan Makki Muhammad Ahmad. *Al-Harakah Al-Islamiyah Fi Al-Sudan, 1969-1985: Tarikhuha Wa-Khatabuha Al-Siyasi.* Khartoum-Sudan: Ma'had al-Buhuth wa-al-Dirasat al-Ijtima'iyah: Bayt al-Ma'rifah lil-Intaj al-Thaqafi, 1990.

(The Islamic Movement in Sudan). In this book al-Turabi talks in detail about the history of the Movement, its relationship with other Islamic movements, and about his own role in transforming the Movement from a small elite group to a mass political force destined to play a major role in shaping Sudanese political life.[68]

An important work about the Movement's early days, particularly in Egypt, was written by Mohammed al-Kheir Abdelgader, one of the founders of the Islamic Movement in Sudan in the 1940s. In his book *Nashat Al-Harakah Al-Islamiyah Al-Hadisa Fi Al-Sudan* (The Beginning of Modern Islamic Movement in Sudan), Abdelgader details the early days of the Movement in Sudan. He describes several venues by which the Brotherhood's ideology infiltrated Sudanese society. The first venue was the Egyptian nationals who worked in Sudan and were members of the Brotherhood in Egypt. These nationals propagated the Brotherhood ideology among their Sudanese colleagues. The second venue was the Sudanese students who studied in Egypt, where they came in contact with the Brotherhood. Upon their return to Sudan during breaks and holidays, these students, according to Abdelgader, worked to spread the Brotherhood ideology, especially among high school students and their families.[69] Abdelgader's book is the only book written by one of the founders of the Movement in Sudan, and it details Movement activities, organizational structure, and recruitment strategies in its early years.

The fourth major work on the Islamic Movement in Sudan entitled *Turabi's Revolution: Islam and Power in Sudan* has been written by Abdelwahab el-Affendi, until recently a long-time member of the Movement. In this book, el-Affendi provides a detailed the history of the Movement, particularly after al-Turabi assumed its leadership in the mid-1960s. El-Affendi explains the reasons that contributed to the unprecedented growth of the Movement in Sudan, such as

---

[68] Hasan al-Turabi. *Al-Harakah Al-Islamiyah Fi Al-Sudan*, Afaq Al-Ghad 8. Kuwait: Dar al-Qalam, 1988.

[69] Mohammed al-Khier Abdelgader. *Nashat Al-Harakah Al-Islamiyah Al-Hadisa Fi Al-Sudan.* Khartoum: Sudan: Sudanese House For Books, 1999.

the declining influence of the Nationalists and Communists in the Arab World following the 1967 war with Israel, the declining influence of the Sudanese Communist Party among Sudanese intellectuals following the party massacre in 1971 at the hands of Nemeri's military regime, and the failure of the two major political parties in Sudan (al-Umma and the DUP) to develop a comprehensive post-independence development program.

Furthermore, el-Affendi attributes the unprecedented growth of the Movement to the accommodationist policy that the Movement used in relation to Nemeri's military regime, and its modernist stand on many issues that are problematic to other Islamic political movements in the region, such as the role of women and non-Muslims in Islamic societies, arts and music in Islam, and working and dealing with non-Islamic secular regimes and political parties.[70]

Most of the works about the Islamic Movement in Sudan have been written by Sudanese Islamists themselves, rare exceptions to the rule are the contributions of Haydar Ibrahim Ali.[71] Through a series of publications, Ali analyzes the history of the Islamic Movement in Sudan, its ideology, and particularly the writings of its main leader Hasan al-Turabi. Ali argues that the rise of the Islamic Movement in Sudan was due in large part to the absence of real political alternatives for Sudanese intellectuals. He also argues that the increasing influence of the Movement in Sudanese public life is due to the unprecedented wealth that the Movement accumulated through the establishment of Islamic banks and other Islamic economic institutions. This is why, Ali argues, that the Islamic Movement in Sudan literally functioned both as a political party and a

---

[70] Abdelwahab El-Affendi. *Turabi's Revolution: Islam and Power in Sudan* London: UK: Grey Seal Books, 1991.

[71] Haydar Ibrahim Ali. *Al-Tayyarat Al-Islamiyah Wa-Qadiyat Al-Dimuqratiyah* / Beirut: Lebanon: Markaz Dirasat al-Wahdah al-`Arabiyah, 1996, *Azmat Al-Islam Al-Siyasi :Al-Jabhah Al-Islamiyah Al- Qawmiyah Fi Al-Sudan* Namudhajan Alexandria: Egypt: Markaz al-Dirasat al-Sudaniyah, 1992, *Lahut Al-Tahrir :Al-Din Wa-Al-Thawrah Fi Al-`Alam Al- Thalith* Alexandria: Egypt: Dar al-Nil, 1993, *Suqut Al-Mashru Al-Hadari* Khartoum-Sudan: Markaz al-Dirasat al-Sudaniyah, 2004.

major employer and lender (where unemployment among college graduates is more than 40%).

The Movement, according to Ali, was functioning as a "State within a State." Besides the Islamic banks, the Movement created an economic empire that was in total control of the Sudanese economy by the mid-1980s. This economic empire consisted of economic and business enterprises, health and non-profit organizations, which provided services for the needy and the poor in all parts of Sudan, educational institutions, such as private Islamic schools and universities, media enterprises that included more than 17 published newspapers and magazines.

A unique work that detailed the history of the Sudanese military establishment and its relations with ideological parties and groups such as the Sudanese Communist Party, Arab Nationalists, and the Islamic Movement was published by Isam al-Deen Mirghani, a former military officer in the Sudanese army. In his book *Al-Gayash Al-Sudani Wa Al-Siyasa* (The Sudanese Military and Politics), Mirghani explains how the recruitment strategy of the Islamic Movement worked among members of the Sudanese military. He identifies the Islamists' early attempts to infiltrate the military establishment. He also shows that the rising influence of Communists and Arab Nationalists coupled with the conflict between the Brotherhood and the army in Egypt limited the Movement's abilities to attract members of the military establishment to its ranks. According to Mirghani, that all changed after the Reconciliation Accord of 1977 between Nemeri and Islamists and later the declaration of Islamic laws in 1983 which resulted in an unprecedented growth of the Movement's influence among the military.[72]

Most of the works in English about the Islamic Movement in Sudan were written after its successful military coup in 1989. These studies are concerned mainly with issues such as the position of minorities, non-Muslims, and women

---

[72] Isam al-Deen Mirghani. *Al-Geash Al-Sudani Wa Al-Siyasa*. Cairo: Egypt: Afrongi For Printing, 2002, 236.

36

under the current Islamic regime in Sudan, the discourse of its leader Hasan al-Turabi and his ideology, or its relations with other Islamic movements worldwide following the September 11th attacks. [73] Yet none of these works attempts to address the central questions of the nature of the Islamic Movement in Sudan and the reasons behind its emergence and development, its internal structure, early history, ideology, recruitment, financial institutions, and the role of its charismatic leader (al-Turabi) in transforming the Movement from a small elite-centered pressure group to a mass social and political movement.

Most of the published works on the Islamic Movement in Sudan in English have focused only on some partial aspects of the Movement, such as the

---

[73] For these contributions see Ibrahim Abu-Rabi. "Arabism, Islamism, and the Future of Arab World." *Arab Studies Quarterly* 22, no. 1 (2000): 91, Korwa G Adar. "Ethno-Religious Nationalism in Sudan: The Enduring Constraint on the Policy of National Identity " In *Shifting African Identities*, edited by Simon; Martine Dodds Bekker & Meshack M. Khosa. Cape Town, South Africa: Human Sciences Research Council, 2001, Amina Alrasheed Nayel. "Sudanese Women in Exile: Islam, Politics, and the State." *Respect* 1, no. 4 (2006): 1-23. Abdullahi Ahmed An-Na`im, ed. *Islamic Fundamentalism and Social Change: Neither The "End of History" Nor A "Clash of Civilizations"*. Edited by Gerrie & Busuttil Haar, James J. The Freedom to Do God's Will: Religious Fundamentalism and Social Change. New York: Routledge, 2002. Abdullahi Ahmed An-Na`im. and Francis M. Deng. "Self-Determination and Unity: The Case of Sudan." *Law & Policy* 19, no. 3 (1997): 199. Roksana Bahramitash. "Myths and Realities of the Impact of Political Islam on Women: Female Employment in Indonesia and Iran." *Development in Practice* 14, no. 4 (2004): 508-20. François Burgat. *The Islamic Movement in North Africa* Austin, TX: Center for Middle Eastern Studies, University of Texas at Austin 1993. Lampi Sorensen Claes-John. "The Islamic Movement in Sudan: External Relations and Internal Power Struggle after 1989." Master, American University Beirut, 2002. Dan Connell. "Political Islam under Attack in Sudan." *Middle East Report*, no. 202 (1996): 34-36.Francis M Deng. "Sudan--Civil War and Genocide." *Middle East Quarterly* 8, no. 1 (2001): 13. John L. Esposito. "Sudan's Islamic Experiment." *The Muslim World* 76, no. 3-4 (1986): 181-202. Carolyn Fluehr-Lobban and Richard Lobban. "The Sudan since 1989: National Islamic Front Rule (Cover Story)." *Arab Studies Quarterly* 23, no. 2 (2001): 1. Sondra Hale. "Sudanese Women and Revolutionary Parties: The Wing of the Patriarch." *MERIP Middle East Report*, no. 138 (1986): 25-30. Sondra Hale. "Gender Politics and Islamization in Sudan." Women Living Under Muslim Laws http://www.wluml.org/english/pubsfulltxt.shtml?cmd%5B87%5D=i-87-2670. Sondra Hale. "Mothers and Militias: Islamic State Construction of the Women Citizens of Northern Sudan." *Citizenship Studies* 3, no. 3 (1999): 373. Sondra Hale. "Activating the Gender Local: Transnational Ideologies And "Women's Culture" In Northern Sudan." *Journal of Middle East Women's Studies* 1, no. 1 (2005): 29-52. Abdullahi Ali Ibrahim. "A Theology of Modernity: Hasan Al-Turabi and Islamic Renewal in Sudan" *Africa Today* 46, no. 3/4 (1999): 195. Mohamed Mahmoud. "Islam and Islamization in Sudan: The Islamic National Front." In *Religion and Peacemaking*. Washington, DC: U.S Institute of Peace, 1997. Judith Miller. "Faces of Fundamentalism. Hasan Al-Turabi and Muhammed Fadlallah." *Foreign Affairs* 73, no. 6 (1994): 123-42.

application of *Shari'a* laws in Sudan in 1983 and the role of Movement leadership in implementing these laws. Following the Movement's successful military coup in 1989, more works about the new "Islamic" government in Sudan have been published.

An example of such works is an edited book by Alexander De Waal titled *Islamism and its Enemies in the Horn of Africa*. In this book De Waal and his collaborators examine the phenomenon of political Islam in the region. They explain how the fundamentalist Islamic ideologies helped create a sense of unity and belonging among the Muslims in the region. Islamic fundamentalist groups according to De Waal were able to deliver vital social and economic services to local populations and thus enhanced their position among the locals. Special attention in this book was given to political Islam and its 'destructive' role in Sudan and Somalia.[74] De Waal and his collaborators mistakenly argued that political Islam played a major role in the collapse of the state in Somalia and in the civil war in Sudan. The weakness of such arguments is that the Somali state collapsed long before the rising influence of Islamists in the country and was largely due to regional and ethnic differences between Somali clans; while in Sudan the first civil war (1955-1972) and the second civil war (1983-2004) were largely the result of long-standing religious, ethnic, and regional differences between the South and the North.

Islam, Sectarianism and Politics in Sudan since the Mahadiyya by Gabriel Warburg is another book that covers the politics of Islam in Sudan. In this book, the author analyzes the history of Islam and politics since the Mahadiyya Revolution in 1881. Great attention is given to the cause of the Mahadiyya revolution which is described by the author as "an anti-colonial movement, seeking to liberate Sudan from alien rule and to unify the Muslim *ummah*

---

[74] Alexander De Waal, ed. *Islamism and Its Enemies in the Horn of Africa*. Bloomington, IN: Indiana University Press, 2004.

(nation)." [75] The author's methodology in examining the politics of Islam in Sudan is a clear manifestation of "society in crisis" and "ideology vacuum" theories that dominate the literature of political Islam.

Warburg argues that the resurgence of political Islam in the 1960s was a direct result of the failure of Nasserism and other popular ideologies following the 1967 war. While this explanation may be true in the case of other Islamic movements in the region, particularly in Egypt, this was not the case in Sudan. In the 1960s the Arab Nationalists, Nasserists, and Communists enjoyed wide support among Sudanese intellectuals. This support reached its culmination in the 1968 parliamentary election when the Sudanese Communist Party (SCP) captured the majority of seats in the Graduate Constituencies which were designated for college graduates only. While the "society in crisis" and the "ideology vacuum" theories can provide some explanations for the rising of political Islam in some countries, they cannot fully explain the phenomenon of political Islam in Sudan.

T. Abdou Maliqalim Simone offers an inside look into the Islamic Movement government in Sudan in his book *In Whose Image?: Political Islam and Urban Practices in Sudan*. Simone examines the rising influence of political fundamentalism during the 1985-89 period of democratic rule in the Sudan. He shows how "the *Shari'a* Movement attempted to shape a viable social order by linking religious integrity and economic development, where religious practice was to dominate all aspects of society and individuals' daily lives."[76] The author argues that because the "Sudanese society is remarkably diverse ethnically and religiously, this often led to conflict, fragmentation, and violence in the name of Islam. Finally, the author provides a comparison between the role of Islam in South Africa, which called for more political unity between different religious groups, and the Sudanese 'Islamic' experiment in the period following the 1989

---

[75] Gabriel Warburg. Islam, Sectarianism, and Politics in Sudan since the Mahdiyya. Madison, WI: UW Press, 2003.

[76] T. Abdou Maliqalim Simone. *In Whose Image?: Political Islam and Urban Practices in Sudan.* Chicago, IL: University of Chicago Press, 1994.

Islamists' coup, which resulted in intensifying the violence between different religious and ethnic groups in the country.

The Root Causes of Sudan's Civil Wars by Douglas H. Johnson is another book that examines the issue of Islam and politics in Sudan and how Islam played a major role in shaping Sudanese identity and thus became one of the causes of the unending civil war in the country is. In this book, Johnson argues there is not one cause of war, but many, and there is not a single war, but a network of inter-related violent conflicts. Johnson successfully rebukes the dominant trend among western scholars who claim religion as the main cause of the civil war in Sudan. He heavily criticizes reductionist explanations of the conflict and calls for a more comprehensive approach to examine the roots of the conflicts in Sudan. Johnson does not eschew discussion of religion or ethnicity, but analyses "how religious affiliation or race determine access to political power and economic opportunity, and how identity and affiliations are forged through these processes."[77] Johnson suggests other causes of wars in Sudan such as nationalism, competition for natural resources –particularly the Nile waters and oil in the south- marginalization, and the politics of neighboring countries: Kenya, Uganda, Libya, Egypt, Ethiopia, and Eritrea.

The main finding of this literature review is that Islamic movements are increasingly becoming important actors in the political arenas of the Islamic world. Approaches to the study of the phenomenon of Islamic movements in the West are generally characterized by limited scope for such important phenomena. The cultural-religious approach, despite its wide acceptance among politicians following the September 11th attacks, failed to uncover the reasons behind the rising influence of Islamic movements. The socio-economic approach which is also widely accepted by academicians, particularly Marxists and leftists, also failed to provide clear explanations for the phenomenon of Islamists and their

---

[77] Douglas H. Johnson. *The Root Causes of Sudan's Civil Wars.* Bloomington, IN: Indiana University Press, 2003.

rising influence. The failure of this approach is due in large part to its reductionist nature as it tries inadequately to explain the Islamists' rising influence only economically while ignoring other important factors such as religion, culture, and history. This study will utilize the broader social movement theory.

Another problem with the western literature on Islamic Movements is its imposing generalizations about the Muslim Brotherhood in Egypt on other Islamic Movements in the region, thus ignoring the historic, socio-cultural differences of the former. It is the objective of this study, therefore, to provide an interpretation for the rising influence of the Islamic Movement in Sudan in the specific historical context of the country and to understand the different factors behind its emergence and development in Sudanese political life. Several factors that contributed to the unprecedented success of the Islamic Movement in Sudan are compared to other Islamic movements in the region. Ideology, organizational design and structure, economic institutions, political maneuvers and flexibility will be examined in great detail. Consequently the perspective taken in this study is unique especially because most of the information gathered for this thesis relies on resources published in Arabic.

CHAPTER II

Methodology

Introduction

The initial problems surrounding the term of Islamic Fundamentalism/Movements and its definition are further compounded by the approaches and theoretical frameworks used to explain the phenomenon. Most explanations evolve around "the society in crisis" theory. As to the nature of these crises and their relation to Islamic Movements, two trends appear to be dominant in the literature, particularly, the Western one. The first of these trends tend to emphasize on Islamic movements as traditional reaction to the impact of Western modernity and modernization on Muslim traditions, culture, social structure, and value systems. This group of writings heavily emphasizes external cultural and ideological factors as major reasons behind the phenomenon of political Islam or the rising influence of Islamic Movements in the Islamic world.

The second trend tends to overemphasize the socio-economic factors of Muslim societies. Islamic Movements, according to the representatives of this trend, represent the political ideology of certain social classes that used Islam and Islamic slogans and symbols to reach power. These two schools of thought are not as mutually exclusive as it may appear, and between these two trends in literature, there is a host of writings and approaches that oscillate between the two main poles.

Another approach that was suggested by some researchers in trying to explain the phenomenon of Islamic movements is the Gramscian approach. Representatives of this approach:

> . . . seek to examine political Islam as an instrument of political protest to de-legitimize the hegemonic or status quo power at both the domestic and international level, according to Gramsci; this is to be accomplished by

creating a revolutionary movement based on a coherent ideology, unified organization, and long-term strategy.[78]

An isolated approach or theoretical framework that tried to explain the phenomenon of Islamic Movements emerged following the 9/11 terrorist attacks on the United States. This approach looks to the phenomenon as a problem with Islam itself. Unlike other approaches and theoretical frameworks, representatives of this approach (mainly outside academia) tend to look to all Islamic groups and movements as one homogenous group that advocates the use of violence to achieve their goals.

The Modernization Explanations

As indicated above the first group of writings explains Islamic Movements as traditional reaction to the challenges of modernization. Lambton, for example, argues that Islam and its rigid character were the main factors behind the clash between Western and Islamic civilizations. She pointed out that Islam unlike Christianity or Judaism is a religion of the book and hence a fundamentalist religion par excellence. The Quran, she argues:

> . . . is believed by Muslims to be the literally inspired word of God. It claims finality in the context of the wider claim that it is the climax of the revelation of Judaism and Christianity. Islam is an ideology of the book and in this sense it is, per se fundamentalist. Judaism and Christianity are not per se fundamentalist, though fundamentalist movements are to be found in both.[79]

Another representative of the "modernization" trend is W. Montgomery. In his work *Islamic Fundamentalism and Modernity*, Montgomery argues along the same line, emphasizing Islamic Fundamentalism as an Islamic negative reaction to the challenge of Western modernity and modernization in general.[80] Montgomery acknowledges that the origin of this reaction was rooted in a

---

[78] Thomas J. Butko. "Revelation or Revolution: A Gramscian Approach to the Rise of Political Islam." *British Journal of Middle Eastern Studies* 31, no. 1 (2004): 141-42.

[79] Lambton, 34.

[80] W. Montgomery. *Islamic Fundamentalism and Modernity*. New York: Routledge, 1988.

particular interpretation of Islam, and not Islam itself, and thus dilutes Lambton's main argument about the contradiction between Islam and modernization.

The problem of the modernization framework is the Eurocentric definition for the term modernity. The concept of modernity, as historically developed by Western thinkers, has initially emerged as an epochal concept. Modernity denotes both the historical transition of Europe from the medieval periods to modern times and the deep cultural and socio-economic transformations that accompanied this transition. Central to these social transformations were Europe's transition from feudalism to capitalism, the separation of state and church as manifested in the Reformation and Renaissance movements, and the new scientific and geographical discoveries that radically changed the history of Europe and the world.[81]

In this scheme, capitalism and the secularization of the state and society have been considered by most modern Western thinkers to be the most central elements of modernization and the scale by which other cultures should be measured. Colonialism, in this context, has been celebrated by modernization advocates as the spearhead of modernity and modernization and as the external motor that would propel stagnant Muslim societies into modernity. The issues of Islamic Movements, accordingly, tend to be addressed from within the ideal –type traditional-modern dichotomy and the phenomenon of Islamic movements is usually reduced to a single, cultural contradiction explainable in terms of the traditionalism –modernity dichotomy.

Many scholars and researchers, therefore, tend to disagree with the view that Islamic movements represent a traditional reaction to modernization and modernity.[82] Dessouki for instance, points out that new revivalism is not

---

[81] Abdullahi Ali Ibrahim. "A Theology of Modernity: Hasan Al-Turabi and Islamic Renewal in Sudan." *Africa Today* 46, no. 3/4 (1999): 195-222.

[82] For example see: Abdelwahab El-Affendi. "Eclipse of Reason: The Media in the Muslim World." *Journal of International Affairs* 47, no. 1 (1993): 163. "The Long March from Lahore to Khartoum: Beyond the 'Muslim Reformation'." *Bulletin (British Society for Middle Eastern Studies)* 17, no. 2 (1990): 137-51. *Turabi's Revolution: Islam and Power in Sudan.* . London: UK: Grey Seal Books 1991. John L. Esposito. *The Islamic Threat: Myth or Reality?* New York:

essentially a rejection of "Westernizing" influence; rather it is basically the product of new thought-forces that have been generated within Islam itself as a result of, and in response to, profound changes in the twentieth century."[83]

Large numbers of Middle Eastern scholars and some Western scholars in opposition to the argument of "modernity" school, such as Esposito, Voll, al-Effendi, and Dessouki, see some of these Islamic movements as agents of modernization in their societies. For example, as noted by John Esposito "many fundamentalist leaders have had the best education, enjoy responsible positions in society, and are adept at harnessing the latest technology to propagate their views and create viable modern institutions such as schools, hospitals, and social service agencies".[84] Voll, in his commentary about the Islamic movement in Sudan, argues that the latter is an important agent of modernization in the country.[85] He suggests that the emergence of the Movement was less a reaction to modernity and modernization than to the superstition and mysticism of what he calls the "popular Islam" of traditional Sufi orders and the two main religious sects (al-Ansar and al-Khatmiyya).[86] Fundamentalist organizations, he contends, were consciously created by young, modern educated, cosmopolitan Sudanese in an important effort to create more cosmopolitan attitudes in Sudan, as well as organizations that were central and national as opposed to rural and local in orientation.[87]

Oxford University Press, 1992. *Political Islam: Revolution, Radicalism, or Reform?* Boulder, Colo.: Lynne Rienner Publishers, 1997. *Voices of Resurgent Islam.* New York: Oxford University Press, 1983. John L. Esposito & Yvonne Y. Haddad. *Islam, Gender, and Social Change.* Oxford: Oxford University Press, 1997. John L. Esposito & James Piscatori. "Democratization and Islam." *Middle East Journal* 45, no. 3 (1991). John L. Esposito. John Obert Voll. *Makers of Contemporary Islam.* New York: Oxford University Press, 2001.

[83] Ali E. Dessouki, ed. *Islamic Resurgence in the Arab World.* New York: Praeger Publishers 1982, 71-72.

[84] John Esposito. *The Islamic Threat: Myth or Reality?*, New York, Oxford University Press, 1992, 7.

[85] Gabriel Warburg & Uri M. Kupferschmidt. *Islam, Nationalism, and Radicalism in Egypt and the Sudan.* Westport, CT: Praeger, 1983.

[86] Ibid.

[87] Ibid.

Voll's argument is also resonant in the writings of Hasan al-Turabi, the leader of the Islamic Movement in Sudan. Al-Turabi suggests that his movement was provoked by Western values that existed in opposition to the Muslim faith. He maintains that his movement is a creation against Communism in particular.[88] Most importantly, the Islamic Movement in Sudan, al-Turabi suggests, is an authentic Islamic response to the corrupting impact of Sufi teachings on the minds of the Sudanese people.[89] Given this fact, Islamic movements might be seen as a reaction to certain modern Western values, but not modernity or modernization. El-Affendi, on the other hand, argues that the Islamic Movement in Sudan is not inherently modern, but is an important vehicle of modernization in Sudan.[90]

The Socio-economic and Political Explanations

The second trend in the literature is represented in large by Marxist writings on the Islamic Movements phenomenon. Representatives of this school analyze the crisis- producing Islamic movements in terms of the crisis of capitalist development in colonized societies. In this context, the class and the character of these political movements are always emphasized. In other words, Islam is always approached as the political ideology of a certain social class or factions of these classes. Examples of social class analysis can be found in the writings of most Marxists and former Marxist scholars in the Middle East such as Falih Abd al-Jabbar, Rifat al-Saeed, and Haydar Ibrahim Ali.[91]

---

[88] Hasan al-Turabi. *Al-Harakah Al-Islamiyah Fi Al-Sudan: Al-Tatawwur Wa-Al-Kasb Wa-Al-Manhaj.* Cairo, Egypt: al-Qari al-`Arabi, 1991.

[89] Ibid.

[90] El-Affendi, *"Turabi's Revolution."*

[91] For example, see: Ali, Haydar Ibrahim. *Al-Ikhwan Wa Al-Askar.* Cairo, Egypt: Markaz al-Hadarah al-Arabiyah, 1993. *Al-Tayyarat Al-Islamiyah Wa-Qadiyat Al-Dimuqratiyah /* Beruit: Lebanon: Markaz Dirasat al-Wahdah al-`Arabiyah, 1996. *Azmat Al-Islam Al-Siyasi :Al-Jabhah Al-Islamiyah Al- Qawmiyah Fi Al-Sudan Namudhajan* Alexandria: Egypt: Markaz al-Dirasat al-Sudaniyah, 1992. *Lahut Al-Tahrir :Al-Din Wa-Al-Thawrah Fi Al-`Alam Al- Thalith* Alexandria: Egypt: Dar al-Nil, 1993. *Suqut Al-Mashru Al-Hadari* Khartoum-Sudan: Markaz al-Dirasat al-Sudaniyah, 2004. Falih Abd al-Jabbar. *Al-Dawlah, Al-Mujtama` Al-Madani Wa-Al-Tahawwul Al-Dimuqrati Fi Al-`Iraq,* Silsilat Dirasat Mashru` Al-Mujtama` Al-Madani Wa-Al-Tahawwul Al-Dimuqrati Fi Al-Watan Al-`Arabi;. al-Qahirah: Markaz Ibn Khaldun bi-al-ishtirak ma`a Dar al-Amin lil-Nashr wa-al-Tawzi`, 1995. "Ayatollahs, Sufis and Ideologues: State, Religion and Social Movements in Iraq." Saqi. *Ma`Alim Al-`Aqlaniyah Wa-Al-Khurafah Fi Al-Fikr Al-Siyasi*

Representatives of this school of thought emphasize political Islam as the political ideology of certain social classes in Muslim societies that have been affected by the transition of pre-capitalist feudal and semi-feudal social formations into capitalism. Representatives of the socio-economic school further argue that Islamic Movements do not express social interests as much as the social fears of the middle classes. Given their rural and agrarian forms of consciousness and their inability to find solutions to the crisis of poverty and problems produced by the rapid and intense process of urbanization, the middle classes increasingly began to look to religion as a refuge.

Ali also suggests that the emergence of political Islam was not only a direct product of the problem of transition to capitalism, but also a strong indication of the failure of the Arab and Muslim bourgeois classes and their inability to develop a rational consciousness. He points out their inability to carry the social mission of industrialization and large scale production in a fashion similar to the European bourgeoisie at the time of its emergence. Ali further argues political Islam today in the Arab world is the ideological expression of an opportunistic bourgeoisie that has used Islam as an ideological disguise to achieve certain class interests. For Ali, political Islam is also the product of the general crisis that Muslims suffer today. It appears in economic, political and cultural dependency on the capitalist centers, poverty, despair, and alienation among the masses, and in political oppression. This general crisis has provided Islamic Movements with the essential conditions to grow, but not to solve this crisis.

Despite the sophistication of Marxist scholars, there nevertheless are many instances of reductionism and imbalance in their writings. Their overemphasis on the class character of this phenomenon prevents them in most cases from developing a comprehensive approach that caters to the multidimensional

Al-'Arabi, Buhuth Ijtima'Iyah ;; 16;. Landan: Dar al-Saqi, 1992. Falih Abd al-Jabbar & Anderson R. Benedict. O'G. *Al-Qawmiyah: Marad Al-'Asr Am Khulasah?* Bayrut, Lubnan: Dar al-Saqi, 1995. Rif'at Al-Sa'id. *Hasan Al-Banna: Mata.. Kayfa... Wa-Limadha?* Cairo: Egypt: Maktabat Madbuli, 1977. *History of the Socialist Movement in Egypt (1900-1925).* Leipzig, Germany: Karl Marx University, 1978.

character of Islamic movements and explains their cross-class character. As well, it fails to explain how this ideology came to be constructed and reconstructed and its relation to Islamic history and tradition. Furthermore, the social backgrounds of individual members of these Islamic political movements demonstrate the incoherence of their arguments. Islamists are neither economically deprived nor do they lack education. They are not loners or marginal individuals searching for the meaning of belonging, or persons unable to get along in modern society. Instead, Islamists come from the most technically advanced sectors of society, often students and graduates of engineering, medicine, and other sciences.

The Gramscian Approach

The Gramscian approach has been applied to the phenomenon of political Islam by few scholars (Butko, 2004 and Usenmez, 2005),[92] but it is an emerging approach in the area of political Islam and it claims to provide better answers and better explanations to the phenomenon of political Islam. According to this approach, "those movements that utilize the ideology of political Islam are not primarily religious groups concerned with issues of doctrine and faith, but political organizations utilizing Islam as a (revolutionary) ideology to attack, criticize, and de-legitimize the ruling elite and power structure on which their authority and legitimacy is based.[93] Also according to the scholars and the advocates of this approach, "since the one-party and military authoritarian state is the norm of most of the Middle East, only Islam has been able to provide the marginalized, alienated, and disgruntled masses with an opposition force capable of articulating their specific grievances and general displeasure with these regimes."[94]

---

[92] See for example Thomas J. Butko. "Revelation or Revolution: A Gramscian Approach to the Rise of Political Islam." *British Journal of Middle Eastern Studies* 31, no. 1 (2004): 141-62., Ozgur Usenmez. "A Neo-Gramscian Approach to the Rise of Political Islam." In *Annual Meeting of the International Studies Association*. Honolulu, Hawaii, 2005.

[93] Thomas J. Butko. "Revelation or Revolution: A Gramscian Approach to the Rise of Political Islam." *British Journal of Middle Eastern Studies* 31, no. 1 (2004): 141-62.

[94] Ozgur Usenmez. "A Neo-Gramscian Approach to the Rise of Political Islam." In *Annual Meeting of the International Studies Association*. Honolulu, Hawaii, 2005.

The Gramscian approach, which is based on the writings of the Italian Marxist Antonio Gramsci (1891-1937), is to some extent similar to the socio-economic approach as both look to the phenomenon of political Islam as a struggle between economically alienated disadvantaged groups or individuals that use religion to express their anger and frustrations and against a state that is controlled by corrupted officials or groups.[95] Both approaches tend to overemphasize the economic factors while minimizing or ignoring other factors that play major roles in shaping the phenomenon of political Islam.

An additional obstacle to theory building in the study of political Islam is its multidisciplinary nature, as noted by Wiktorowicz (2003):

> Multidisciplinary research in Islamic activism is not unified by a shared research agenda. Scattered among a variety of disciplines, publications on Islamic Activism tend to follow narrow sets of research questions, theoretical frameworks, and methodologies, each determined by a particular disciplinary focus. Political scientists, for example, are mostly concerned with how Islam impacts the state and politics; sociologists are interested in exploring the demographic roots of Islamist recruits; religious studies scholars predominately focus on the ideas that motivate Islamic activism; and historians detail the histories of particular Islamic groups. The result is that disciplinary fragmentation has produced greater understanding about each particular element of Islamic activism without developing models or frameworks that explain how all these elements fit together, interact, and influence patterns of Islamic contention.[96]

Toward an Alternative Approach

Any serious theoretical framework for understanding the rise of political Islam in Sudan must keep all above mentioned theoretical deficiencies in mind. It must start by rejecting the highly idealistic, reductionist, and economistic interpretations of the phenomenon that are currently present in the literature. It must also recognize the diverse nature of the phenomenon of political Islam or

---

[95] Antonio Gramsci. *The Antonio Gramsci Reader: Selected Writings, 1916-1935.* Edited by David Hobsbawm & Forgacs J. Eric. New York: New York University Press, 2000.

[96] Quintan Wiktorowicz, ed. *Islamic Activism: A Social Movement Theory.* Bloomington, IN: Indiana University Press, 2003, 3.

Islamic fundamentalism. This phenomenon is by no means monolithic, nor does it possess a coherent ideology that can be analyzed under one master theory across the Muslim societies. It involves a multiplicity of ideologies and movements. Understanding these requires each of the movements and ideologies to be approached and studied as a unique entity and in relation to the specific context of its emergence.

Using a wider theoretical framework and recognizing the gaps that exist in studying political Islam, this study will utilize the Social Movement Theory (SMT)[97] in examining the rise of political Islam in Sudan (1945-1989) as it is represented by the Movement led by Hasan al-Turabi. SMT can provide a more comprehensive understanding of the Islamic movement in the Sudan by exploring the Movement's understudied mechanism of contention, including the tactical use of social networks and family ties; strategic framing designed to facilitate mobilizations, particularly, the selective usage of language and symbols, organizational structure; recruitment among students; women, workers; military personnel and merchants; the economic institutions; the usage of media; the ideology and political alliances and agreements, and tactical consideration in the use of violence and accommodation.

According to Nicholas (2007), the earliest scholars (1920s to 1960s), such as Ralph Turner, Talcott Parsons, Neil Smelser, and Herbert Blumer who studied social movements, largely viewed them as irrational or semi-rational responses to

---

[97]The term "social movements" was introduced in 1850 by the German Sociologist Lorenzo von Stein in his book "*History of the French Social Movement from 1789 to the Present* (1850).For detailed information about Social Movement Theory (SMT) see: Donatella Della, & Mario Diani, *Social Movements: An Introduction* 2nd ed. Ames, IA Blackwell Publishing Limited, 2006.Marco Giugni, Doug McAdam & Charles Tilly, ed. *How Social Movements Matter* Minneapolis, MN: University of Minnesota Press, 1999. John D. McCarthy & Mayer N. Zald,. "Resource Mobilization and Social Movements: A Partial Theory." *The American Journal of Sociology* 82, no. 6 (1977): 1212-41. Aldon Morris. "Reflections on Social Movement Theory: Criticisms and Proposals." *Contemporary Sociology* 29, no. 3 (2000): 445-54. Sidney Tarrow. *Power in Movement: Social Movements and Contentious Politics*. 2nd ed. Cambridge: UK: Cambridge University Press, 1998.Charles Tilly. *Social Movements, 1768 - 2004*. Boulder, CO Paradigm Publishers 2004. Quintan Wiktorowicz. "Islamic Activism and Social Movement Theory: A New Direction for Research." *Mediterranean Politics* 7, no. 3 (2002): 187-211. *Islamic Activism: A Social Movement Theory* Bloomington, IN: Indiana University Press, 2003.

malfunctioning institutions and norms; collective behavior and related theories constituted the dominant paradigm that guided research of social movements.[98] These theories argued that social movements were a form of collective behavior that emerged when significant social and cultural breakdowns occurred. As a form of collective behavior, social movements were considered spontaneous, unorganized, and unstructured phenomena that were discontinuous with institutional and organizational behavior. In this view, emotions and irrational ideologies were central because movements occurred in highly charged contexts characterized by mass enthusiasm, collective excitement, rumor, social contagion, and eventual mass hysteria. Thus, social movements and movement participants were viewed as irrational, given the unpredictability and heavy emotional content of these movements. Collective behavior theory assumed a direct link between emotions and irrationality.[99]

The Civil Rights Movement and the movements it helped spawn were the major catalysts that shattered the intellectual viability of collective behavior theory. When the principal formulators of those theories sought to understand such movements, they found it necessary to reject the collective behavior model and its imagery of the emotional crowd. In so doing, resource mobilization and political process theorists (e.g., McCarthy and Zald 1977; Gamson 1975, Tilly 1978, Mc Adam 1982, and Oberschall 1973) have generated a rich plethora of social movement concepts that will continue to yield theoretical insights. They argued that self-interested individuals cooperate in contentious political activities because it is the only way to ensure sufficient resources (money, labor, and knowledge legitimacy) to press their claims within the state. [100]

[98] Walter J. Nicholls. "The Geographies of Social Movements" *Geography Compass* 1, no. 3 (2007): 607-22.

[99] Donatella Della Porta & Mario Diani. *Social Movements: An Introduction* 2nd ed. Ames, IA: Blackwell Publishing Limited, 2006, 11.

[100] Aldon Morris. "Reflections on Social Movement Theory: Criticisms and Proposals." *Contemporary Sociology* 29, no. 3 (2000): 445-54.

Social movements are collective forms of contentious politics activated for the purposes of achieving political goals through nontraditional means (e.g. protest, boycotts, and public campaigns) versus strictly electoral politics, (McAdam et al. 2001). They are collective in the sense that individuals and organizations establish networks with one another in the hopes of attaining their common objective. They are contentious because in putting forth their claims, they come into conflict with the interests of others. And they are political because the state in one way or other is involved in this process, either as an object of claims, allies of certain forces, and/or monitors of contention.[101]

Social movements are also defined as "a collective attempt to further a common interest or secure a common goal, through collective action outside the sphere of established institutions."[102] A revolutionary social movement aims at radical change, but not always by radical methods. Three characteristics differentiate social movements from other types of collective behavior (crowds, or mobs, or terrorist groups): a high degree of internal organization; typically longer duration, often spanning many years; and the deliberate attempt to reorganize society itself.[103] By these definitions the Islamic Movement in Sudan is a revolutionary social movement since it evidently has all the necessary characteristics: the Movement has a pyramid structure of command with the General Secretary and the *Shura* Council at the top of the Movement; the Movement has existed for more than 60 years; and it aims at radical changes of Sudanese society.

In other words, social movements have not been examined as objects of inquiry in their own right. Years ago however, sociologists and political scientists, embarked on a research program that resulted in a series of concepts and theories that helped to reveal the complex processes and mechanisms involved in making social movements (McAdam 1982; McAdam et al. 2001; McCarthy and Zald

---

[101] Charles Tilly. *Social Movements, 1768 - 2004*. Boulder, CO: Paradigm Publishers, 2004.

[102] Anthony Giddens. *Sociology*. 4th ed. Cambridge: UK: Polity Press, 2001, 24.

[103] John J. Macionis. *Sociology*. 7th ed. New Jersey: Prentice Hall, 1999.

1977; Melucci 1996; Tarrow 1989, 1998; Tilly 1986 and Touraine 1981).[104] This literature showed that although people may be discontented with economic and political processes, they do not automatically form into political collectivities to transmit their grievances to the political sphere. For this to occur, people must perceive problems as presenting a threat to their common interests, resources need to be pooled and organized, beliefs in the cause must be constructed, political openings need to be available to advance the cause, etc. This literature, in other words, directly assessed the complex steps involved in translating grievances into collective action.[105]

Also, because political Islam is a very dynamic phenomenon, SMT can provide the needed tools to study this phenomenon and its dynamic nature. Social movements like the Islamic Movement in Sudan are in reality highly dynamic entities, being in constant flow and motion. Like Edward Thompson's notion of social class, a social movement is not just a thing; it is primarily a process, and should be studied as a historical phenomenon in a span of time.[106] A narrative of the movement, which perceives it as a process, offers a more comprehensive idea about its particular character. One cannot comprehend the Islamic Movement in Sudan, for instance, if one does not recognize its historical dynamics. Considering social movements in motion is a crucial issue, because the concern's focus, and even the direction of the movements, may change over time as a result of both internal and external factors. Factors such as demonstration effect, repression, internal rifts, change in economic or political conditions, and expansion in their social base are likely to influence the direction of social movements.[107]

Using the SMT to analyze the phenomenon of political Islam is not by any means a unique approach. Several leading scholars and researchers have called for the incorporation of world views on Islamic movements into broader debates of

---

[104] Morris, 445-54.
[105] Tilly, 2004.
[106] Edward Palmer Thompson. *The Making of the English Working Class*. London: Penguin, 1963.
[107] Asef Bayat. "Islamism and Social Movement Theory." *Third World Quarterly* 26, no. 6 (2005): 891-908.

social movement theory and successfully used them in providing better explanations to the phenomenon of Islamic activism.[108] In their works, these scholars and researchers used Social Movement Theory as a unifying framework that provided an effective model for inquiry that furthered the boundaries of research on Islamic movements.

There are several theories that explain conditions in which social movements arise such as structural-functional theory, political opportunity theory, and resources mobilization theory.[109] This study presents a set of concepts and propositions that articulate the resource mobilization approach as the major theory that explains the conditions that led to the unprecedented rise of the Islamic Movement in Sudan. I chose this approach over the other two approaches (structural-functional theory and political opportunity theory) because resource mobilization theory deals in general terms with the dynamics and tactics of social movement growth, decline, and change. As such, it provides a corrective to the practical theorists, who naturally are most concerned with justifying their own tactical choices, and it also adds realism, power, and depth to the truncated research on and analysis of social movements offered by many social scientists.[110]

Resource mobilization theory emerged in response to the shortcomings of the early socio-psychological approaches to social movements. Rather than viewing social movements as constituted by irrational or psychologically deprived individuals, who join in response to structural strains, resource mobilization theory, views social movements as rational, organized manifestations of collective

---

[108] See the works of Quintan Wiktorowicz, ed. *Islamic Activism: A Social Movement Theory* Bloomington, IN: Indiana University Press, 2003. Quintan Wiktorowicz. "Islamic Activism and Social Movement Theory: A New Direction for Research." *Mediterranean Politics* 7, no. 3 (2002): 187-211. Emmanuel Karagiannis. "Political Islam and Social Movement Theory: The Case of Hizb Ut-Tahrir in Kyrgyzstan." *Religion, State & Society* 33, no. 2 (2005): 137-49. Asef Bayat. "Islamism and Social Movement Theory." *Third World Quarterly* 26, no. 6 (2005): 891-908. Munson Ziad. "Islamic Mobilization: Social Movement Theory and the Egyptian Muslim Brotherhood " *The Sociological Quarterly* 42, no. 4 (2001): 487–510.

[109] Emmanuel Karagiannis. "Political Islam and Social Movement Theory: The Case of Hizb Ut-Tahrir in Kyrgyzstan." *Religion, State & Society* 33, no. 2 (2005): 137-49.

[110] John D. McCarthy & Mayer N. Zald. "Resource Mobilization and Social Movements: A Partial Theory." *The American Journal of Sociology* 82, no. 6 (1977): 1212-1241.

action. As an approach, its central contention is that while grievances are ubiquitous, movements are not. As a result there must be intermediary variables that translate individualized discontent into organized contention.

For resource mobilization theory, resources and mobilizing structures, such as formal social movement organizations, are needed to collectivize what would otherwise remain individual grievances. Movements are not seen as irrational outbursts intended to alleviate psychological distress, but rather as organized contention structured through mechanisms of mobilization that provide strategic resources for sustained collective action.[111]

The resource mobilization approach emphasizes both societal support and constraint of social movement phenomena. It examines the variety of resources that must be mobilized, the linkages of social movements to other groups, the dependence of movements upon external support for success, and the tactics used by authorities to control or incorporate movements. The shift in emphasis is evident in much of the work published in this area (J. Wilson 1973; Tilly 1973, 1975; Gamson 1975; Oberschall 1973; Lipsky 1968; Downs 1972; Mc-Carthy and Zald 1973, Buechler, Klandermans, 1984, Marullo, 1988, Fox, 1991, 1999, Kendall, 2005). This approach depends more upon political, sociological and economic theories than upon the social psychology of collective behavior.

In general, resource mobilization theory claims that social movements are unlikely to emerge without necessary resources. It argues that grievances are a crucial but not sufficient condition for the rise of a social movement. In fact, there are grievances everywhere in the world, many of which never lead to the formation of a social movement. The real question then is what besides grievances is needed for the emergence of a social movement? According to the resource mobilization theory, social movements must be able to mobilize key resources if they are to emerge. Its focus, therefore, is on how social movements recruit and mobilize individuals, raise money and build economic institutions,

---

[111] Quintan Wiktorowicz. "Islamic Activism and Social Movement Theory: A New Direction for Research." *Mediterranean Politics* 7, no. 3 (2002): 187-211.

train members, frame their messages, and present their ideology and so on.[112]

Rather than viewing social movements as consisting of angry or alienated individuals who join together in response to economic deprivations or challenges of modernization, this theory approaches them as rational, organized, manifestations of collective action.[113] While for the most part, social movement theory tends to downplay the role of ideology in mobilizing collective action. Ideology encompasses ideas, beliefs, values, and symbols, which can motivate individual participation and give coherence to collective action.[114] The Islamic Movement in Sudan provides a good test case of the importance of ideology in mobilizing the population. The unprecedented rise of the Islamic Movement in Sudan will be argued in this study to be a direct result of the Movement's abilities to mobilize all key resources (recruitment, organizational structure, finance, ideology, media, etc) and to act as a cohesive social movement for more than 60 years.

---

[112] Ibid., 195-96.

[113] Ibid., 196.

[114] John Wilson. *Introduction to Social Movements*. New York: Basic Books, 1972.

CHAPTER III

Sudan: Historical Background

Introduction

The history of the Sudan is as diverse as its people. However, much of its ancient history is either poorly known or dimly seen through the lens of oral tradition. Most available information concerns the development of the central and northern areas of the Nile Valley, but even for these areas much remains to be learned. In the 1960s considerable information came to light from archeological efforts to study sites in the Nubia before they were covered by waters of the Aswan High Dam, Lake Nasser reservoir built in 1970.[115] The boundaries of the contemporary Sudanese state were established by the British in the wake of their conquest in 1898. Before the nineteenth century, the territory was the eastern reaches of what medieval Arabs called *bilad al-Sudan* (the land of black people), a broad band that extended through central Africa.[116]

The Islamic States

The period between the sixteenth and nineteenth centuries witnessed the rise of two Islamized kingdoms: the Funj Sultanate which dominated much of the Sudanese Nile Valley, and the Fur Sultanate which controlled western Sudan (present-day Darfur).

The Funj Sultanate (1504-1820)

At the same time that Ottomans brought northern Nubia into their orbit, a new power, the Funj, had risen in southern Nubia and had supplanted the remnants of the old Christian kingdom of Alawa. The Funj Sultanate was

---

[115] Richard A. Lobban Jr., Robert S. Kramer, Carolyn Lobban-Flueher. *Historical Dictionary of the Sudan.* Lanham, MD: The Scarecrow Press, Inc., 2002, IXXX.

[116] Ann Mosely Lesch. *The Sudan--Contested National Identities.* Bloomington, IN: Indiana University Press 1998, 25.

established in the central and northern Sudan in the early sixteenth century with its capital at Sinnar. The origins of the Funj are still the subject of scholarly dispute.[117] The state that they established followed traditional African patterns of kingship, although Islam rapidly became an important political and cultural force and the Funj converted to Islam.[118] They defeated the earlier major Arab state of the "Abdallab" and incorporated that group into the Funj political and administrative systems as viceroys of the Northern provinces. The founder of the Funj Sultanate, also known as *al-Saltanah al-Zargah* (Black Sultanate), was Amara Dongos (1504-1533).

The Funj ruled directly over some parts of their kingdom such as al-Gezira, southern Blue Nile, and established tributary relations with other territories that came under their jurisdiction by virtue of conquest or necessity. Although the Funj royalty embraced Islam in the early days of the Sultanate, their political system closely resembled the Meroitic and Nubian kingships and was in a way a continuation of their traditions.[119]

The political system of the Funj Sultanate included a loose confederation of sultanates and dependent tribal chieftaincies drawn together under the leadership of Sinnar's *mek* (Sultan). As overlord, the *mek* received tribute, levied taxes, and called on his vassals to supply troops in time of war. Vassal states in turn relied on the *mek* to settle local disorders and resolve internal disputes.[120] The last decades of the Funj era were characterized by dynastic and inter-dynastic

---

[117] For further discussions on the origins of the Funj, see: P. M. Holt. "Funj Origins: A Critique and New Evidence." *The Journal of African History* 4, no. 1 (1963): 39-55. *The Sudan of the Three Niles: The Funj Chronicle, 910-1288/1504-1871.*Boston, MA: Brill Academic Publishers 1999. "A Sudanese Historical Legend: The Funj Conquest of Suba." *Bulletin of the School of Oriental and African Studies, University of London* 23, no. 1 (1960): 1-12. Jay Spaulding. "The Funj: A Reconsideration." *The Journal of African History* 13, no. 1 (1972): 39-53.

[118] Jay Spaulding. "The Funj: A Reconsideration." *The Journal of African History* 13, no. 1 (1972): 39-53.

[119] P. M. Holt. "A Sudanese Historical Legend: The Funj Conquest of Suba." *Bulletin of the School of Oriental and African Studies, University of London* 23, no. 1 (1960): 1-12.

[120] P. M. Holt. "Funj Origins: A Critique and New Evidence." *The Journal of African History* 4, no. 1 (1963): 39-55.

disputes and wars. The end came when Sinnar was conquered by the invading Turco-Egyptian army in 1821.

The Fur Sultanates (1596-1874 and 1899-1916)

The Fur, who were probably related to some tribes of Western Bahr al-Ghazal in the south, were the largest non-Arab tribe in Darfur. While the early history of Darfur is obscure and unknown, at least two states were known to have ruled the region between the thirteenth and sixteenth centuries: the Daju and the Tunjur. After a period of internal wars and unrest the Kayra clan, led by Sulayman Solonge prevailed. Solonge declared Islam as an official religion of the kingdom and united the Fur and non-Fur people in his kingdom. By the eighteenth century, the Kayra Sultanate consolidated its power over the whole region of Darfur and from the present Sudan-Chad border in the west to the White Nile in the east, covering approximately the combined area of the present-day Darfur and Kordofan.[121]

The political system in Darfur resembled that of the Funj to the east and the tradition of the Sudanic kingdoms in West Africa. The Kayra dynasty played a major role in strengthening Islamic teachings in Darfur and Kordofan and in spreading Islam in West Africa. They ruled Darfur from the early seventeenth century to 1874 when they lost their independence to the Turco-Egyptian rule.[122] Kayra's rule was restored again by Ali Dinar (1898-1916) who maintained the kingdom's independence until 1916 when Darfur was conquered by the British and annexed to the Condominium Sudan.

According to Sidahmed and Sidahmed (2005), its under the Funj and Fur Sultanates, the northern and western parts of Sudan became Islamized and largely Arabaized. Arabization and Islamization of these parts came through a lengthy peaceful process that involved demographic movements, particularly the migration of Arab tribes and their settlements in different parts of Sudan,

---

[121] Abel Salam Sidahmed & Alsir Sidahmed. *Sudan.* London, UK: RoutledgeCurzon, 2005, 5.
[122] Ibid., 6.

commercial contacts, and preaching and educational efforts of individual Muslim scholars.[123]

The Turco-Egyptian Rule (1821-1885)

In 1820 Mohammed Ali (1769-1849), the viceroy of Egypt, which was nominally a province of the Ottoman Empire, invaded the Sudan regions with two armies that penetrated the Nile Valley and western Sudan. Muhammad 'Ali was interested in the gold and slaves that the Sudan could provide and wished to control the vast hinterland south of Egypt. By 1821 the Funj and the sultan of Darfur had surrendered to his forces, and the Nilotic Sudan from Nubia to the Ethiopian foothills and from the Atbarah River to Darfur became part of his expanding empire. The Turco-Egyptian rule of Sudan expanded the country's borders to cover the western coast of the Red Sea and its ports, and the southern Sudan up to northern Uganda and Darfur. That is to say, the Sudan with approximately its current political borders came into existence during the Turco-Egyptian period.[124]

The Turco-Egyptian rule of the Sudan established a centralized administration system of government that was supported by a regular army with garrisons in major cities and strategic locations. The new administration divided the country into provinces under the *hikimdar* (governor-general). Each province was administered by a *mudir* (provisional governor) and subdivided into districts. A well-trained bureaucracy developed under Egyptian rule as specialized *diwans* (departments) dealing with administration, accounts, mining, etc. were established in Khartoum and the provinces. Mainly Egyptian clerical and administrative employees staffed these *diwans*. A centralized judiciary system based on Shari'a laws that dealt primarily with personal affairs was established under the auspices of *qadi umum al-Sudan* (Chief Justice for the Sudan). [125]

---

[123] Ibid., 6.
[124] Ibid.,9.
[125] Ibid.,9.

The Turco-Egyptian era also witnessed the introduction of new technologies such as modern means of transportation and communication, building of new irrigation systems, and the introduction of advanced methods of cultivating lands. The major impact of the Turco-Egyptian period was that for the first time in its history the Sudan came into existence as one political entity with clearly defined political borders. The new regime brought together under a single administration the domains of the Funj and the Fur sultanates, the region of Nuba Mountains, and southern Sudan, as well as the country of the Beja in eastern Sudan and the Nubian territories in the far north. [126]

With regard to religious institutions, the era witnessed two important developments: the growth and consolidation of centralized Sufi Brotherhoods and the rising influence of the newly emerging class of *ulama* (religious scholars) who received their training locally and at the famous al-Azhar University in Egypt. By the start of the nineteenth century the Sudan began to receive representatives of Sufi reformism groups which began in Hijaz (Saudi Arabia) and other parts of the Islamic world during the eighteenth century. Chief among these movements were the Sammaniyya and al-Khatmiyya.

The Sammaniyya was introduced in the Sudan by Ahmed al-Tayyib al-Bashier (1742-1824). On the eve of the Turco-Egyptian conquest, the Sammaniyya had spread widely in al-Gazera. Al-Khatmiyya, on the other hand, was established in Sudan through the teachings of Mohammed Osman al-Mirghani (1793-1852) who visited Sudan in 1817-1818 preaching the teachings of his Sufi *tariqa* (order). Both Sufi *tariqas* grew and expanded during that era but al-Khatmiyya *tariqa* was favored by the ruling government because of its ties to Egypt.[127] The rivalries between the two Sufi *tariqas* would play a major role in determining the country's future in later years, as al-Khatmiyya became more closely allied to Egypt and thus called for the Sudan to become part of the

---

[126] Ibid.,9.
[127] Ali Salih Karrar. *The Sufi Brotherhoods in the Sudan*. London, UK: Munster, 1992, 46.

Egyptian state, while the Sammaniyya clearly advocated a creation of an independent Sudanese state.

By the 1880s Turco-Egyptian rule was growing unpopular. Corruption and excessive taxation forced many Sudanese to relinquish their lands and to voice their opposition to the regime. Religious leaders in the North also became increasingly hostile toward the government in Khartoum as a result of its policy that encouraged the appointment of Europeans to political positions in Sudan and its policy concerning the opening of South and the Nuba Mountains to Christian missionaries.

The Mahdia State (1885-1898)

The accumulated grievances and discontent generated over the years by the Turco-Egyptian occupation and its policies erupted in a rebellion in 1881 led by a young religious man named Mohammed Ahmed al-Mahdi (1844-1885). After a series of battles al-Mahdi and his followers, who came to be known as al-Ansar, succeeded in ousting the Turco-Egyptian regime and establishing an independent state in 1885. The success of the Mahdi Revolution could be largely attributed to its charismatic leader, al-Mahdi who created a wide coalition that consisted of heterogeneous forces, each having their own grievances against the Turco-Egyptian regime. As a movement, the Mahdiyya relied on tribal and religious loyalties. Through utilization of these tribal and religious bonds, the Mahdist movement achieved its mass character, and was able to realize its immediate goals of ousting the Turco-Egyptian regime and establishing an independent state.

Al-Mahdi died six months after the capture of Khartoum. His successor, Khalifa Abdullah (1846-1899), from western Sudan led the process of transformation of Mahdia from a revolution to a state. Khalifa Abdullah faced the task of consolidating and protecting the new state while keeping diverse factions unified. He fought the Ethiopians in the East and was able to put down several mutinies against his regime in the West and the North.

Drawing upon a loyal coterie and utilizing an administrative structure and personnel largely taken from the former Turco-Egyptian regime, the Khalifa in general achieved a measure of security and stability for the Mahdist state by the early 1890s. However, by then a major threat to the state had already been developed at the Berlin Conference of 1884-1885, where the partition of Africa by dominant European powers was approved. Great Britain, France, and Italy all had interest in Sudan, though it was the British who ultimately succeeded, neutralizing Italian ambitions in Eritrea and French ambitions in the Upper Nile.

In 1898 the British invaded the Mahdist state with an Anglo-Egyptian army. The invasion faced meager opposition in the north and finally the decisive battle was fought at Karari, north of Omdurman in September 1898, where the British machine guns massacred over 10,000 of al-Ansar. The Khalifa managed to retreat from Omdurman before it was occupied. A year later, in a final battle in Um-Dibikrat in 1899, the Khalifa was killed with a group of his followers.

Despite its short-lived existence the Mahadia state played a major role in spreading Islam in Sudan and strengthening its teachings, particularly in the west and the south where Islamic teachings were frequently mixed with local traditions and beliefs. The Mahdia state also helped create a Sudanese identity with its distinctive characteristics. Before the Mahdia, Sudanese tribes and people looked to themselves as an extension of Arab tribes from Arabia or African tribes from West Africa, the Mahdia revolution emphasized the distinctive characteristics of the Sudanese identity which is a mix of Arab and African bloods and traditions.

The Anglo-Egyptian Condominium (1898-1956)

The new administration in Sudan, which was defined by the Anglo-Egyptian agreement of 1899, gave Egypt a limited influence in Sudan while the actual control of the country was laid in the hands of British officials. The organization of the new government relied on the nineteenth century Turco-Egyptian precedents for central and provincial organization. The early years of British rule were occupied mainly by establishing military control and maintaining order. The Mahdist writings and teachings were outlawed; nonetheless, many Sudanese cherished their adherence to Mahdism, and the Mahdi's posthumous son Sayyid Abdel Rahman (1885-1959) provided the locus of their loyalty. Abdel Rahman was a pragmatic leader who decided to cooperate with the British in order to be able to reorganize his followers.[128] The British were also interested in his cooperation in order to limit the rising influence of Egyptian loyalists in Sudan represented by al-Khatmiyya *tariqa*.

By 1920 a relatively small and articulate Sudanese educated class started to emerge and gradually to replace Egyptian officials in Sudan. Also, Gordon College, which was established in 1901 in Khartoum, started to expand its programs in order to meet the need for more trained Sudanese clerics and low-ranked government officials. By the mid-1930s and after early cooperation with the colonial system, the emerging Sudanese educated class began to grow dissatisfied with their prospects and the lack of possibilities for self-rule. With the emergence of an educated class of Sudanese, resistance to British rule began to shift away from traditional leadership to nascent political parties. [129]

The Sudanese educated class succeeded in creating the Graduate Congress (GC) in 1938. In the beginning Members of GC concentrated their efforts on the expansion of modern education in the country and on other social issues. By the mid-1940s, and with the increasing numbers of Sudanese students inside and outside Sudan, particularly in Egypt, the GC became active politically.[130] In 1942 the leadership of GC submitted a memorandum to the Governor in Khartoum calling for self-determination for Sudan. The struggle within the GC over what appropriate political course to take led to its split into two groups. The first took the slogan 'Sudan for Sudanese' and was supported by the leftists and Sayyid Abdel Rahman al-Mahdi and his Al-Ansar sect, whereas the other group rallied behind the slogan 'Unity of Nile Valley' and enjoyed the support of Sayyid Ali al-

---

[128] Sidahmed & Sidahmed, 19.

[129] Lobban Jr., Kramer, and Lobban-Flueher, 409.

[130] Tim Niblock. Class and Power in Sudan: The Dynamics of Sudanese Politics, 1898-1985. Albany, NY: State University of New York Press, 129.

Mirghani and his al-Khatmiyya *tariqa*. The years after World War II saw increasing political activities and the emergence of new political groups such as the Sudanese Communist Party (SCP) and the Muslim Brotherhood. The culmination of these political activities was the country's independence in 1956.

CHAPTER IV

The Leading Ideologues of Contemporary Political Islam

Historical Background

The issues of renewal and religious resurgence are not intellectually and historically unexpected in Islamic historic experience. The Islamic creed considers resurgence, renewal, and revival to be an original part of its assumptions, starting with Islam itself which is regarded as a revival of Abrahamic monotheism.[131] According to the leading Muslim scholar, Yousif al-Qaradawi, renewal for Muslims is not only a demanding necessity, it is a religious obligation. He often quotes Prophet Mohammed's *hadith* that proclaims: "At the start of each century, Almighty God will send to this *umma* someone to renew its religion."[132]

The issues of renewal of Islam and Islamic institutions during the last two centuries came as result of the challenges that faced Muslim rulers during that time. These challenges could be divided into two parts. The first was the "materialistic" challenge which was the lure of Western civilization and the material benefits it offered such as advancement in technology, education, medicine, and military. The second was a "moral" challenge. As Muslims pondered the secret of Western material superiority which was becoming more and more compelling, they were faced with the possibility that European societies could have been based on higher moral principles. The West also posed as a

---

[131] Emirates Center for Strategic Studies and Research. *Islamic Movements: Impact on Political Stability in the Arab World.* Abu Dhabi, UAE: Emirates Center for Strategic Studies and Research, 2003, 12.

[132] Yusuf al-Qaradawi. *Islamic Awakening between Rejection and Extremism.* 2nd ed. Herndon, VA: The Institute of Islamic Thought, 1991.

teacher on human rights, and how they should be better protected, as well as how societies should be organized on fairer and more humane bases. [133]

The moral challenge was the most devastating and demoralizing, especially to a community that for so long believed itself to be most virtuous and self-sufficient. However, the moral challenge was at first subordinate to the material one. At first it was only the desire to attain the material benefits associated with the process now known as modernization and the fear of Western armies and navies that pushed Muslim rulers to adopt Western ways. [134]

The initial response to the European challenge arose within the political and intellectual elite, but was more practical than intellectual. Rulers who found themselves threatened by the ascendancy of the West moved to acquire what they thought was the secret of the West, "military technology." Special military schools were set up in different parts of the Ottoman Empire, Egypt, Iran, and Tunisia to train soldiers and technicians and to translate European works on science. For the first time, some Muslims students were sent to study abroad, particularly in France and England. Armies were modernized along European lines.

These early attempts to modernize Muslim societies failed to achieve their goals and objectives, and in the long run led directly to the subordination of these societies to the powers they wanted to compete with. [135] The reasons for this failure are complex, but it deepened the crisis within Muslim societies, and led to calls for some drastic solutions. The response to this failure came this time from outside the political establishment in the Islamic world. This response could be divided into two periods, before the establishment of the Muslim Brotherhood in Egypt in1928 and 1928 to present.

Before 1928 the call of renewal by Muslim thinkers was concentrated mainly on how to reform the political and religious institutions, education

---

[133] Osman. "The Political and Ideological Development," 13.

[134] Ibid., 13.

[135] Ibid., 14.

systems, and society within existing political institutions. Thinkers of this period were not organized in groups and did not attempt to challenge existing political regimes. Representatives of this period believed that modernization and political reforms were needed but absolute rule in Muslim countries obstructed modernization. These representatives adduced Islamic values to support their advocacy of democracy and the accountability of government. They genuinely believed that Islam supported reform. However, their main concern was to succeed in modernizing their society. They concentrated their efforts on providing advice and ideas to the ruling class about the importance of reform in order to meet the challenge of the West (at that time Britain, France, and Russia). As a result, their messages and calls for reform were mainly spread among the elite and they lacked any public support. The most prominent thinkers of this period were Jamal al-Din al-Afghani (1838-97), Mohammed Abduh (1849-1905) and Rashid Rida (1866-1935).[136]

The writings of the intellectual school representatives influenced the next generation of "organized" Islamic thinkers, particularly their writings about the dangers of the rapid influence of Western civilization and culture which deeply influenced Hasan al-Banna, the founder of the Muslim Brotherhood in Egypt. As al-Affendi accurately observes:

> there is no doubt that general legacy of this intellectual school, including its main principles and concerns- such as resisting colonialism and regaining the glory of the nation, and their call for establishing the basis of *shura*, and the reforming of government, religious reform and the renewal of religion – constituted the bases for the emergence of the modern organized Islamic movements.[137]

Renewal and reform during the second period (1928-Present) were greatly influenced by the transformations that occurred in the Middle East as a result of World War I, such as:

---

[136] Ibrahim M. Abu-Rabie. *Intellectual Origins of Islamic Resurgence in the Modern Arab World*, SUNY Series in near Eastern Studies. Albany, NY: State University of New York Press, 1996.

[137] Emirates Center for Strategic Studies and Research, 19.

- The political "vacuum" created in the Islamic world as a result of the abolition of Caliphate at the hands of Kamal Ataturk in 1924. The crisis over the Caliphate led Islamic thinkers to develop different ideas regarding the relationship between religion, politics, and state.[138]

- The Europeans, who already had colonized much of the Ottoman Empire in the 19th century, completed the takeover with the territories of Arabia, Iraq, Syria, Lebanon and Palestine following World War I.

- The emergence of modern political boundaries of individual nation-state in the Middle East under the control of France and Britain.

- The emergence of Arab and Turk Nationalist Movements such as Saad Zagloul Movement in Egypt 1918 and Ali Abdellatif Movement in Sudan in 1924.

- Challenges of modernization and cultural hegemony of the West that resulted from rapid industrialization and technology revolution in Western countries.

- The rise (after World War II) of the influence of Communism in the Middle East, particularly in Egypt and Sudan.

Representatives of this period argued that Islam faced imminent threat and challenge from Western colonizing countries such as France and Britain and called for governments or organizations that could unite Muslims. They believed the creation of such governments or political and social organizations was possible only through a dedicated education campaign among the masses. The most prominent thinkers of this period were Hasan al- Banna (1906–1949), Abul A'la al-Mawdudi (1903-1979), and Sayyid Qutb (1906-1966).

---

[138] Lia Brynjar. *The Society of the Muslim Brothers in Egypt: The Rise of an Islamic Mass Movement 1928-1942.* Dryden, NY: Ithaca Press, 2006.

Organized Islamic Movements

The principles and teachings of early reformers such as al-Afghani, Abduh and Rida are followed by those who succeeded them since 1928. While the goals and the objectives remained the same, the post-1928 reformers heavily emphasized the importance of political Islamic groups that could play a leading role in mobilizing Muslim societies to face the rising influence of Western culture and to establish a new Islamic state governed by *Shari'a* and the principles of *shura*. The most prominent thinkers of this period are: Hasan al- Banna, Abu A'la al-Mawdudi, and Sayyid Qutb.

Hasan al-Banna (1906-1949)

Soon after the abolition of the Islamic Caliphate in 1924, the Islamic revival, which until that time was only intellectual, entered into the movement phase. Motivated by his antipathy toward the British Protectorate in Egypt, which was partially ended in 1922, Hasan al-Banna founded *al-Ikhwan al-Muslimoon* (Muslim Brotherhood) in 1928, the largest and the most influential Islamic revivalist organization in the 20th century. Al-Banna was influenced by the writings of al-Afghani and Abduh in believing that Europeans had been able to dominate the Muslim World because Muslims had strayed from following the true path of Islam. But it was Rida who most influenced al-Banna. Al-Banna was a dedicated reader of *al-Manar*, the magazine that Rida published in Cairo from 1898 until his death in 1935. Al-Banna also shared Rida's central concern with the decline of Islamic civilization relative to the West. He, too, believed that this trend could be reversed only by returning to an unadulterated form of Islam, free from all the accretions that had diluted the strength of its original message.

Like Rida at the end of his life, al-Banna felt that the main danger to Islam's survival in the modern age stemmed less from the conservatism of Islamic schools and centers such as al-Azhar (which he criticized) than from the ascendancy of Western secular ideas. The Muslim Brotherhood became the first mass-based overtly political movement to oppose the ascendancy of secular and

Western ideas in the Middle East. Hasan al-Banna saw these ideas as the main cause of the decay of Islamic societies in the modern world; he called for the return to Islam as a solution to the ills that had befallen Muslim societies.

Unlike his predecessors, al-Banna was more of a brilliant organizer and charismatic leader than a thinker and ideologue. He was able, in a short period of time, to establish the Muslim Brotherhood as a major political and social group in Egypt. By the late 1930s, it had established branches in every Egyptian province. A decade later, it had 20,000 active members and as many sympathizers in Egypt alone, while its appeal was now felt in several other countries as well. The society's growth was particularly pronounced after al-Banna relocated its headquarter from Ismailia to Cairo in 1932.[139]

The single most important factor that made this dramatic expansion possible was the organizational leadership provided by al-Banna. He endeavored to bring about the changes he desired through institution-building, relentless activism at the grassroots level, and a reliance on mass communication. He proceeded to build a complex mass movement that featured sophisticated governance structures: sections in charge of furthering the society's values among peasants, workers, and professionals; units entrusted with key functions, including propagation of the message, liaison with the Islamic world, and press and translation; and specialized committees for finance and legal affairs.

In anchoring this organization into Egyptian society, al-Banna skillfully relied on pre-existing social networks; in particular, those built around mosques, Islamic welfare associations, and neighborhood groups. This weaving of traditional ties into a distinctively modern structure was at the root of his success. Directly attached to the brotherhood, and feeding its expansion, were numerous businesses, clinics, and schools.[140] In addition, members were affiliated with the movement through a series of cells, revealingly called *usar* (families). The material, social and psychological support thus provided was instrumental in the

---

[139] Brynjar,96.
[140] Ibid.,109-112.

movement's ability to generate enormous loyalty among its members and to attract new recruits. The services and organizational structure around which the society was built were intended to enable individuals to integrate themselves into a distinctly Islamic setting, shaped by the society's own principles.[141]

Rooted in Islam, Al-Banna's message tackled important issues including colonialism, public health, educational policy, natural resources management, Marxism, social inequalities, the weakness of the Islamic world on the international scene, and the growing conflict in Palestine. By emphasizing concerns that appealed to a variety of constituencies, al-Banna recruited from among a cross-section of Egyptian society, although modern-educated civil servants, office employees, and professionals remained dominant among the organization's activists and decision makers.

In his writings, which are known as *al-Rasael* (Messages), al-Banna tried to avoid giving details about the Muslim Brotherhood understandings of the Islamic state, the Islamic economy, or its position on minorities (non-Muslims) in Egypt. His writings took a general nature, as he clearly understood that any detailed programs or explanations of how to achieve these goals could jeopardize the future of his organization. His writings took more general historical-preaching characteristics that relied heavily on glorifying the Islamic past with extensive usage of citation both from the Quran and the *Sunna* of the Prophet Mohammed.

Hasan al-Banna's greatest achievement was his ability to create a sophisticated organizational structure which translated his vision into reality. However, what distinguishes the Muslim Brotherhood from other Egyptian political groups which were established in the twenties and afterwards, such as Communist groups and *Hizb Misr El-Fatah* (Young Egypt) Party, is the former's holistic approach. The Muslim Brotherhood was not merely a social, political or religious association or group. It was described by antagonists as a state within a

---

[141] Ibid.,109-112.

state.[142] Following its unprecedented growth and expansion in Egypt, the ideology of the Muslim Brotherhood and the teachings of its founder began to transcend national borders into countries such as Syria, Jordan, and Palestine in 1930s, and in the 1940s and 1950s to other Muslim countries such as Sudan, Tunisia, Libya, and some of the Gulf countries.

Abul A'la al-Mawdudi (1903-1979)

The same factors, both locally and internationally that played a major role in establishing the Muslim Brotherhood in Egypt, were also decisive in the formation of the *al –Jamah al-Islamyyia* (Islamic Group) by Abul A'la al-Mawdudi in 1941 in India. Unlike al-Banna in Egypt whose concerns were predominately social, al-Mawdudi's concerns were political in nature and revolved around the political status of Muslims in India. Al-Mawdudi's strong feelings against the second class status of Muslims in the Indian State led him to agree with the call that the poet Mohammed Iqbal launched and which was carried by the Islamic League, namely, the establishment of a separate state for Muslims.[143]

Al-Mawdudi was highly critical of the apologetic approach of modernists, which he believed, started as a result of the Western domination over Muslim societies during the colonial rule. He saw modernization together with the different character traits and norms associated with it, such as rationalism, positivism, nationalism, and scientism, as expressive of the deeply rooted desire of man to dominate man by ever-shifting ideological concepts. He declared that Islam stands in absolute opposition to all these ideologies since in Islam man is taught to submit only to God and to discard all other masters. He wrote "to dominate is to play God and to accept domination is to worship a Golden Calf."[144] Al-Mawdudi insisted: "Whenever man finds himself in a position, from which he can dominate, tyranny, excess, intemperance, unlawful, exploitation and

---

[142] Ibid.

[143] Emirates Center for Strategic Studies and Research, 21.

[144] Cited by Abbott Freeland. *Islam and Pakistan.* Ithaca: Cornell University Press, 1968, 175-176.

inequality reign supreme."[145] Modernism, therefore, appeared to al-Mawdudi as an ideology of domination by the scientifically and technologically advanced nations of the world over the rest of mankind; and so he stood firmly opposed to it.

Al-Mawdudi criticized the Westernized educated class in the Islamic world and other advocates of modernity for their lack of understanding of the meaning of the religion. According to him:

> All these earlier writers and so-called modernizers had accepted the Western notion of religion without realizing that the Western viewpoint on religion had been obtained from Christianity and not Islam. Without critical analysis they had accepted the Western proclamation that religion was in actuality a private matter and had nothing to do with the experience of society as a whole. These Islamic apologists had taken Western philosophies and ideologies to be the criteria of truth and therefore, had started remaking Islam. They had attempted to shape everything in Islam to agree with Western criteria and whatever could not be shaped had to be deleted from history and if it was unable to be eradicated excuses had to be advanced for it before the world.[146]

Al-Mawdudi also criticized traditionalist Muslims as follow:

> These traditionalists who had attempted to conserve the earlier heritage of the Islamic disciplines without any consideration of good or bad elements in it, they did not embrace any influence from the modern successful civilizations, they did not think it was useful to understand the West, nor did they try seriously to analyze their own past legacy and discover what was worth preserving and what was to be discarded from it. Similarly, they failed to study the nature of the Western civilization to recognize what could be gained from it and try to find out the weaknesses in Muslim thought and performance. These traditionalists also ignored the force of science that gave the British the ability to dominate India.[147]

Al-Mawdudi favored borrowing Western technology and machines but not Western culture as he was a staunch opponent of both Western secular democracy and socialist doctrines. He thought that both secular democracy and socialism were based on the assumption that men were free to decide their worldly affairs

---

[145] Ibid., 176.
[146] Abul A'la al-Mawdudui. *Come Let Us Change the World.* Translated by Kaukab Siddique. Washington: The Islamic Party of North America, 1972, 21-22.
[147] Ibid., 22-23.

independent of religion. Al-Mawdudi rejected democracy as the "sovereignty of the masses," and called for the establishment of an ideological Islamic state based on God's sovereignty *(hakimiyya)* and on Shari'a. He also described the current state of Muslims as *Jahilliyya* (the period before Prophet Mohammed), this term *(Jahilliyya)* would later be popularized and emphasized by Sayyid Qutb one of the most influential figures in contemporary political Islam.

Sayyid Qutb (1906-1966)

Sayyid Qutb was by far the most influential thinker among the Islamists, not only in Egypt, but also in the entire Islamic world. His views on Islam and society spread widely, and were accepted especially among radical *(Jihadists)* groups. Qutb's writings and intellectual contribution to the cause of Islamic revivalism could be divided into two periods. The first period is before 1954 and the second period is from 1954 to 1966, during which he suffered imprisonment and torture at the hands of Nasser's regime until his execution in 1966.[148]

During the 1930s and 1940s, Qutb was a member of Egypt's literary elite, as well as of Egypt's nationalist Wafd Party and a civil servant in the Egyptian Ministry of Education. Already, however, he was becoming wary of the head-long pro-Westernization of many other Egyptian intellectuals. In 1947 he was sent by the Egyptian Ministry of Education to the United States for further education. He stayed in the United States for the period between 1947 and 1950 where he earned his Master of Arts (Education) in Colorado.[149] During his stay in the United States, Qutb published his first major work on Islam *Social Justice in Islam* (originally published in Arabic as *Al-'Adalah al-ijtima'iyah fi'l Islam*). Hamid Algar suggests, in his excellent introduction to this volume, that Sayyid Qutb's stay in America 1947-1950" may have been decisive in turning him fully to Islam as a total civilizational alternative."[150]

---

[148] Moussalli, 1999.
[149] Ibid.
[150] Sayyid Qutb. *Social Justice in Islam.* Translated by John B & Algar Hardie, Hamid. Revised edition: Islamic Publications International, 2000.

Social Justice in Islam was published while Sayyid Qutb was still in America. He was also in the U.S. when Hassan Al-Banna, the founder and leader of the Muslim Brotherhood, was assassinated in February 1949. On his return to Egypt, having decided not to remain in the U.S. for a doctorate, he immediately became involved in the Muslim Brotherhood. Algar suggests also that Sayyid Qutb's entry into the ranks of the Muslim Brotherhood provided the organization with its first true ideologue and led ultimately to a radicalization of the whole Islamic movement in Egypt.[151]

The events of the later years of Qutb's life are well known. During the Muslim Brotherhood's brief flirtation with Jamal Abdul Nasser and the Free Officers' revolution in 1952, Qutb was among those who resisted attempts to draw the Muslim Brotherhood into the emerging structures of the Nasserist state. In January 1954, following an assassination attempt on Nasser by a member of the Muslim Brotherhood, the Muslim Brotherhood was outlawed and Qutb was jailed for the first time. Nasser released him two months later, evidently hoping that the Islamic movement would have learned to be more co-operative. He was wrong. In October the same year, Nasser used a supposed Muslim Brotherhood's attempt on his life as a pretext to crack down on the Muslim Brotherhood once more, and Qutb was among those arrested. Six of the Muslim Brotherhood leaders were hanged and Qutb was sentenced to 15 years imprisonment. He was to spend the rest of his life in jail, except for eight months of restricted liberty in 1964-65, before being hanged on August 29, 1966.

It was in jail that Qutb wrote many of his most important works, including the 8-volumes Quranic commentary *Fi Zilal al-Qur'an* (In the Shade of the Quran', 1962) and *Ma'alim fi'l Tariq* (Milestones, 1964). Qutb's *Milestones* has inspired some of the most extreme expressions of Islamic revivalism, such as *al - Takfir wa al- Hijra* (Condemnation and Migration) and Islamic Jihad in Egypt. One of the central concepts of the book is *Jahilliyya* (the period before Prophet

---

[151] Ibid.

Mohammed in Arabia). Qutb gives an interesting twist to the idea of *Jahilliyya*. *Jahilliyya* for Qutb is the sovereignty of man over man, socio-political orders where men have power over other men, to institute legislation and determine principles of right and wrong. The Quran is explicit in postulating Islam as the antithesis of *Jahilliyya*. By redefining *Jahilliyya* to encompass modern secular systems of political organization, Qutb is basically decreeing that all existing systems are unacceptable and even antithetical to the spirit of Islam. Thus the dichotomy, Islam and *Jahilliyya* includes both the Islamic and the anthropocentric way of doing things, and Islamic regimes and the existing non-Islamic regimes in Muslim lands.

His understanding of the obligation of *Jihad* -- struggle in the path of *Allah* -- is also a significant departure from traditional understanding. To him *Jihad* takes many different forms, depending upon the stage of development of the Muslim community. Thus at the earliest stage, it implies the struggle to assert the principle of *tawhid* (monotheism) against all odds. Further along the journey of Islamization, it means defending communities' right to "freely practice Islamic beliefs," even if it entails the use of force. He challenges those Muslim writers who argue that *Jihad* is restricted to self-defense only. Qutb argues that *Jihad* is a mandatory proactive activity that seeks to establish *Allah's* sovereignty on earth.[152]

Qutb also developed the theory of *talia* (vanguard) which is similar to Lenin's theory about the role of the Communist Party as a vanguard in leading the masses and the proletariat to the socialist revolution. According to Qutb, the revival of Islam requires a vanguard movement. This vanguard movement must be determined and capable of leading the Muslim community into a *Jihad* that would transform the entire world from *Jahilliyya* to Islam. This vanguard ought to be capable of isolating itself from the ignorance of the world, and after establishing the Muslim community, it ought to confront the ignorance itself and

---

[152] Sayyid Qutb. *Milestone*. Cedar Rapids, IA: The Mother Mosque Foundation, 1981, 47-48.

rise against it.[153] Qutb also advocated the use of force by this "vanguard movement" in order to establish the Islamic state. As Qutb explained:

> Since this movement comes to conflict with the *Jahilliyya* which prevails over ideas and beliefs, and which has a practical system of life and a political and material authority behind it, the Islamic movement has to produce parallel resources to confront the *Jahilliyya*. This movement uses methods of preaching and persuasion for reforming ideas and beliefs; and it uses physical and Jihad for abolishing the organizations and authorities of *Jahili* system which prevent people from reforming their ideas and beliefs and force them to obey their aberrant ways.[154]

The writings of the early Islamists such as al-Afghani, Abduh and Rida were known to the Sudanese educated class, particularly those who frequently visited Egypt or received their education there. However, they did not play any significant role in formulating the ideological base for the Islamists in Sudan. It is the writings of al-Banna, al-Mawdudi, and Qutb that played a major role in shaping the Islamic Movement in Sudan in its early days. Like many other Islamic movements in the region, the Islamic Movement in Sudan looked to the intellectual contributions of al-Banna as its major source for guidance, but unlike other movements in the region, the Islamic Movement in Sudan was less influenced by the writings of al-Mawdudi, and Qutb, because at that time it witnessed the emergence of al-Turabi as a major thinker and ideologue for the movement in Sudan.

---

[153] Ibid., 47-48.
[154] Ibid., 55.

CHAPTER V

The Islamic Movement in Sudan 1945-1989

Introduction

This chapter looks at the history of the Islamic Movement in Sudan between 1945 and 1989. Unlike many other Islamic movements in the region, the Islamic movement in Sudan during this period changed its name, goals, and strategies to adapt to changes in the country. Following its establishment in 1945 the Movement, which at the time was heavily influenced by the Brotherhood organization in Egypt, adopted the name of the Muslim Brotherhood. Following the October Uprising in 1964, the Movement's leadership changed the name to the Islamic Charter Front (ICF) in order to rally support among members of traditional parties and Sufi groups for its proposed Islamic constitution. Following Nemeri's military coup in 1969, the Movement functioned in secrecy and its members referred to themselves as Islamic Path advocates within the one-party system that was established by the regime. Following the April 1985 Uprising, the Movement changed its name to the National Islamic Front (NIF). The newly created front included the Movement's members, Sufi groups, tribal leaders, and independent intellectuals who were concerned about the rising influence of Sudanese Communist Party (SCP) and those who advocated a greater role for Islam in public life.

The ability to transform itself and adapt to political changes gave the Islamic Movement more flexibility in maneuvering against its political rivals. It also helped the Movement avoid any confrontation with Nemeri's regime thus allowing it to quietly infiltrate government institutions. In general the Movement history between 1945 and 1989 could be divided into six periods: The Early Years (1945-1954), The Formative Years (1955-1963), The Islamic Charter Front (ICF)

(1964-1968), The Movement and Nemeri (1969-1976), The Expansion Years (1977-1984), and The National Islamic Front (NIF) (1985-1989).

The Early Years (1945-1954)

The Second World War gave rise to decolonization movements in Asia and Africa; and Sudan was not an exception. Following the War, Sudanese intellectuals were able to organize themselves around a united political front which came to be known as the Graduates Congress (GC). The GC became the recognized voice of the Sudanese people in their demands for the self-determination, a self-determination that was promised to them by the British government during World War II. By the late 1940s a division among GC members occurred as some of its members interpreted self-determination as the creation of an independent Sudanese state, while others favored unity with Egypt. As a result, the GC split into two factions, the Unionists who later organized the Democratic Unionist Party (DUP) and relied on the support of al-Khatmiyya sect and those who advocated the slogan of "Sudan for the Sudanese" and who later organized the al-Umma Party which relied on the support of the al-Ansar sect (followers of Imam Mohammed Ahmed al-Mahdi). [155]

In their attempts to attract more Sudanese intellectuals to the idea of unity with Egypt, the Egyptian government started to invite large numbers of Sudanese students to study in Egypt. Upon their arrival in Egypt, these students found themselves in the center of the political struggle that dominated the Egyptian political arena at that time. The major political forces in Egypt in the 1940s were Egyptian nationalists led by Mustafa al-Nahas Pasha (1879-1965) and his Wafd Party; the Muslim Brotherhood (MB) led by the charismatic leader Hasan al-Banna; and several Marxist groups with considerable influence among Egyptian intellectuals. The majority of Sudanese students became more attracted to the latter two groups and several of them, such as Sadiq Abdallah Abdel Magid,

---

[155] Mohamed Omer Bashier. *Al-Harakah Al-Wataniyah Fi Al-Sudan 1990-1969*. Translated by Henry Riad, William Riad & Omer, Aljneed A. Sudanese House For Books, 1977, 220-221.

Gamal al-Deen al-Sanhouri, and Kamal Madani became members of the Muslim Brotherhood organization in Egypt.[156]

At the same time several Egyptian civil servants who worked in Sudan and who were members of the Muslim Brotherhood in Egypt, started to spread the Brotherhood's teachings among their Sudanese colleagues and friends. The culmination of these activities was the arrival of Salah Abdel-Seed, an Egyptian lawyer and an active member of the Brotherhood in Egypt, to Sudan in 1944-1945 where he lectured at the GC club in Omdurman explaining the message and the teachings of the Brotherhood. His message was met with great enthusiasm among GC members and some of them immediately established the first MB group in 1945.[157] It included prominent Unionists such as Ibrahim al-Mufti, Badawi Mustafa, Ali Talb Allah, and Mohammed Ismail. According to Hasan Makki, the MB group was not effective in spreading the Brotherhood's ideology because it was a clear attempt by the Unionists to control the new organization.[158]

To show the importance of Sudan in Egyptian politics, the leadership of the Egyptian MB decided in 1946 to send two of its prominent members to Sudan. The mission of Abdel Hakim Abdeen and Gamal al-Deen al-Sanhouri was to strengthen the presence of Brotherhood ideology in Sudan and also expand membership. Another major concern for the delegation was also to explain to Sudanese Unionists that the position of the MB in Egypt was in favor of unity between the two nations and not opposed to it as was widely thought by many leading Unionists in the Sudan.[159] The delegation arrived in Sudan in 1946 and visited most political and religious leaders of the country, explaining to them their teachings and their position regarding the question of unity with Egypt. They also

---

[156] Ibid., 241-244.

[157] Ahmad, "*Harakat Al-Ikhwan Al-Muslimin Fi Al-Sudan, 1944-1969,*" 17.

[158] Ibid., 17.

[159] The position of the Muslim Brotherhood in Egypt toward the issue of unity with Sudan at that time was that the Sudanese people must decide whether to unite with Egypt or to establish their own independent state. The Egyptian MB clearly favored unity with Sudan but that unity must come from Sudanese consensus and not by force or negotiation between Egypt and Britain. This position was interpreted by the Unionists in Sudan as an anti-unity position.

traveled to the different parts of Sudan where they were able to establish more than 25 branches in all areas of Sudan.[160]

Despite all these activities, the MB in Sudan continued to function as a loose organization with no established organizational structure or clear leadership like its counterparts in Egypt and in other Arab countries. In 1948 Ali Talb Allah was appointed by Hasan al-Banna as the General Guidance (GG) for the MB in Sudan.[161] The appointment of Ali Talb Allah laid the first precedent for the appointment of the GG by the Egyptian MB and not by the Sudanese organization, and this would have a great impact on the future of the MB in Sudan. As a result of his energetic work, Talb Allah opened the first MB meeting club in Omdurman in 1953.[162] Despite Talb Allah's attempts to create a strong organization in Sudan, the perceived pro-unionist position of the MB limited the Movement's influence among the Sudanese educated class, who at that time were becoming overwhelmingly in favor of establishing an independent Sudanese state. Like many other MB movements in the region, the Sudanese MB relied heavily on al-Banna's teachings and followed the same organizational structure as the Egyptian MB.

By the late 1940s large numbers of Sudanese students who were educated in Egypt started to return to Sudan. Those who had been exposed to the MB ideology and joined the MB in Egypt started to propagate its ideology among the Sudanese educated class. They concentrated their efforts among Sudanese students in high schools such as Hantoub and Wadi Saydna. Two of those contacted in Hantoub were Babiker Karar and Mohammed Yousif Mohammed. They were approached by their former teacher, a member of the MB in Egypt, and asked to set up a branch for the MB in Hantoub. They both rejected the idea after they saw some of the MB literature which they interpreted as pro-Unionist literature.

---

[160] Ahmad, *"Harakat Al-Ikhwan Al-Muslimin Fi Al-Sudan, 1944 -1969,"* 18.
[161] Ibid., 23.
[162] Ibid., 24.

Upon their arrival to Gordon Memorial College (GMC) the following year, they were surprised by the dominant role Communists were playing there. Faced with this situation Karar started to gather his friends and drafted a constitution for a new movement which was called *Harkat al-Tahrir al-Islami* (The Islamic Liberation Movement--ILM).[163] The Movement's main objectives were the revival of Islam and the establishment of a new world order transcending the prevalent East-West dichotomy.[164] Despite its differences in programs from the MB, the ILM was immediately labeled by Communists at GMC as a new terrorist branch for the MB in Sudan.[165] The ILM repeatedly denied any connections with the MB in Egypt, but the need for support to counteract the rising influence of Communists in Sudan among the educated class and trade union members forced the ILM to establish contacts with various MB-affiliated groups outside GMC. In 1951 Karar met Talb Allah and explored the possibility of future work between the two organizations.

In 1951 a group of GMC students that included many members of ILM visited Egypt and were able to meet the Egyptian MB leadership who introduced them to MB history, objectives and its position regarding the future of Sudan. The introduction of ILM members to MB ideology, coupled with the arrival of a student named Abdel Bagi Omar Atiyya, a member of the MB who returned from Egypt that year and joined ILM, played a major role in bridging the gap between the ILM and the MB in Sudan. The gradual and informal integration of the two groups took place because the ILM itself lacked any clear organizational structure or well-defined leadership except that of Karar dominant role. In 1953, al-Rashid

---

[163] Osman, "The Political and Ideological Development," 92.

[164] Ibid., 92.

[165] The description of "terrorists" by Communists in Sudan was largely due to the conflict between MB in Egypt and the Egyptian government at that time. As a result of that conflict, the military wing of the MB engaged in several violent acts against the government which included the assassination of Egyptian Prime Minister Mahmud Fahmi al-Nograshi in 1948 by Brotherhood member and veterinary student Abdel Meguid Ahmed Hassan, in what is thought to have been retaliation for the government crackdown on the MB. For detailed information about the Egyptian MB military wing, see: Abdelazeem Ramadan. *Al-Ikhwan Al-Muslemeen Wa Al-Tanzeem Al-Siri.* 2nd ed. Cairo: Egypt: Egyptian General Establishment For Books, 1993.

al-Tahir, an ILM member and president of the GMC Students Union, visited Egypt by invitation from the new revolutionary government. During his stay in Egypt, al-Tahir held a series of meetings with the MB leadership; upon his return, al-Tahir became an ardent supporter of integration with the Egyptian MB.[166]

Despite its limited success in counteracting Communist influence among the Sudanese educated class, the ILM faced numerous challenges that led to factionalism within the Movement. First, the ILM needed to decide on the new name of the organization, despite their clear differences from the MB in Egypt, many of the ILM members started to refer to themselves as members of the MB in Sudan. Second, the ongoing battle with Communists forced the ILM into establishing close relations with MB affiliated groups outside GMC and eventually with the Brotherhood in Egypt. Third the ILM also needed to find a compromise position between al-Rashid al-Tahir and the majority of the ILM members who advocated the immediate unification of the ILM with MB-affiliated organizations in Sudan led by Talb Allah, and Babiker Karar and his small group who vowed to keep ILM as an independent organization or at least if they joined with the Talb Allah MB group, then the new group must have a different name than the MB and not become part of the Egyptian organization. Finally, the ILM also needed to address the issue of their relationship with the Egyptian Brotherhood if the merger of the two groups in Sudan was approved.

To settle all of these differences and to avoid the possibility of a split which started to loom, the leadership of the ILM and the MB affiliated organizations in Sudan, led by Talb Allah, agreed to meet on what came to be known as the *Eid* Conference in 1954 -- because it was held during the *Eid* (religious festival following Ramadan on 1373 of the Islamic calendar) holiday.[167]

The conference convened in the Omdurman Cultural Club on 21 August 1954. Among those who attended the Conference was Hasan al-Turabi who represented the student body of the Islamists. In spite of Talb Allah's objections,

---

[166] Osman, "The Political and Ideological Development," 101.
[167] Ahmad. "*Harakat Al-Ikhwan Al-Muslimin Fi Al-Sudan, 1944 -1969*," 47.

those who attended the conference "approved the resolutions which would give the Islamic Movement in Sudan its shape."[168] First, it was decided to adopt officially the name of *al-Ikhwan al-Muslimoon* (Muslim Brotherhood--MB). The adoption of the new name clearly indicated the triumph of those who advocated a close relationship with the Egyptian Brotherhood. Second, Talb Allah was removed from his position as the General Guidance of the Movement in Sudan. Third, the Movement decided to function as an independent political group and to campaign for an Islamic constitution. Finally, an Executive Office was elected to run the Movement and Mohammed al-Kheir Abdel Gadir was elected as the Secretary of Executive Office.[169]

A few members of the ILM led by Karar, rejected the Conference resolutions, especially the new name, and decided to create their own organization, *al-Jamaa al-Islamyyia* (the Islamic Group), which adopted a radical program with strong socialist overtones.[170] Talb Allah and his conservative pro-Egyptian group also rejected the Conference resolutions and tried to find support from the main organization in Egypt, but the MB in Egypt at that time was busy with its first bloody conflict with Nasser. Years later a final compromise was reached between Talb Allah and the new leadership. As a result of that compromise, Abdel Gadir resigned from his leadership position and al-Rashid al-Tahir was elected the new leader for the MB in Sudan.[171] He was designated as *al-Muraqib al-Aam* (the general supervisor), the first time such a title was given to an elected leader of Sudanese MB, thus signifying a major step in the development of the movement.[172]

The Eid Conference was a significant step in the creation of the contemporary Islamic Movement in Sudan as it ended the unequal relationship with the main organization in Egypt and laid the foundation for an independent

---

[168] Osman, "The Political and Ideological Development," 103.
[169] Ahmad, "*Harakat Al-Ikhwan Al-Muslimin Fi Al-Sudan, 1944 -1969*,"48.
[170] Osman, "The Political and Ideological Development,"103.
[171] Ahmad, "*Harakat Al-Ikhwan Al-Muslimin Fi Al-Sudan, 1944 -1969*,"54.
[172] El-Affendi, "*Turabi's Revolution*,"54.

Sudanese Islamic Movement that elected its leader and functioned as an independent national movement rather than a branch of the main organization in Egypt. The election of the new leadership by the Sudanese members of the MB was also a significant departure from the MB traditions where the leadership of the MB organizations in countries such as Syria, Iraq and Jordan was appointed by the GG of the Egyptian MB who was considered to be the General Guidance of all MB organizations in the Arabic world. The independent course of the Sudanese Movement was due in large to the colonial legacy of Egypt in Sudan and the anti-Egyptian sentiments that were widely spread among Sudanese people.

The Formative Years (1955-1963)

Despite the split of Karar and his group, the MB in Sudan led by its new *al-Muraqib al-Aam*, al-Tahir, gradually became a dominant political movement especially among the students of GMC. The execution of several Egyptian MB leaders by Nasser's regime in 1954 resulted in the dramatic shift of the Sudanese Islamists from the pro-union camp to the independence camp. This dramatic shift greatly influenced MB growth among GMC students and the Sudanese educated class who became overwhelmingly in favor of an independent Sudanese state. The brutality of Nasser's regime against Islamists, Communists, and the Wafd Party members, who either opposed the new regime or expressed their concerns or reservations regarding the new direction of the country, also swayed many unionists in Sudan toward the independence camp.

After it became clear that the country was headed toward independence, the MB started to concentrate their efforts on two fronts: the expansion of the movement's support among the educated class and the establishment of an Islamic order in Sudan. To achieve its first goal, the new leadership of the MB worked hard to publish a newspaper to carry the message of the movement to the public. Despite its limited financial resources, the MB was finally able to publish its first newspaper in 1956. It was given the title *The Muslim Brotherhood* with

Sadiq Abdallah Abdel Magid as its first general editor. Despite its limited circulation of 3,000 copies the new newspaper played a significant role in introducing MB ideology to the Sudanese educated class, particularly high school and college students.[173]

Aware of their very limited influence in politics of the country, the MB approached the two major political groups al-Ansar and al-Khatmiyya in a bid to fulfill the MB's main goal, the establishment of an Islamic order in Sudan. In December 1955 the MB declared the formation of the Islamic Front for the Constitution (IFC). The new organization was to be an open organization for all individuals who favored an Islamic constitution. The creation of an "Islamic Front" was a clear indication of the MB's familiarity with SCP tactics and organizational structure in Sudan. The SCP was known to favor the creation of several "democratic fronts" to work simultaneously among students, women and workers, a strategy that seemed to have impressed the MB enough for it to try and emulate.[174]

The IFC also produced a "model constitution" which called for the establishment of a parliamentary system with regional devolution in a unitary state. It also paid great attention to economic organization, reflecting the influence of the "socialist phase" of the movement. It called for land reform, public ownership of mineral resources, and nationalization of banks, in addition to specifically Islamic reforms such as the prohibition of *riba* (interests on loans).[175] Despite their efforts IFC members failed to rally needed support among the educated class for the Islamic constitution when in 1957 the Constitution Commission (CC) rejected the proposal of IFC by a decisive margin (21 to 8).[176]

In the 1958 election the MB decided not to run its own candidates but pledged its support to any candidate who advocated their call for an Islamic constitution. As a result a split developed within the IFC when non-MB members

---

[173] Ahmad, "*Harakat Al-Ikhwan Al-Muslimin Fi Al-Sudan, 1944 -1969,*"63

[174] El-Affendi, "*Turabi's Revolution,*" 57.

[175]Osman, "The Political and Ideological Development,"113.

[176] Ibid., 114.

wanted to run for election. The differences between the MB and IFC leadership over the election, coupled with the differences between al-Rashid al-Tahir (the MB leader) and Omer Bakheit al-Awad (the IFC leader), who resigned his MB leadership position over the role of the MB within the IFC, led eventually to the collapse of the IFC.[177]

During the same period the MB continued to build its internal structure. The Sudanese MB adopted the Egyptian Brotherhood's internal structure of *usar* (families). Khartoum was divided into three *usar* councils: Omdurman, led by Sadiq Abdallah Abdel Magid; Khartoum North, led by Mohammed Yousif; and Khartoum, led by Omer Bakheit al-Awad.[178] During this time also the MB started to campaign among workers and trade unions in unsuccessful attempts to counteract Sudanese Communist Party (SCP) influence among these groups. A Workers Office (WO) was established in Omdurman to supervise the work of the MB among workers and trade unions, but lack of experience in working with workers and the elitist nature of the MB at that time, coupled with the strong presence of the SCP among these groups, resulted in total failure by the MB cadres in establishing a strong presence among these groups.

During this same period the MB became engaged in international issues of concern to Muslims. In 1952 the MB newspaper called for Sudanese political figures boycott the French Embassy in Khartoum and devoted several issues to the cause of the Algerian Revolution. The MB leaders also played an active role in the creation of the Sudanese Front for Solidarity with Algerian People. They also supported the Iraq Revolution of 1958, which overthrew the pro-Britain monarchist regime of Nuri al-Saeed. As for Sub-Sahara, the MB expressed support for Kwame Nkrumah's pan-Africanism ideas.[179]

The continuing political instability that dominated the Sudanese political scene after 1954, the rivalry between the two major political parties, al-Umma and

---

[177] Ibid., 116.

[178] Ahmad, "*Harakat Al-Ikhwan Al-Muslimin Fi Al-Sudan, 1944 -1969,*"71.

[179] Ibid., 68-69.

the DUP, and the rapid spread of the civil war in the South, led to the first intervention in politics by the Sudanese military establishment. On November 17, 1958, General Ibrahim Abboud, the Commander-in-Chief of the Sudanese armed forces, moved his forces to topple the government of the Prime Minister Abdallah Khalil. The MB, and all other political parties, except the SCP, welcomed the new military regime.[180]

The MB was treated as a "religious group" by the new military government at the beginning, but a year later, and as a result of several articles critical to the government, the MB newspaper was suspended. The MB leadership, represented by al-Rashid al-Tahir, was plotting more drastic action against the military junta. Al-Tahir started to contact several officers in the army in an attempt to topple Abboud's regime. The countercoup was eventually carried out on 9 November 1959 and failed. Al-Tahir was arrested, trialed and was sent to prison for five years while five officers were executed.[181] The attempted coup of al-Tahir created a deep rift within the MB because many of its leaders expressed their anger and concern about the way that the MB was functioning and how al-Tahir was able to commit the movement to a military coup without the MB leadership's approval or knowledge. Following the coup MB activities became limited to its student branch at the University of Khartoum.

After al-Tahir's imprisonment, Sadiq Abdallah Abdel Magid became the MB leader. The MB leadership, which became very concerned about the undemocratic nature of the MB's internal structure decided to establish a new form of governing for the movement. Thus, in 1962, in an attempt to avoid any future temptations by its leaders, the MB leadership decided to create a collective leadership to run the movement. The MB leadership elected Sadiq Abdallah Abdel Magid, Malik Badri, Mohammed Yousif, and Mubarak Gism Allah to serve as the new collective leadership.[182]

---

[180] Osman, "The Political and Ideological Development,"121.
[181] Ibid., 124.
[182] Ahmad, "*Harakat Al-Ikhwan Al-Muslimin Fi Al-Sudan, 1944 -1969*,"98.

In December 1959, following the failed coup in which the MB leadership represented by al-Tahir was implicated, and under the pressure of the SCP and other progressive groups at the University of Khartoum (formerly GMC), the MB-controlled Khartoum University Students Union (KUSU), led by Gafaar Sheikh Idris, handed the military junta a memorandum that called for the return to civilian rule and the lifting of any restrictions on political parties and newspapers. The KUSU memorandum was a clear reflection of the MB position at the University of Khartoum but not the position of the MB leadership.[183]

In 1962 Hasan al-Turabi temporarily returned from France where he was pursuing his Ph.D. in constitutional law. Al-Turabi, who was heavily influenced by the role of students and trade unions in politics in France in 1960s, started to question the MB's general strategy, recruitment strategies, political maneuvers, and its relations with other political parties. For example, he asked whether the MB wanted to continue as a pressure group or become a political party. And, if the latter, did they want to be an elitist party, as they had remained hitherto, or did they want to become a mass movement? Did they want to achieve their aims by force or stick to the democratic process?[184]

Al-Turabi convinced the MB leadership to take a strong stand against Abboud's military regime because "it is based on tyranny, oppression, and espionage and denial of *shura* (consultation)."[185] As for resistance tactics against the military regime, al-Turabi rejected a countercoup because of its violent nature; instead he suggested "peaceful and protracted popular resistance."[186] The MB leadership accepted al-Turabi's proposal about the importance of toppling the military regime in Sudan and directed all its members to work closely with other political groups to create a united front against the military regime. The KUSU which was dominated by MB members was the key instrument in rallying support against the military junta.

---

[183] Ibid., 122.
[184] Osman, "The Political and Ideological Development,"126.
[185] Ibid., 126.
[186] Ibid., 126.

The Islamic Charter Front (ICF) (1964-1968)

Al-Turabi returned from France in 1964 after he finished his education. He was appointed Dean for Faculty of Law at the University of Khartoum. During the same year the MB decided to conduct its sixth conference in order to further discuss the movement's strategies and to resolve the issue of the collective leadership, which many leading members considered inappropriate and impractical for movement work, particularly in the current political situation. Al-Turabi and his supporters also wanted the conference to adopt some organizational reforms that were designed to eliminate preoccupation with secrecy inherited from the Egyptian Brotherhood (which insisted on individual recruitment and the rigorous formation of individual members).[187] Al-Turabi's ideas were met by fierce resistance from the MB old guard who forced him to back down. Al-Turabi's suggestions, which were aimed to make the movement more open by lifting restrictions that required members to be subjected to a long period of indoctrination before they could have full rights, including aspiring for leadership positions, were rejected.

On October 21, 1964 following a political discussion that was organized by KUSU at which al-Turabi was the main speaker, spontaneous student demonstrations started at the University of Khartoum. The security forces of the military junta fired at the students killing at least three of them. The incident sparked an outrage throughout the country which culminated in an open strike by all trade unions and professional associations. The strike, coupled with the threat of junior members of the Sudanese military forces to the junta, resulted in the collapse of the military regime.

Following the October Uprising a transition government led by Sir al-Khatim al-Khalifa was formed in order to prepare the country for an election within one year. All parties and trade unions were represented at that government.

---

[187] Ibid., 128.

The MB was represented by Mohammed Salih Omer who became the Minister of Animal Resources. As for al-Turabi, he emerged from the October Uprising as a hero. In November 1964 he was overwhelmingly elected as the Secretary General of the MB.

Understanding its limited influence among the public, and in order to push for their Islamic state call, the MB decided to revive its old IFC organization by the creation of a new umbrella organization for those individuals and organizations that shared the MB stand on the creation of an Islamic state in Sudan. In 1964 the newly created organization was named the Islamic Charter Front (ICF) and al-Turabi was elected as a General Secretary for the ICF.[188] The formation of ICF represented a major departure for the MB from its Egyptian-style secrecy organization and also can be considered a major victory for al-Turabi and his supporters who actively advocated the importance of the creation of an open organization that would work with other individuals and groups that shared its values and objectives.

In early 1965 the ICF published the *Islamic Charter*, a document that outlined the Islamic order as envisaged by the MB at the time. In addition to their usual demands for the implementation of *Shari'a* laws and other Islamic related demands, the ICF called for the establishment of a presidential system and an economic system that fostered social justice without compromising democracy.[189] Unlike the 1958 elections where the IFC supported those candidates who advocated the Islamic order, the ICF leadership decided to run its own candidates for the April 1965 elections. A total of 100 candidates represented the ICF in that election (85 candidates in geographic districts and 15 in the Graduate Constituencies). The ICF won seven seats, of which two (including al-Turabi's) were from Graduate Constituencies. Its total share of votes was 5.1%, coming

---

[188] Ahmad, "*Harakat Al-Ikhwan Al-Muslimin Fi Al-Sudan, 1944 -1969*,"105.

[189] Osman, "The Political and Ideological Development,"151.

mainly from Khartoum (11.6%). The ICF was outdone by the SCP which won 11 seats in the Graduate Constituencies.[190]

After the 1965 election, which resulted in overwhelming victory for the country's traditional forces represented by al-Umma and the DUP, a new constitution drafting committee was established with the purpose of writing a new constitution for the country. The ICF was represented with three out of forty-four members on that committee. The constitution committee which was dominated by representatives of traditional parties, decided to draft a new constitution "which reflects the Islamic heritage of Sudanese people."[191] During that time the ICF moved closer to the al-Umma party led by young Sadiq al-Mahdi (whose sister al-Turabi later married). The new alliance between al-Turabi and al-Mahdi was mainly directed to counter the rising influence of the SCP, especially following the 1965 election.

In 1965 and following statements by a student at the Faculty of Education at the University of Khartoum in Omdurman, which attacked Islam and the Prophet Mohammed, the ICF organized massive demonstrations in the capital demanding the disbanding of the SCP and the outlawing of its activities. The mass protests organized by ICF members forced the parliament to vote to ban the SCP and expel its members from the parliament. After deliberations lasting one year, the Supreme Court ruled the ban to be unconstitutional; another court subsequently ruled the expulsion of SCP MPs invalid. The Council of Ministers and the Parliament refused to obey the court's orders and as a result the head of the Supreme Court resigned. The matter remained unresolved until the 1969 military coup.

The years 1964-1969 were generally characterized as a period of political stagnation and political instability by Sudanese political observers. All major parties were subjected to splits and divisions. For example, the DUP was divided into two factions; the first group was led by Ismail al-Azhari, the first Prime

---

[190] Ibid., 152.
[191] Ibid., 154.

Minister of the country following independence, and the second group was led by Ali Abdelrahman. Al-Umma was also divided into two groups; the first one was led by al-Hadi al-Mahdi and Mohammed Ahmed Mahjoub while the other group was led by Sadiq al-Mahdi.[192] The leftists started to became more radical following the SCP ban, as they clearly understood that any attempts to reform the country's political and economic structure could be achieved only through a military coup as the traditional parties showed no concern for the democratic process and the rule of the law.

The ICF was not an exception. Despite its limited success following the election of 1965, the ICF was facing numerous challenges, most notably the future of the MB within the ICF. The ICF leadership publicly insisted that there was no MB within the movement and that the MB must be completely dissolved within the ICF. Al-Turabi was a major supporter of this argument as he consistently favored the open organization form for the movement. Following the ICF's limited success in the 1965 election, the dissatisfaction among some MB members inside the ICF grew. In their efforts to undermine al-Turabi's leadership, the opposing elements within the MB pushed for the separation of the posts of the General Secretary of the MB and ICF. Thus, al-Turabi was forced to resign his position as the MB leader and Mohammed Salih Omer was elected as the new MB leader.[193]

After the 1968 election in which the ICF won only 4 seats compared to seven seats in the previous election, the opposition to al-Turabi's leadership, and to the ICF as the future organizational structure for the movement, started to mount among MB members led by Gafaar Sheikh Idris. Al-Turabi's open and liberal approach toward many political issues such as the role of women in public life and the importance of working within the society for change, were met with stiff resistance from Idris and his supporters, who were greatly influenced by al-Mawdudi's and Qutb's writings.

---

[192] Bashier, "*Al-Harakah Al-Wataniyah*."
[193] El-Affendi, "*Turabi's Revolution*,"87.

In April 1969 MB members gathered in a general conference to resolve the dispute. The ideological arguments at the conference centered around the purpose and main task of the organization. The dissidents, who came to be known as the "educationalist school," wanted to maintain the elitist nature of the movement, with membership restricted and intensive indoctrination administered, preferably in isolation from society.[194] They rejected ICF and its open format. The pro-al-Turabi group, known as the "political school," countered that Islam could be better served by an open organization accessible to all and not only to exclusive groups. Al-Turabi's groups also argued that political activism did not need to be preceded by indoctrination or education, since the service of the people, in politics, trade unions, etc., was in itself the best education. ICF, as a receptacle for the collective energies of the largest possible numbers of Muslims was, according to them, a necessity.

At the end, al-Turabi's charisma and leadership skills played a major role in persuading MB members to support his arguments and positions. Al-Turabi was again elected as the General Secretary for the MB and the ICF. The educationalists accepted the conference resolutions with the exception of a few, who were expelled from the movement. [195] Before the new strategies suggested by al-Turabi were put in place, the radical elements of the SCP and other leftists groups decided to strike. On the morning of 25 May 1969 a military coup led by Colonel Gafaar Nemeri overthrew the civilian government and dissolved all political parties in the country including the ICF and the MB.

The Movement and Nemeri (1969-1976)

The military coup of May 25, 1969 was clearly planned and carried out by leftist elements within the Sudanese army. The newly created Revolutionary Council (RC) consisted mainly of Communist, Arab Nationalist, and Socialist officers. The ICF immediately opposed the new regime and started to rally other

---

[194] Ibid., 87.
[195] Ibid., 87.

parties against the regime. Sadiq al-Mahdi, who at that time was a close ally of the ICF, was first selected to lead the opposition group that included representatives of other parties such as the DUP, led by al-Sharief Hussien al-Hindi. As a result of their activities, most of the ICF leadership was arrested including al-Turabi.

In 1970 after the bloody clash between the Sudanese army and al-Hadi al-Mahdi on the island of Abba, al-Sadiq al-Mahdi was placed under arrest and the leadership of the opposition went to al-Hindi who was in Lebanon during the military coup. Al-Hindi started to organize opposition to the regime with the support of countries such as Libya and Saudi Arabia, which feared the further influence of the Communists on the new regime. Talks with representatives of the MB and the al-Umma party led to the formation of the National Front (NF), in which the MB was represented by Osman Khalid Mudawai who served as its Secretary General.[196] The NF charter advocated the creation of a democratic order in Sudan with an Islamic orientation.

Following the May coup the ICF ceased to exist and the bulk of opposition work was handled by the MB, particularly at the university branch which led fierce resistance to the new regime. The SCP support of the new regime clearly undermined their influence among university students who supported a democratic form of governance for the country. Dissatisfaction among university students transferred into overwhelming support for MB candidates in student union elections. By 1973, the Nemeri regime had moved from success to success. After crushing the Communist challenge to his rule in July 1971, Nemeri was elected president. In March 1972, the Addis Ababa Agreement was signed between Nemeri and the rebels in the South ending 17 years of civil war in the country.[197] The early economic and political successes of the Nemeri regime made it difficult for the opposition to find allegiance among Sudanese people, who at

---

[196] Ibid., 105.
[197] Ibid., 107.

that time overwhelmingly supported the regime, especially after the ending of the civil war in the south.

In 1973 the government introduced new economic policies that were aimed to cut the deficit in the general budget; some of these policies included raising prices on some essential products such as gas and sugar. These new policies were met by stiff resistance particularly among students. The NF thought to exploit the situation. The MB and other NF parties directed their members to join students in an attempt to create momentum for a popular uprising similar to the one of October 21, 1964. The NF attempt was a total failure as the Nemeri regime moved quickly to crush demonstrators.

Following the failure of the students' uprising, the dominant members of the NF decided to prepare for an armed showdown with the regime, a position which was earlier rejected by al-Turabi. An unsuccessful military coup led by Hassan Hussein against Nemeri regime in 1975 led to another boost for the military option. During this time the MB leadership was freed from jails and quietly started to rebuild the movement. Hundreds of MB, DUP, and al-Umma members were directed to join training camps in Ethiopia.

In July 1976 the NF began its military operation against the regime in Khartoum. After several days of bloody street fights, NF forces were defeated and thousands of NF members were killed or summarily executed. The military failure of the NF signaled its collapse as the differences between al-Hindi and al-Mahdi on how to further proceed literally crippled the NF. In 1977 al-Mahdi started secretly to negotiate with the Nemeri regime. Al-Mahdi's attempts were first met by a strong opposition from both the DUP and the MB, but later the MB leadership in London, under pressure from al-Turabi, decided to join al-Mahdi in the negotiation process.

During the period 1969-1976 the MB was struggling to keep their organization going despite repression and arrests by the Nemeri regime. Notwithstanding these difficulties, ironically, the 1969 military coup helped the movement to stay united as it temporarily stopped the internal rift between the educationalists and the pragmatists led by al-Turabi. In 1974 al-Turabi introduced complete internal reforms aimed to strengthen his position within the organization. The complete democratization of the structures of the movement gave power to thousands of young members who joined in the late 1960s and deeply admired al-Turabi.[198] The young generation of leaders dominated the leading offices of the MB thus depriving the old guard of their hold on the organization.

The Expansion Years (1977-1984)

The culmination of al-Mahdi and MB leadership negotiations with the Nemeri regime was the signing of the National Reconciliation Accord (NRA) of 1977 which was brokered by the Saudi government represented by Prince Mohammed al-Faisal (the founder of Faisal Islamic Bank—FIB). The leadership of the MB justified its joining the NRA citing the changing climate in international circumstances, especially on the Sudanese borders, particularly in Ethiopia and Libya which were the main supporters of the Sudanese opposition (NF).

In Ethiopia a new Marxist regime led by Mengistu Haile Mariam (1974-1987) was becoming more hostile toward NF forces because of their historical ties with Eritrean rebels, and in Libya Muammar al-Qaddafi, who was the principal supporter and arms supplier of the NF, became closely allied with the Soviets. These changing circumstances forced the leadership of the NF to speed the process of peace negotiations with Nemeri's regime.[199] The only group within NF that rejected the NRA was the DUP and its leader al-Hindi, who vowed to continue his struggle against Nemeri's regime

Following the signing of the NRA by NF leaders, many MB prominent figures returned to Sudan, such as Osman Khalid, Gafaar Sheikh Idris, Ahmed

---

[198] Ibid., 113.

[199] Zakaria Bashier. *The National Reconciliation in the Sudan and Its Aftermath*, Seminar Papers 12. Leicester, England: Islamic Foundation, 1981, 14.

Abdel Rahman, Ahmed al-Turabi, and Rabi Hassan Ahmed. As a part of the NRA arrangements, all political prisoners were released. Also, al-Mahdi and al-Turabi were both appointed members of the political bureau of the Sudanese Socialist Union (SSU), the highest political authority in the country. Al-Turabi was later appointed as an assistant of the Secretary General of the SSU for foreign affairs and information. Soon afterwards he was appointed as political commissioner of the Western province of Darfur and ultimately appointed as a justice minister in 1979.[200] Then the Second People's Assembly (parliament) was dissolved, ostensibly to make room for newcomers to be represented in a new Assembly. During that election, the Islamists won about 18 seats out of more than 300 seats. They were all members of the single party of the SSU.[201]

Internally, after the NRA, the leadership of the MB approved an ambitious plan to rebuild the movement. Understanding the complexity of working under the constant surveillance of Nemeri's security forces, the MB leadership approved a plan that called for complete decentralization to make the movement more efficient and more resistant to regime crackdown. Decentralization was enhanced by setting up numerous satellite organizations loosely affiliated to the Movement. The late seventies and early eighties saw the emergence of the Society of Renaissance Vanguards, the Youth Society for Construction, the Association of Southern Muslims, the Association of Sudanese *ulama* (religious scholars), the Islamic *Dawa* (Propagation) Organization, the African Islamic Relief Agency, the Namariq Literary and Artist Society, and the Union of Muslim Literary Men, to mention only the most prominent. [202]

The leadership of the MB during that period also started aggressive recruitment campaigns to increase the Movement's membership, especially among women and trade union members. Al-Turabi's writings played a crucial role in presenting the movement as a liberal progressive Islamic movement. His

---

[200] Ibid., 16.
[201] Ibid., 16.
[202] El-Affendi, *"Turabi's Revolution,"* 115.

writings about the role of women in society, arts and Islam, *shura*, and the position of non-Muslims in Islamic societies, provided needed ideology to counter Communists, who despite their bloody clash with Nemeri in 1971, still enjoyed a considerable support among women and trade unions members. Some of al-Turabi's ideas about women, *Ijtihad*, and relations with secular regimes were controversial and were met with strong opposition from the old guard, "the educationalists." The differences between al-Turabi, who enjoyed the wide support of the MB membership, and the educationalists continued to mount; and finally in September 1980 a small group of MB leaders, led by Sadiq Abdallah Abdel Magid declared their split from the movement, citing their dissatisfaction and objection of the Movement relationship with Nemeri's secular regime. Abdel Magid and his group also voiced their opposition to some of al-Turabi's religious views and his rejection to the role of the Egyptian-controlled International Order of the Muslim Brotherhood which controlled and coordinated the work of Muslim Brotherhood organizations around the world.

As part of their grand strategy for expansion following the NRA, the MB leadership directed its members to infiltrate all government ministries and agencies. Understanding the importance of finance to the movement work, the movement convinced Prince Mohammed al-Faisal to open branches of his Faisal Islamic Bank (FIB) in Sudan. The opening of FIB in Sudan, which was followed by the openings of several other Islamic banks and investment companies, helped the movement accumulate great wealth as it controlled the operations of all newly created Islamic enterprises. That wealth was used in expanding Movement work around the country and in establishing several Islamic non-profit organizations (INGOs) in the areas of education and health.

By the mid-1980s the newly established Islamic enterprises were able to dominate the Sudanese economy. Hundreds of MB members who previously were teachers, engineers, lawyers, or physicians became the wealthiest business people in the country. INGOs expanded to all areas of Sudan and after the drought and the famine that struck Sudan in the early 1980s, these INGOs literally replaced the government in providing educational, social, and health services for the Sudanese people, especially in the Darfur region.[203]

In the early 1980s the economic situation in the country started to decline and thousands of Sudanese professionals started to leave the country for the Gulf region when job opportunities became available there. This was particularly true for those who were constantly harassed by Nemeri's security forces because of their opposition to the regime. At the same time the newly created Islamic enterprises and the relatively peaceful relationship between the regime and the MB guaranteed MB membership full access inside Sudan to employment and prosperity. With Communists and other opposition individuals leaving the country for better employment opportunities outside the country and the MB professional cadres remaining in the country, the MB controlled most of the professional associations and the workers' unions.

In 1983, in an attempt to please some of his Southern political allies from small tribes who wanted to end the Dinka domination of southern politics, Nemeri decided to divide the Southern region into three provinces, which was a clear violation of the 1972 Addis Ababa Accord that called for a one regional government in the South.[204] The move was interpreted by Dinka representatives as an attempt to weaken their dominant position in the South and the civil war renewed in the south again.

In September 1983, in an attempt to suppress the rising dissatisfaction among the Sudanese people, Nemeri declared the implementation of *Shari'a* laws in the country. Despite the flaws associated with these laws, the MB leadership

---

[203] For full details of the impact of Islamic finance on the movement work see pp.161-171.

[204] The Dinka tribe constitutes the largest tribe in the South (more than a million). Dinka are also the most educated and well-connected in the South because of their historical ties with the British colonial administration which favored them over other tribes, thus giving them some access to education. By having the South as one region, Dinka's representatives controlled the whole South. Dividing the South into three regions limits the Dinka control to only one region in which they are concentrated. Other Southern large tribes such as the Nuer and Shuluk constantly resisted Dinka hegemony in the region and frequently looked to the North as a major ally against the Dinka.

decided to support Nemeri's Islamic reforms. Hundreds of MB cadres were appointed in specially created Islamic courts that handled criminal and civil cases. The MB cadres in these badly organized courts used them against their political adversaries. In 1985 one of these courts sentenced Mahmoud Mohammed Taha the founder of the Sudanese Republican Party (1909-1985), to death mainly because of his opposition to the Islamization path that Nemeri took. Mahmoud Mohammed Taha was accused of apostasy and was publicly executed on January 18, 1985.[205] Later it was reported that the body was buried in a shallow hole in the desert west of Omdurman.

Following the declaration of *Shari'a* law the influence of MB members within the SSU and other government organs became visible. Large numbers of Nemeri supporters who were suspicious of MB activities started to voice their concerns to Nemeri and he started to pay attention to them. Nemeri became more isolated after the declaration of *Shari'a* laws, which also escalated the situation in the south as more southern leaders started to join the newly formed Sudanese People's Liberation Movement (SPLM) led by John Garang. During their long association with Nemeri, the MB managed to acquire some vital assets; chief among these was the infiltration of security forces and the army. On March 9, 1985 when Nemeri ordered his security forces to crack down on the MB, security contacts tipped off the MB leadership off which gave them a few hours notice. Key underground cadres were whisked away into hiding and preparations were hurriedly made for a long struggle with the regime.[206]

By April 1985 opposition against Nemeri's regime was mounting. Political parties, trade unions, student unions, and professional associations started to meet regularly and discuss plans to topple the regime. The MB leadership was never invited to these meetings as it was deemed unworthy of

---

[205] Abdullahi Ahmed An-Na`im. "The Islamic Law of Apostasy and Its Modern Applicability: A Case from Sudan." *Religion, State & Society*, no. 16 (1986): 197-224.

[206] El-Affendi, *"Turabi's Revolution,"*129.

trust. The culmination of these activities was the April 6, 1985 Uprising which toppled Nemeri's regime and established civilian rule in Sudan.

The National Islamic Front (NIF) (1985-1989)

After the collapse of Nemeri's regime, the MB emerged as an isolated political group as it was condemned by all political parties because of its role in Nemeri's regime. Despite this isolation the MB leadership optimistically looked to the next election which was planned for the year of 1986. In April 1985 al-Turabi suggested the creation of a new Islamic political body to unite all 'Islamic' forces in the country and during the same month the National Islamic Front (NIF) was chartered. The formation of the NIF represented the ultimate triumph of the pragmatic line advocated by al-Turabi since 1962.[207] The creation of the NIF represented a great challenge for traditional parties and the SCP, which clearly underestimated the political and economic power that Islamists had gained during their cooperation with Nemeri's regime. The core membership of the NIF was MB members. Large numbers of 'Islamists,' Sufi groups, and tribal leaders who benefited from the services of INGOs in their regions also joined the new political organization.

The organizational structure of the newly created NIF rested in four bodies: the General Congress, the General *Shura* Body, the Executive Organ, and the Secretary General. The ultimate authority was vested in the General Congress that convened every three years. The General Congress then elected the General *Shura* Body which consists of 361 members. The General *Shura* Body was the highest authority after the General Congress and met every six months. The Executive Organ was a body comprising 114 members of whom 76 were elected by the General *Shura* Body, while the rest consisted of members of executive offices. The Executive Organ met every three months and was presided over by the Secretary General who was elected by the General Congress.[208]

---

[207] Osman, "The Political and Ideological Development,"284.
[208] Ibid., 321.

Membership for the new movement was more open and less restricted. There were no requirements for education or indoctrination. Al-Turabi was elected as the General Secretary of NIF. To the surprise of many observers, Ali Osman Mohammed Taha, who was relatively young (the current vice president in Sudan) was elected as the second person in the NIF. The *Shura* Council (the highest authority of the NIF) consisted mainly of members who were loyal to al-Turabi and also included some members of the dissolved SSU who sympathized with the cause of the NIF and who had good relations with MB leaders during their cooperation with Nemeri. NIF branches enjoyed considerable autonomy with little or no interference from the central organs of the NIF who handled the propaganda, finance, and support for these regions. The NIF also enjoyed the work of well-trained communication, journalist, and computer cadres sent to the leading western universities during the 1980s. These cadres gave the NIF a major advantage in mass communication and political advertisements. By late 1985, the NIF published more than seven daily newspapers including the NIF official newspaper al-Raya.

The elections of April 1986 confirmed the emergence of the NIF as a major political power in the country. NIF candidates dominated the Graduate Constituencies (GC) winning all of the 21 GC seats in the North plus two in the South, while the SCP won only one GC seat in the South; whereas in the 1968 election the SCP won 11 GC seats out of 13 while the MB won only one seat. The NIF achieved great success in the geographic Constituencies winning 28 seats out of 236 compared to four seats in the 1968 election. NIF gains came mainly in urban areas. It won 13 seats in Khartoum, the capital. The 1986 election results confirmed the decline of secularist forces in the country represented by the SCP which won only three seats. It also confirmed the emergence of the NIF as the third political force after al-Umma party led by al-Mahdi, which won about 100 seats, and the DUP which won about 63 seats.[209] The elections also signaled the

---

[209] Ibid., 305.

major shift that occurred among Sudanese intelligentsia and Sudanese educated women as it appeared that they shifted their allegiance to the NIF rather than the SCP.

After the election a new government led by al-Mahdi was formed in alliance with the DUP. In the period between 1986 and 1988 al-Mahdi's reign of power was characterized by corruption and governmental inability to solve the problems deemed to be crucial to the public, such as negotiating with the rebels who were growing strong in the South, introducing new laws to replace Nemeri's Islamic laws, and developing new economic policies for the country. Unable to face these challenges and fearing that his party alone would be blamed for the failure to solve these problems, al-Mahdi decided to invite the NIF to form a new coalition. The NIF leadership, who clearly understood the importance of having a foothold in government to protect their Islamic banks and other economic and political entities, which were increasingly coming under harsh attack from leftists and traditional parties, decided to join the coalition government. The DUP rejected the new government and remained in opposition.

The newly-created coalition government between al-Mahdi and al-Turabi met with stiff resistance from the left and the DUP. The left was able to mobilize trade unions and professional associations against the new government. The deteriorated economic situation and the inability of the new government to rally needed support for its economic and political programs resulted in a total chaos in the country. On the other hand the SPLM in the south was rapidly gaining strength. By 1988 the Sudanese army in the South was rapidly losing ground to the SPLM.

On February 1989 the Sudanese commander-in-chief and 150 high-ranking military officers gave Prime Minister al-Mahdi a week to form a new government from representatives of all parties and work to end the nation's civil war.[210] The army's ultimatum came as a result of al-Mahdi's rejection of the peace

---

[210] Mirghani, 202-206.

proposal negotiated by DUP leadership with the SPLM. Fearing further escalation with the army al-Mahdi formed a new national unity government that included representatives of all political parties and trade unions with the exception of the NIF which refused to join. The newly created government approved the peace proposal between the DUP and the SPLM, which called for ending military operations in the South, freezing Islamic laws, and preparing for a constitution conference to solve all the country's problems.

The NIF rejected the new arrangements especially the freezing of Islamic laws which was viewed by its leadership as a clearly anti-Islamic measure. The NIF also saw the creation of a new government and the call for the constitution conference as an attempt by the leftists, SPLM, and traditional parties to limit its influence. With the preparations for the constitution conference underway, the NIF leadership decided to move quickly. In the subsequent months a small group of the NIF leadership led by al-Turabi started to discuss a military option for replacing the current government and establishing an Islamic state; finally, the group approved a plan for a military takeover of the government.[211]

The NIF military wing in the Sudanese army had grown tremendously after the NRA and especially after Nemeri's Islamization program in which large numbers of MB members were recruited to lecture in army colleges and barricades. On June 30, 1989 the military wing of the NIF, led by Brigadier Omer Hassan al-Bashier, with the support of many NIF loyal members who were dressed in military uniforms, struck down the capital and within hours they controlled all important military units. The political orientation of the coup leaders remained unknown to many Sudanese people who thought it was just a move by patriotic army officers to end the corruption and the political instability in the country. Other army officers in the region who supported the coup at the beginning thought it was the army high-ranking leadership in the capital who

---

[211] Abdelrahim Omer Mohi Eldeen. Al-Turabi Wa Al-Ingaz Siraa Al-Hawia Wal Al-Hawa: Fitnat Al-Islameen Fi Al-Sultah Mein Muzakirat Al-Ashrah Ela Muzakirat Al-Tafahum Maa Garang. 3rd ed. Khartoum, Sudan: Marawi Bookshop, 2006, 177.

authorized the move after the failure of al-Mahdi to meet their demands.[212] The only political party which correctly described the coup as a pro-NIF coup was the SCP.

[212] Mirghani, 296.

CHAPTER VI

Factors that Influenced the Rise of the Islamic Movement

in Sudan

Introduction

In the four decades between the Movement's emergence in 1945 and its military coup in 1989, the Islamic Movement in Sudan transformed itself from a tiny elite-centered pressure group to a massive political organization that eventually became the third largest political force in the country behind al-Umma Party and the Democratic Unionist Party (DUP). It also became the dominant political force among the country's educated elite who previously were heavily influenced by Marxist and Arab-nationalist ideologies. This chapter looks at the factors that influenced the unprecedented rise of the Islamic Movement in Sudan.

The first factor is the Movement's ideology as presented by its chief ideologue and leader, Dr. Hasan al-Turabi. Al-Turabi presented the Movement as a modern political force that while calling for the establishment of an Islamic state in Sudan, still views Islam in more progressive ways than any other contemporary Islamic political movement in the Islamic world. Al-Turabi's writings about modernity, art, music, economics, relations with secular regimes and women played a significant role in expanding the Movement's membership especially among young Sudanese intellectuals and women who previously overwhelmingly supported the Sudanese Communist Party (SCP). His writings on issues such as *ijtihad* (interpretation of Islamic jurisprudence), *ijmaa* (consensus), and *tajdid* (renewal) in Islam, art, democracy, music, and theatre also helped the Movement to expand to new territories which previously were considered unthinkable.

The second factor is the Movement's changing views on women's role in public life. The Movement's position toward the role of women in Sudanese society was greatly influenced by al-Turabi's liberal views on women. Al-Turabi argues in favor of a greater role for women in the Movement and in society in general. He advocates greater opportunities for women in work and education and also calls for their full participation in the Movement's activities and in the country's political process. Al-Turabi's views on women revolutionized the Movement's work among women and heavily influenced the outcome of the Sudanese student union elections as more women started to vote regularly for Movement members, thus enhancing their position in higher education institutions.

The third factor is the Movement's presence among students who became the Movement's major supporters of. It also explains how the Movement's strategy in directing its membership to join the teaching profession, particularly in high schools, helped the Movement in expanding its support among young students before they entered colleges and universities, thus avoiding competition with other political groups that traditionally recruited only at the college and university level. The Movement's newly graduated cadres were encouraged by the Movement leadership to serve a few years as high school teachers for the purpose of exposing young students to the Movement ideology; later these professionals returned to their original professions. Also, the linkage between emerging Islamic institutions and the Movement's student cadres played a significant role in helping the Movement keeps its student cadres following their graduation.

The fourth factor is the emergence of Islamic economic institutions such as Faisal Islamic Bank (FIB), and how these financial institutions changed the political landscape in the country in favor of the Movement. The discussion of the fourth factor details how the Movement controlled these institutions and utilized them in building a solid economic base in the country, particularly in the foreign trade area, which traditionally was controlled by foreigners and supporters of the DUP. The newly created economic institutions enhanced Movement presence among students, women, trade unions, and professional associations because they provided needed services and products for these groups. Newly created Islamic institutions also helped the Movement in the creation of a large network of Islamic Non-Government Organizations (INGOs), which also enhanced the presence and the visibility of the Movement, particularly in the regions where these INGOs were able to provide much needed services such as educational and health services.

The fifth factor is the Movement's organizational structure, its development, and how this structure has evolved throughout the Movement's history in order to meet the needs of each period. The MB moved away from traditional rigid hierarchal structure inherited from the main organization in Egypt into an open and flexible system responsive to change. For example, student organizations in their colleges and universities, and large regional bodies such as the Movement's organization in Darfur, were guaranteed full autonomy from the Center in running their local affairs.

Additionally, the Movement developed a new and more effective strategy of recruiting army officers. Historically, military rule played a major role in shaping the political process in the Middle East and Africa. Sudan was no exception. Throughout the history of the country the military was at the center stage of the country's politics. It intervened in 1958 under General Abboud, then again in 1969, in a Communist-sponsored military coup led by Nemeri, and finally in an Islamist-sponsored coup in 1989 led by al-Bashier.

Furthermore, the Movement developed a new strategy toward trade unions and the labor movement in Sudan. Traditionally, trade unions and the labor movement played a major role in the country's politics and were heavily influenced in the beginning by pro-Egyptian unionists and later by the Communists. The Movement's strategy toward these organizations falls into two stages. In the first stage, the Movement's main concern was to limit or eradicate the (SCP) influence among members of these organizations. The second stage was to initiate intensive recruitment campaigns among members of both organizations which would enable the Movement to take control in the end.

Al-Turabi's Intellectual Contributions

Hasan al-Turabi was born in 1932 in the city of Kassala in the eastern part of Sudan. His family had a long tradition in academia and Sufism.[213] His father, Abdalla Dafa'alla al-Turabi (1889-1990), was a *qadi* (*Shari'a* judge) of the Shari'a Division of the Sudan Judiciary, which he joined in 1924 during the British colonial administration. Al-Turabi's father, who was very suspicious of the "secular" education system in the country encouraged his son to study traditional Islamic subjects besides the Arabic language.[214] As a son of a *qadi*, al-Turabi grew up under colonial policies which restricted Islam to the realm of family practice. Shari'a was confined to Muslim personal law, away from arenas of politics and business.[215]

After his graduation from high school, al-Turabi entered the Faculty of Law at Khartoum University College (KUC) –later University of Khartoum- and graduated with a BA in Law four years later. A year later, he was sent by the KUC to Britain where he obtained his LLM in Law from the University of London in 1957. Upon his return to Sudan, he joined the Faculty of Law at the University of Khartoum as an assistant lecturer. In 1959 he was sent again by the University of Khartoum to France, where he earned his PhD in Law from the Sorbonne University in 1964. His dissertation was entitled "States of Emergency in Constitutional Jurisprudence." [216]

Upon his return from France, al-Turabi was appointed dean of the Faculty of Law at the University of Khartoum. During his short-lived academic career, al-

---

[213] Ahmad S. Moussalli. "Hassan Al-Turabi's Islamist Discourse on Democracy and Shura." *Middle Eastern Studies* 30, no. 1 (1994): 52.

[214] Ibrahim, "A Theology of Modernity,"194-222.

[215] Ibid., 199.

[216] Ibid., 217.

Turabi played a major role in overthrowing Abboud's military regime. He was a vocal critic of the military regime and frequently called for the return of the military to their barracks and the restoration of democracy in the country.[217] In October 1964, after a public political gathering about the situation in the South, organized by Islamists' dominated Khartoum University Students Union (KUSU), a spontaneous strike was declared by most professional associations and the military regime of General Abboud collapsed.

Al-Turabi's role in the "October Uprising," and his election in the same year as the General Secretary for the Muslim Brotherhood in Sudan, marked the beginning of al-Turabi's political career. By late 1964 al-Turabi resigned his post as dean of Faculty of Law and in 1965 was elected to the parliament from the Graduate Constituencies as the only successful candidate from the Brotherhood's list. While the October Uprising could be considered a watershed in al-Turabi's political career, Al-Turabi had been involved in politics since 1954 when he took part in the founding of the Sudanese Muslim Brotherhood. During his studies in Britain he served as the secretary general of the Sudanese Student Union, while in France he was the secretary general of the Islamic Society for the Support of the Algerian Cause.

Al-Turabi's election as the leader for the Movement literally revolutionized its works. During his European stay in the 1960s, al-Turabi witnessed the emergence of powerful social movements such as the Students' Movement in France, the rising influence of the left in Europe, women organizations, and trade unions. He clearly understood the important role that these social movements can play in shaping political life, not only in European countries, but also in other countries including Sudan. He became more convinced about the importance of such movements and organizations after the October Uprising of 1964 when trade unions, professional associations, and student unions

---

[217]Hasan Makki Muhammad Ahmad. *Al-Harakah Al-Islamiyah Fi Al-Sudan, 1969-1985: Tarikhuha Wa-Khatabuha Al-Siyasi.* Khartoum-Sudan: Ma'had al-Buhuth wa-al-Dirasat al-Ijtima'iyah: Bayt al-Ma'rifah lil-Intaj al-Thaqafi, 1990, 105.

played a major role in overthrowing the military regime in Sudan. Al-Turabi was determined to reconstruct every aspect of the Movement in Sudan. This included its organizational structure, recruitment strategies, ideology, and relations with other political parties.

Despite his western educational background in Britain and France, many of his critics and western scholars dismiss his contact with modernity as superficial. For them, al-Turabi is a renegade who turned his back on his Western education to engage in politicizing religion. Peter Kok finds it difficult to believe that the intellect which produced a PhD dissertation, heavily shot through with Cartesian logic and August Comet's positivism, could seriously accept the dogma and assumptions of Islamic fundamentalism.[218] At best al-Turabi is represented as irreparably torn between Islam and Western culture. Ali (1992) traces his duality to the time al-Turabi spent in a colonial school pursuing a modern career. Europe, suggests Ali, colonized his intellect, which was considered a threat.[219] Al-Turabi, he argues, exudes Europe in language, dress, and political skills of mass mobilization, but loathes its traditions of rationality, liberalism, and freedom.[220] Other detractors from within the Islamic Movement criticize al-Turabi for exuding too much modernity for their liking, denouncing him as a secularist in Islamic garb.[221]

Despite his critics, who pictured him "sitting astride modernity and tradition,"[222] and based on his numerous pamphlets and books, written mostly in Arabic,[223] al-Turabi, in fact, sees no conflicts between "tradition" and "modernity"

---

[218] Peter Nyot Kok. "Hasan Abdulla Al-Turabi." *Orient* 33, no. 2 (1992): 185-92.

[219] Haydar Ibrahim Ali. *Azmat Al-Islam Al-Siyasi: Al-Jabhah Al-Islamiyah Al- Qawmiyah Fi Al-Sudan*. Namudhajan Alexandria: Egypt: Markaz al-Dirasat al-Sudaniyah, 1992.

[220] Ibid.

[221] Ibrahim, "A Theology of Modernity,"196.

[222] El-Affendi, "Turabi's *Revolution*,"179.

[223]See his works, Hasan al-Turabi. *Al-Harakah Al-Islamiyah Fi Al-Sudan*, Afaq Al-Ghad 8. Kuwait: Dar al-Qalam, 1988. *Al-Harakah Al-Islamiyah Fi Al-Sudan: Al-Tatawwur Wa-Al-Kasb Wa-Al-Manhaj*. Cairo: Egypt: al-Qari al-`Arabi, 1991. *Al-Iman : Atharuhu Fi Hayat Al-Insan*. Kuwait: Dar al-Qalam, 1974. *Al-Islamiyun Wa-Al-Masalah Al-Siyasiyah*. Silsilat Kutub Al-Mustaqbal Al-`Arabi 26;. Beirut: Sudan: Markaz Dirasat al-Wahdah al-Arabiyah, 2003. *Al-Ittijah Al-Islami Yuqaddimu Al-Marah Bayna Taalim Al-Din Wa-Taqalid Al-Mujtama»*. Jeddah:

as he understands the term. His concern is not with the dichotomy of tradition and modernity because Islam, for him, is not a tradition that helplessly second-guesses its worth in the face of transient realities such as modernity. Islam, al-Turabi argues:

> Not only finds nothing in modernity against which to quarrel, but is divinely endowed to humanize these realities, bless them, and harness them for a more intimate worshipping of God. In short, his theology is about the coming together of the traditional and modern.[224]

Al-Turabi articulates a theology of modernity which reconciles his seemingly divided cultural experience through the concept of *ibtila* (challenges posed by God to test Muslims' faith).[225] He uses this concept, which means experiencing life as a perpetual challenge posed by God to test a Muslim's faith, as synonymous with "modernity," this being the specific test set for contemporary Muslims. According to al-Turabi modernity is *ibtila* of the times for Muslims. Al-Turabi presents the need to come to grips with modernity as a calling similar to American Puritanism.[226]

According to professor Ibrahim, there is no contradiction between modernity and Islamism. He writes:

KSA: al-Dar al-Sa`udiyah lil-Nashr wa-al-Tawzi`, 1984. *Al-Marah Bayna Al-Usul Wa-Al-Taqalid*. Khartoum: Sudan: Markaz Dirasat al-Marah, 2000. *Al-Mashrue Al-Islami Al-Sudani: Qiraat Fi Al-Fikr Wa-Al-Mumaasah*. Khartoum: Sudan: Ma`had al-Buhuth wa-al-Dirasat al-Ijtima`iyah, 1995. *Al-Musalahat Al-Siyasiyah Fi Al-Islam*. Beirut: Lebanon: Dar al-Saqi, 2000. *Al-Salah Eimad Al-Din*. Jeddah: KSA: al-Dar al-Sa`udiyah lil-Nashr wa-al-Tawzi`, 1984. *Al-Shura Wa-Al-Dimuqraiyah*. Khartoum: Sudan: Alam al-Alaniyah, 2000. *Al-Siyasah Wa-Al-Hukm: Al-Nuzum Al-Sultaniyah Bayna Al-Usul Wa-Sunan Al-Waqi»*. al-Tab`ah 1. ed. Bayrut: Dar al-Saqi, 2003. *Islam, Democracy, the State and the West : A Round Table with Dr. Hasan Turabi, May 10, 1992*. Beirut: Lebanon: al-Dar al-Jadid, 1995. "*Islamic Fundamentalism in the Sunni and Shia Worlds.*" Islam For Today, http://www.islamfortoday.com/turabi02.htm. . *The Islamic State*. Princeton, N.J.: Films for the Humanities & Sciences, 1994. Videorecording Videocassette (VHS tape. "*Principles of Governance, Freedom, and Responsibility in Islam.*" The American Journal of Islamic Sciences 4, no. 1 (1987): 1-11. *Tajdid Al-Fikr Al-Islami*. Al-Rabat: Morocco Dar al-Qarafi lil-Nashr wa-al-tawzi, 1993. *Tajdid Usul Al- Al-Islami*. Beirut: Lebanon: Dar al-Jil, 1980. *Women in Islam and Muslim Society*. London, U.K: Milestones Publishers, 1991. *Islam, Democracy, the State and the West: A Round Table with Dr. Hasan Turabi, May 10, 1992, Wise Monograph Series; No. 1*. Tampa, Fla., U.S.A: World & Islam Studies Enterprise, 1993.
[224] Ibrahim, "A Theology of Modernity,"196.
[225] Ibid., 201.
[226] Ibid., 202.

For al-Turabi, modernity is simply a God-given reality, whose manipulation leads to a more profound worship of God. Contrary to the common popular piety, which sees modernity as a delusion, al-Turabi sees it as a corridor to God. Urbanization, for example, urges Muslims to humanize the sprawling rabbit warrens of cities through recognizing difference, imparting civility to the madding crowd, and soothing loneliness with peace of mind. Only weak Muslims would shun urbanity for its evils, lure, and materialism. Looking nostalgically toward a familiar rustic rurality, he argues, is a disservice to God, who unleashed urbanity on us to test our love for him. In worshipping God, Muslims need not be intimidated by the ungodly concepts by which modernity is perceived or articulated. Like the Prophet Mohammed who usurped pagan Arabic idioms to preach monotheism, Muslims have the duty to engage modern concepts and to gear them toward glorifying God.[227]

Al-Turabi also rejected the claim that government servants and other graduates from modern schools inside and outside Sudan are the custodians par excellence of modernity. For him, their acceptance of colonialism, the armed extension of modernity as described by Ashis Nandy (1983), made them unable to interrogate modernity as Muslims.[228] In their disbelief in Islam, this class of influential state functionaries has cut all connections with their Muslim "subjects" and equated modernity with the secular, nationalist, and socialist regimes of the post-colonial era. These elite, he suggests, have been too influenced by colonial definitions of modernity to realize that, in Peter Taylor's words, "there are different modern times and different modern spaces in a world of multiple modernities."[229]

After his election as a new leader of the Movement, Al-Turabi suggested the creation of a united front of pro-Islam political parties and groups to work for the establishment of an Islamic state in Sudan and for the drafting of a new "Islamic" constitution for the country. Al-Turabi's idea of creating this front was met with fierce resistance from the Movement's old guard who favored the elite-centered form of organization. Finally, al-Turabi's view about the importance of

---

[227] Ibid., 202.
[228] Ibid., 202
[229] Ibid., 197.

the creation of such a front was supported and the Islamic Charter Front (ICF) (1965-1969) was established under his leadership.

Al-Turabi declared that membership in the ICF was open to everyone who believed in establishing an Islamic state in Sudan and in accepting the idea of the Islamic constitution. The ICF infiltrated the two political parties (Umma and DUP) as some of their members joined the ICF. The ICF achieved a limited success in its campaign for the Islamic state and the Islamic constitution. In the 1965 parliamentary elections the ICF won only seven seats, five in the geographical constituencies and two (out of 15 seats) in the Graduate Constituencies, the other 11 seats went to the SCP. Al-Turabi received the highest number of votes in the Graduate Constituencies (about 7,000). In general the ICF captured only 5.1% of the general vote.[230]

Al-Turabi also argued in favor of changing the Movement's recruitment strategy. His move to change the recruitment strategy was met with stiff resistance from the Movement's old guard, while it was welcomed by the Movement's students and new recruits. The Movement's old guard, who came to be known as the "educationalists," wanted to maintain its elitist, tight-knit nature, with membership restricted and intensive indoctrination administered, preferably in isolation from society. They also objected to what they saw as the unprincipled approach of the ICF leadership dictated by political expediency. The ICF, they argued, made unacceptable expedient alliances such as the one with the Christian-dominated Sudan African National Union (SANU). One of the leading figures among the old guard was Malik Badri. In his letter to Abul A'la al-Mawdudi (1903-1979) he writes:

> In the Sudan, a group of brothers influenced by Dr. al-Turabi came to the conclusion that the methods of *tarbiyyah* (education) of Movement, in spite of its weaknesses, were too slow and inefficient to quickly help the Movement gain political authority in the Sudan. If the time and effort 'wasted' in *tarbiyyah* were devoted to political struggle, Dr. al-Turabi argued, then much time would have been saved, since we would have the

---

[230] Ahmad, "*Harakat Al-Ikhwan Al-Muslimin Fi Al-Sudan, 1944 -1969*,"111-113.

power to change more people in a much faster way with our achieved authority.[231]

Al-Turabi and his supporters, on the other hand, countered that Islam could not be served by exclusive groups, but by an open organization accessible to all. Political activism did not need to be preceded by indoctrination or education, since service to the people, in politics, trade unions etc. was itself the best education.[232] They advocated creation of an open organization and less restrictive requirements for Movement membership. Al-Turabi and his supporters also stressed the important role that the ICF played in introducing the Movement's leadership and its ideology and program to the public. In the end, al-Turabi's charisma prevailed and his new reforms were accepted. [233] Al-Turabi's reforms resulted in unprecedented growth in the Movement's membership in the second half of the 1960s, especially among university students and professionals. Later, during the period of 1977-1989, the Movement's membership expanded to include diverse segments of Sudanese society.

Al-Turabi's anti-elite views may be traced to his childhood. As a son of a *qadi*, al-Turabi lived in the same neighborhood with *effendis*. In his interview with professor Ibrahim, al-Turabi described the *effendis*, who were a class of junior Sudanese staff of the colonial administration, "as rootless as their superiors in outlying administrative postings, they presented themselves as the country's social elite and frequently imitated their colonial-master life's style."[234] According to al-Turabi "they spoke Arabic heavily influenced with English to make it unintelligible to Arabic speakers; they acquired the leisure habits of the British, such as drinking, playing cards, and going to clubs."[235] They literally isolated themselves from the people. On the other hand, despite his father's

---

[231] Malik B. Badri. "A Tribute to Mawlana Mawdudi from an Autobiographical Point of View." *Muslim World* 93, no. 3/4 (2003): 487.

[232] Osman, "The Political and Ideological Development," 177.

[233] Ahmad, "*Al-Harakah Al-Islamiyah Fi Al-Sudan, 1969-1985*," 141-145.

[234] Ibrahim, "A Theology of Modernity," 201

[235] Ibid., 201

limited education, his house was always full of people and he was in contact with people all the time while attending wedding contract ceremonies and leading Friday and funeral prayers.[236]

Unlike the *effendis*, people had no fear in approaching al-Turabi's father's and ask questions about religious practices, seek resolution of a family disputes, mediate in a social conflict or conduct religious ceremonies.[237] For al-Turabi these *effendis* had not only fallen short of addressing the problems that faced the country after independence, but also they were not even aware or conscious of such problems, since the departure of the colonial masters guaranteed them the long-waited leadership positions in the country. The fear of creating a new Islamist "*effendis*" class who would present themselves to the public as the ultimate holders of truth and knowledge and who would isolate themselves from the public, played a major role in al-Turabi's rejection of an organization that was elite-centered and for his call to broaden Movement recruitment among workers, farmers, Sufi groups, and the general public.

Al-Turabi's greatest contribution to the Movement was his intellectual writings on issues that historically had represented great challenges to the Islamists, not only in Sudan, but also in other Islamic countries. These issues include: nationalism, *tawhid* (monotheism) and modernity, the relation between Islamists and their society on one side and their relation with secular governments in the Islamic world on the other side, the position of Islamists toward *shura*, democracy and elections, questions about *ijtihad* (interpretation of Islamic jurisprudence), *ijmaa* (consensus), *fiqh* (Islamic jurisprudence.) and *tajdid* (renewal) in Islam.

Al-Turabi, like most Islamic scholars, opposed the concept of nationalism; he considered it an import from Europe that is incompatible with Islamic universalism. He writes, "We don't believe in nationalist values that divide people on bases of color, geography, or national interests. These are values

---

[236] Ibrahim, "A Theology of Modernity,"201.
[237] Ibid., 201.

fundamentally at odds with Islam; our firm beliefs is mankind is one community."[238] He accepts the nation-state as the framework of the Islamic Order. He does not envisage national-states being absorbed eventually in a universal *umma* state, but recommends their being incorporated as entities. He writes

> The nation state is thus a primary entity, although it may incorporate subsidiary entities. But it must direct itself toward a wider, more comprehensive state. However, the national state must not be considered a transitional phase, awaiting the stage when it would be absorbed in the *umma* state. We have, instead, to incorporate it as an entity, just as the individual is incorporated in the group, and the family in society.[239]

His descriptions of what the Islamic state should be are similar to some extent to the descriptions of other major Islamic scholars. The ideological foundation for his rejection of nationalism, and for his understanding of what constitutes an Islamic state, lies in the doctrine of *tawhid* as a comprehensive and exclusive program of worship. Al-Turabi argued:

> This fundamental principle of belief has many consequences for an Islamic state: first it's not secular. All public life in Islam is religious being permitted by the experience of the divine, second an Islamic state is not a nationalistic state because ultimate allegiance is owed to Allah and thereby to the community of all believers, the *ummah*, third an Islamic State is not absolute, and fourth an Islamic state is not primordial; the primary institution in Islam is the *ummah*. The phrase "Islamic state" itself is a misnomer. The state is only the political dimension of the collective endeavor of Muslim life.[240]

Al-Turabi used the concept of the *tawhid* as the basic foundation for his theory of liberation or freedom in Islam. According to al-Turabi, human submission to divine *tawhid* makes freedom meaningful and paves the way for individuals to liberate themselves from enslavement to others. Without *tawhid*, humankind has no superior doctrine to liberate it, since human liberating philosophy serves to free people from one ideology only to have them enslaved

---

[238] John L. Esposito. *Voices of Resurgent Islam.* New York: Oxford University Press, 1983.

[239] El-Affendi, "Turabi's *Revolution*,"178.

[240] Hasan al-Turabi. "Principles of Governance, Freedom, and Responsibility in Islam." *The American Journal of Islamic Sciences* 4, no. 1 (1987): 1-11.

by another.[241] *Tawhid* is, then, a doctrine that liberates humans from humans and connects them to a higher level of responsibility. Al-Turabi further argues that the actual, or rather the political, aspect of *tawhid* is not living a specific, traditional way of social and political life; instead, it is living a life that centers around the unity of humankind and, more specifically, the unification of Muslims as a starting point. It is the practical fulfillment of the universal *rabaniyya* (lordship) of God which ties together patterns of living and worship and liberates them from human methods.[242]

Al-Turabi's interpretations of *tawhid* is different from other Muslim scholars, such as Mohammed Ibn Abdelwahab (1703-1792) who saw *tawhid* as a return to the uncorrupted bygone religious community that declined due to foreign innovations (*bidah*). Particular emphasis by Abdelwahab is given to "un-Islamic" practices that were widespread in Arabia among Muslims at that time, such as visiting graves of the Prophet's companions or famous religious scholars, and celebrating annual feasts for Sufi spiritual figures. Abdelwahab condemned these practices and considered them a form of polytheism (*shirk*).

Al-Turabi's writings on issues such as the relation between the Islamists and society and the Islamists and secular governments in the Islamic world were a major departure from al-Mawdudi and Qutb's rejectionist positions that dominated Islamic movements in the 1960s and the 1970s. Al-Turabi saw the Islamic Movement as a force in advocating Islam from within the system. His view was in contrast to al-Mawdudi and Qutb's thesis that described existing Islamic societies as *Jahili* (the period before Islam in Arabia), and suggested that "real" Muslims must isolate themselves from these *Jahili* societies then attack them from outside as the only moral ideal to establish the Islamic state. He discarded the use of coercion to achieve Islamic reforms and argued for the possibility of peaceful transition from within Islam, thus rejecting Qutb's main

---

[241] Ibid.
[242] Ibid.

contention about the *Jahilliyya* of current Islamic societies.[243] Unlike Qutb, al-Turabi rejected the idea of withdrawing from society and encouraged cooperation with other organizations and political groups for the common good of the people. He repeatedly used such tactics to achieve Movement goals, as in the creation of the ICF and the Movement's collaboration with other parties, including the SCP, in the 1964 Uprising to topple Abboud's military regime. For al-Turabi, Islamization is a gradual process where the emphasis is on the transformation of individuals rather than the transformation of society as whole.

Al-Turabi's views on working within the existing secular political establishment were put in place in 1977 when he convinced the Movement's leadership to accept the conditions of the National Reconciliation Accord (NRA), which granted the Movement the freedom of operation in exchange for its political support of Nemeri's military regime.[244] After the signing of the NRA accord, al-Turabi was appointed as a member of the Politburo of Nemeri's ruling party the Sudanese Socialist Union (SSU). Later when he was appointed as the country's attorney general, he led the Committee charged with the Islamization of the Sudanese Laws. That Committee systematically examined the existing legal codes to check for conformity with Islamic law and recommended appropriate amendments or new laws.[245] During the period of national reconciliation (1977-1984) al-Turabi transformed his Movement from a tiny small elite-centered organization to one of the most powerful Islamic political organization in the Islamic world.

Al-Turabi's views on *shura* and democracy were also revolutionary. Al-Turabi believed that, if the *shura* and democracy are viewed outside their historical conditions, then they will be used synonymously to indicate the same idea. While it is true that ultimate sovereignty in Islam belongs to Allah, practical

---

[243] Lamia Rustum Shehadeh. *The Idea of Women in Fundamentalist Islam.* Jacksonville; FL: University of California Press, 2007.

[244] Zakaria Bashier. *The National Reconciliation in the Sudan and Its Aftermath*, Seminar Papers 12. Leicester, England: Islamic Foundation, 1981.

[245] Ibid.

and political sovereignty centers on the people. For al-Turabi, therefore, *shura* does not take away communal freedom to select an appropriate course of action, a set of rules or even representative bodies.[246] Thus, al-Turabi reserves the ultimate political authority to the community which, in return, concludes a contract with individuals to lead the community and organize its affairs. Al-Turabi accepts any state order that is bound by and is based on contractual mutuality, where the ruler never transgresses against the individual or communal freedom provided by the Quran. Al-Turabi further argues that the main Quranic discourse is not primarily directed to the state but to the people, and more specifically to the individual.[247]

Al-Turabi's views on *ijtihad* (interpretation of Islamic jurisprudence), *ijmaa* (consensus), and *tajdid* (renewal), Islam, and art and music are also revolutionary. The Islamic political ideology in general is based on four pillars, the Quran, *Sunna*, *ijmaa*, and *ijtihad*. Al-Turabi's views on the first two (the Quran and the *Sunna*) are to some degree similar to the views of traditional Muslim scholars. As for the *ijmaa* and the *ijtihad* his view could be considered a major departure from the traditional Muslims scholars' thoughts.

Al-Turabi starts his arguments about the need for new thinking and *ijtihad* by figuratively lashing against traditional Islamic *ulama*. He describes them as having a virtual monopoly over Islam and being conservative in their attitudes. According to him, "They are not conscious of developments, and they never renew religious spirit and religious thoughts from time to time."[248] He further argues these traditional *ulama* failed to understand the dire necessity not only to consider new answers to new problems but also to reconsider how to revitalize the methodology of *usul al-Fiqh al-Islami* (Source Methodology in Islamic jurisprudence). Hence, *usual al-Fiqh al-Islami*, for al-Turabi depended on a continuous renewal of ideas to be able to provide answers to current problems, and thus transform religious jurisprudence into political doctrine. In emphasizing

---

[246] Hasan al-Turabi. *Tajdid Usul Al- Al-Islami*. Beirut, Lebanon: Dar al-Jil, 1980.

[247] Ibrahim, "A Theology of Modernity," 194-222.

[248] Lamia Rustum Shehadeh. *The Idea of Women in Fundamentalist Islam*. Jacksonville; FL: University of California Press, 2007, 145.

the central role of knowledge in Islamism, al-Turabi expands the original meaning of *alim* (religious scholar) to designate anybody who knows anything well enough to relate to Allah. Since all knowledge is divine, specialists of all domains (medicine, engineering, chemistry, law, economics, etc) are *ulama*.[249]

Al-Turabi constantly advocates the usage of *ijtihad* as the only way to adapt *Shari'a* rules to changing societal circumstances. He further emphasizes the need for a comprehensive *ijtihad* by stating that "The most serious thing we have found is that most of the Islamic literature has been written centuries ago, and much of it is not relevant today, in the fields of economics, law, politics, government, etc. Therefore, a great deal of *ijtihad* is required."[250] For changes in circumstances necessitate changes in religious expression, the only exceptions to change being "the eternal principles of the divine message."[251] According to al-Turabi, Muslims may vary the practices of the prototype community of the Prophet to meet changing realities, but they must always retain the meaning behind the original model.

Al-Turabi further argues that because there is no clergy in Islam, *ijtihad* is open to anyone who is qualified for it. No one can monopolize the understanding Islam. In other words, there is no official spokesperson for Islam. In the past, Muslims practiced *ijtihad* in very effective and creative ways. There was a time in which *ijtihad* was the general rule and the exception was the *taqleed* (following rules declared by a person who did *ijtihad*). During that era, Muslims were attached to the text (Quran and the *Sunna*), not to the scholars. And even the scholars used to teach the people that they should abandon their (scholars') own opinion if they found an evidence (from the Quran and the *Sunna*) stronger than theirs.[252]

Al-Turabi's views on *ijmaa* are also unique and different from the views of other Islamic scholars. Traditionally, *ijmaa* is understood as the consensus of

---

[249] Ibid., 145.
[250] Ibid., 145.
[251] Ibid., 145.
[252] Ibid., 146.

ulama, or the consensus of the orthodox religious leaders. Al-Turabi argues that the difficulty of achieving popular consensus on most issues led the *ulama* to neglect the central role of Muslim public opinion in legislation. This was compounded by the fast spread of Islam, leading to the existence of masses of Muslims not properly educated in matters of faith. *Ulama* thus assumed "guardianship" over these masses.

The natural thing, according to al-Turabi's views, is to have democratic representative governments and an enlightened public. Al-Turabi further defines *ijmaa* as the consensus of a community or the people. Al-Turabi argues, unlike in Christianity, *ulama* in Islam were not given any exclusive roles; they are part of the *umma* and hold the same duties and responsibilities as the public.[253] Al-Turabi further expands the concept of *ulama* to include any person who is knowledgeable and educated. Thus, important public issues are undertaken by representatives of the people and not by religious authority, which according to al-Turabi does not exist in Islam.

Tajdid is al-Turabi's most treasured idea. The call for the revival and renewal of Islam continued to be the trumpet call of all activists since al-Afghani.[254] In a lecture at the University of Khartoum in Januray 1978, al-Turabi argued

> "Islam needs to be re-thought radically. It is not true, he says, that Islam is eternal and cannot change. There are eternal principles in Islam which are commonly known as *ibadat* (worships) and there is *fiqh* (the classical exposition of religious law inherited from earlier generations of Muslims), which is a more human endeavor, representing the cumulative understanding of earlier Islamic thinkers of religious truths and commands. *Fiqh* could be reevaluated freely by today's Muslim."[255]

According to al-Turabi, traditionalIslamic thought shifted the responsibility in this rethinking to a mythical savior of the faith referred to

---

[253] Muhammad al-Hashimi Hamidi. & Hasan al-Turabi. *The Making of an Islamic Political Leader: Conversations with Hasan Al-Turabi.* Boulder, Colo.: Westview Press, 1998.

[254] Osman, "The Political and Ideological Development," 387.

[255] Ibid., 387.

normally as al-Mahdi.[256] In truth, however, it is the responsibility of the community as a whole, and should be undertaken in our time by a movement or a large group, since it has become a very complex task which can not be undertaken by individuals.[257]

Tajdid (renewal) is also an ongoing exercise that needs to be undertaken continuously. According to al-Turabi:

> Tajdid is not a transcendence of religion, but a response to the demands of religiosity in an evolving situation. The way to achieve this tajdid, according to al-Turabi, is to go back to the basic principles of Islam. This must not be interpreted as a call to return to the forms of earlier religious expressions or even to the study of earlier texts. This latter attitude is an aberration caused by isolation within the old forms of thinking expressed by the so-called Salafiyya movement (movement attempting to go back to the 'roots' of 'true' Islam), which saw the highest religious achievements in following what the salaf (ancestors) had done. [258]

These people were oblivious of the fact that some of the earlier forms of religious expression, if forced on a different reality, could lead to the opposite of what was intended and could jeopardized the true mission of Islam. The true Muslims must constantly view their heritage critically and not dogmatically, and subject it to the eternally revealed principles, which are the objects of their attempt to realize the ideals of religion. For fulfillment of the demands of true religion, al-Turabi maintains it's the duty of every generation of Muslims to make its own original contribution to religious life.[259]

Al-Turabi also called for tajdid al-Fiqh, "renewal of laws." He argued that the traditional fiqh was adapted to a life where the individual led a largely autonomous life, while today's Muslims are faced with a more closely-knit social existence created by intensive urbanization and socialization of life.[260] These new changes need a new way of thinking, supplemented by the findings of the social

---

[256] Ibid., 388.
[257] Ibid., 388.
[258] Ibid., 392.
[259] Ibid., 392.
[260] Ibid., 389.

sciences and the philosophy of sciences. New *fiqh*, according to al-Turabi, should concentrate on social rather than individual issues.[261]

Al-Turabi also called for developing a new method for interpreting Islam. According to him, modern interpretations of Islam tend to be timid and display a gross lack of methodology.[262] This created a great gap between Muslims' thought and the needs of their actual life. This according to el-Affendi:

> ... divided Muslims between rigid traditionalists and timid reformers. The traditionalists, who wanted to restrict new interpretations by demanding stringent qualifications for anyone deemed fit to pronounce independent opinion on religious matters, espouse safeguards and precautions that now conflict with the needs of Muslim society. They thus tended to divide Muslim society into a majority that was excluded from thinking about religion, and a clique which monopolized religious secrets. Timid modernizers, on the other hand, are still intimidated by ready accusations of heresy in presenting their new ideas, while all the time looking in ancient books for ideas that may remotely resemble theirs.[263]

Another problem with modern Islamic thinkers according to al-Turabi was their lack of methodological consensus. There is no consensus on methods, and the search for an implicit methodology only reveals total methodological confusion.[264] The remedy for such confusion suggested by al-Turabi was

> ... the creation of well-informed public opinion to resolve the disputes, or a political authority that would organize procedures to determine what a legitimate consensus is. Both the Muslim public and the political authority in the lands of Islam are in no position to fulfill this role, because of the lack of knowledge and direction. There is thus no alternative but for the intellectuals to develop a methodological consensus according to which all interpretations would be judged and evaluated. [265]

The new methodology that should be developed by Muslim intellectuals must be based on *tawhid*, and governed by the balance it creates between

---

[261] Ibid., 389.
[262] Ibid., 393.
[263] Ibid., 394.
[264] Ibid., 394.
[265] Ibid., 395.

individual and group, society and state, conscience and practice, and reason and revelation.[266]

Unlike *Salafiyya* groups who were consistently in conflict with Sufi groups and frequently accused them of being *mushrik* (Islamic concept of the sin of polytheism) because they believe that their sheikhs (leaders) hold some forms of mystical powers from God, al-Turabi called on Sufi leaders to abandon some of their teachings and practices that clearly contradicted Islam. He never accused them of being *mushrik*, as he clearly understood the important role that these groups had in spreading Islam, not only in Sudan, but also in Africa. Al-Turabi's views on Sufism and Islamic traditional scholars were greatly influenced by his background. Al-Turabi's ancestors, including his father, were members of Sufi groups and when he was child, these Sufi groups were frequent visitors to his home.[267] Al-Turabi views helped the Movement expand its base among these groups. The Movement further instructed its members to keep their membership with Sufi groups and correct what they thought contradicted Islam, instead of leaving their Sufi group once they join the Movement.

Another area of traditional Islamic thinking which al-Turabi revolutionized was the relation between religion, art and music. He criticized the intense hostility of the traditional scholars toward art and music and condemned them as *haram* (forbidden) in Islam. Al-Turabi introduced the concepts of "Islamic art" and "Islamic music" mainly in the fields of theatre, painting, and Islamic singing. Al-Turabi tried to liberate the issue of art and music from controversies about what is permissible and what is not that have occupied Muslim scholars for centuries.[268]

Al-Turabi approach was innovative and radical. He first defined art as "the creation of beauty" and then proceeded to show that beauty was recognized in Islam as a supreme gift from God that is to be enjoyed in gratitude. Art and music

---

[266] Ibid., 395.
[267] Ibrahim, "A Theology of Modernity,"194-222.
[268] El-Affendi, "Turabi's *Revolution*,"175-176.

could, therefore, in themselves become a great aid to religiosity or a great handicap to it.[269] For al-Turabi, "art is an activity laden with symbolic content that transcends reality and gives added impetus from imagination and feeling to the movement toward God."[270] Al-Turabi further argues that art must be used to serve the cause of Islamic revival. In the case of music, he called for integrating music and singing into religion. This could be achieved by the creation of art and music that are directed toward worshipping God. According to him "the greatest challenge for Islamists today is therefore to re-conquer art and music for religion and thus end the western philosophical domination in the field of art and music."[271]

Al-Turabi views created much controversy, especially when he tried to interpret some commands of the Prophet and the Quranic verses in a manner at great variance with what traditional Islamic scholars believed. For example, using some Quranic verses, he rejected the stoning of adulteresses as an obligatory rule in Islam. He also voiced his objection to condemning an apostate to death and declared such a sentence was not mandatory but conditional on his engaging in war against the Muslim community.[272] Such pronouncements caused a great deal of anger even within the ranks of the Movement and were the basis of the split that occurred in the mid-1970s. They were also the reason for a strong campaign launched from the centers of traditionalism in Saudi Arabia, Egypt, and the International Muslim Brotherhood movement. Despite these fierce campaigns by centers of traditionalists in Egypt and Saudi Arabia, al-Turabi's theoretical contributions have played a major role in enhancing the position of the Islamic Movement not only in Sudan, but also in the Islamic world.

Al-Turabi's charisma and leadership skills were also important in bridging the generation gap within the Movement. Unlike the main Brotherhood in Egypt,

---

[269] Osman, "The Political and Ideological Development," 402.

[270] Ibid., 402.

[271] Ibid., 404.

[272] Hasan Al-Turabi. Islam, Democracy, the State and the West: A Round Table with Dr. Hasan Turabi, May 10, 1992 Beirut: Lebanon: al-Dar al-Jadid, 1995.

which was consistently undergoing rifts between the old guard of the organization and its younger members, the presence of al-Turabi in the Sudanese Movement guaranteed its cohesiveness. Al-Turabi is often described by observers as a man of high intellect and incredible charisma. He is articulate in English, French and Arabic and at ease in both Western and Sudanese dress. According to Peter Kok, al-Turabi is "Machiavellian, dynamic, and ruthless, a forceful and charismatic personality."[273] One of his followers is purported to have said, "Al-Turabi's genius is most apparent in his ability to hover on the borderline between numerous antagonistic positions. He sits astride modernity and tradition, pragmatism and idealism, calculation and faith."[274] As a charismatic leader, al-Turabi masters the game of power politics. In his appeal to the educated elite, he resorts to reason and, when necessary, "moral persuasion."

The Movement's theoretical contributions in the period between 1962 and 1989 were eagerly studied and often accepted by Islamic movements in other countries. Al-Turabi's philosophical thoughts influenced a new generation of Islamic thinkers such as Rashid al-Ghanoushi of Tunisia who built on al-Turabi's innovative approaches to issues such as *tajdid, ijmaa,* and *shura.* Al-Turabi's view on working within the society, rather than attacking it from outside as suggested by Qutb, shaped the future of many other Islamic movements in the region. The Egyptian Brotherhood, for example, gradually became more involved in the political process and by the mid-1980s started to run candidates in the country's parliamentary elections. The same transformations in the attitude toward secular governments occurred in Kuwait, Bahrain, Palestine, and Algeria where Islamic Movements gradually became part of the political process.

---

[273] Peter Nyot kok. "Hasan Abdulla Al-Turabi." *Orient* 33, no. 2 (1992): 185-92.
[274] Osman, "The Political and Ideological Development," 189.

Women

The issue of women in Islam is highly controversial. Many materials on this subject lack objectivity and clarity, some writers often confuse Islamic teachings about the role of women in society with the local customs in some Muslim countries that limited that role. Another major problem with the literature about women in Islamic countries is the fact that writers on the subject are not always able to recognize the diversity within and between Islamic countries. This is also true in the case of the Islamic Movement's position toward women. Several authors, particularly feminist activists, tend to incorrectly describe the Movement's position toward women as reactionary and anti-women.[275]

One example of these misunderstandings is the issue of *hijab*." The *hijab* (veil) is the form of scarf covering the hair commonly worn by Muslim women. Many western researchers, especially feminist activists, view it as oppressive and as a symbol of a Muslim woman's subservience to men. As a result, it often comes as a surprise to Western feminists that the veil has become increasingly common in the Muslim world and is often worn proudly by college girls as a symbol of an Islamic identity, freeing them symbolically from neo-colonial Western cultural imperialism and domination.[276]

There are a few exceptions to this trend; chief among them is the book by Esposito and Haddad, *Islam, Gender, and Social Change.* In this book Esposito and Haddad discuss the impact of the Islamic resurgence on gender issues in Iran,

---

[275] For example see the works of Sondra Hale. "Activating the Gender Local: Transnational Ideologies And "Women's Culture" In Northern Sudan." *Journal of Middle East Women's Studies* 1, no. 1 (2005): 29-52. "Gender Politics and Islamization in Sudan." Women Living Under Muslim Laws http://www.wluml.org/english/pubsfulltxt.shtml?cmd%5B87%5D=i-87-2670 Accessed 01/17/2007. "Mothers and Militias: Islamic State Construction of the Women Citizens of Northern Sudan." *Citizenship Studies* 3, no. 3 (1999): 373. "Sudanese Women and Revolutionary Parties: The Wing of the Patriarch." *MERIP Middle East Report*, no. 138 (1986): 25-30.

[276] "Women in Islam: Muslim Women." Islam, Islamic Studies, Arabic, Religion. Available at http://www.uga.edu/islam/Islamwomen.html. Accessed 02/15/2007. Another article that discusses the impact of political Islam on the role of women is Roksana Bahramitash. "Myths and Realities of the Impact of Political Islam on Women: Female Employment in Indonesia and Iran." *Development in Practice* 14, no. 4 (2004): 508-20.

134

Egypt, Jordan, Sudan, and other Islamic countries. The book as a whole militates against the stereotype of Muslim women as repressed, passive, and without initiative. At the same time it acknowledges the very real obstacles to women's initiatives in most of these societies, as well as the fact that not all Islamic Movements are reactionary in their views of women's role in public life. Indeed some movements such as the Islamic Movement in Sudan since the mid 1960s clearly advocated greater roles for women in the public life.[277]

Another exception is the writings of Professor Carolyn Fluehr-Lobban, who is an acknowledged authority on Sudan, especially with regard to women. She writes:

> When I began working in the Sudan in 1970 I was struck by the sharp contrast between the passive and controlled Muslim woman I had expected from my readings about Arab and Islamic society, and the reality which I encountered in my relationships with Sudanese women. These women presented a strong exterior with a certain toughness of mind and spirit combined, like most Sudanese, with dignity and generosity...In the public arena the movement and activity of women in the urban areas is much less circumscribed than in the past or in more conservative Muslim societies. In the rural areas the confinement of women has rarely been the norm...Veiling and confinement are features of urban bourgeois life in the Arab world and the former is not a cultural tradition in Sudan.[278]

Professor Fluehr-Lobban has also charted the economic emancipation of Sudanese women: "Women are moving into many areas of society from which they were by tradition excluded - in factory work, government bureaucracy, and the professional fields - and this slow transformation has met little resistance."[279] She has also noted the unique position Sudanese women have attained in the legal field - once again in contrast to many other Islamic and Arab countries:

> In 1970 the Sudan...took a bold step when the Grand *Qadi* (similar to a Chief Justice) of the Islamic courts, *Sheikh* Mohammed el-Gizouli,

---

[277] John L. Esposito & Yvonne Y. Haddad. *Islam, Gender, and Social Change.* New York: Oxford University Press, 1997.

[278] Carolyn Fluehr-Lobban. "Women in the Political Arena in the Sudan." In *7th Annual Middle East Studies Association Meeting.* Milwaukee, WI, 1973.

[279] Ibid.

appointed the first woman justice in a Shari'a legal system. Since that time three other women justices have been appointed by the Honorable *Sheikh* el-Gizouli, the only ones, to my knowledge, in the contemporary Islamic world. The Sudan, like most Muslim areas, is undergoing change and is evolving its own set of values that are indigenous and Muslim, and that represent a modernist approach to the improvement of the status of women. [280]

The only Arab countries that have followed Sudan's lead are Lebanon, Jordan, Morocco, Syria, Tunisia, and more recently Egypt.

In its early years, like many other Islamic Movements in the region, the Islamic Movement in Sudan relied on the writings of Hasan al-Banna and other leading figures in the Egyptian Muslim Brotherhood to find answers to the challenges that they faced. One of the great challenges that faced the Islamic Movement in Sudan in its early years was the question surrounding the role of women in public life in general and the role of Sudanese women in the Movement in particular. Thus, in order to clearly understand the position of the Islamic Movement in Sudan in its early years towards women's role in public life, it is essential to understand the response of the main organization in Egypt to this challenge.

Since its establishment at the hands of Hasan al-Banna in 1928, the Muslim Brotherhood organization has given attention to woman's participation. Al-Banna established a Muslim Sisterhood section and assigned it the task of spreading the idea of his Movement among Muslim women in order to raise a generation of women who could shoulder part of the burden carried by the men of the "Muslim Brotherhood" as they endeavored to spread al-Banna's message. Although women participated in certain activities as family members or relatives of the Brothers, the active membership of the female sector of the Brotherhood, the Society of Muslim Sisters, was rather small, never exceeding the peak number

---

[280]Carolyn Fluehr-Lobban. "Challenging Some Myths: Women in Shari'a Law in the Sudan." *Expedition*, no. Spring (1983): 33-34

of 5,000. Despite al-Banna's appeals, the Muslim Brotherhood failed in attracting educated women, who at that time (1930s-1960s) were more attracted by the ideas of the feminist movement from the West and the Eastern Block represented in the works of Egyptian Communists who championed the call for greater women's rights.[281] The failure of the Muslim Brotherhood in Egypt to attract Egyptian women to their ranks was largely due to al-Banna and his early successors relatively conservative views on the role of women in public life. In his tract, 'Toward the Light' in *Five Tracts of Hasan al-Banna,* Al-Banna writes:

> Following are the principal goals of reform grounded on the spirit of genuine Islam...Treatment of the problem of women in a way which combines the progressive and the protective, in accordance with Islamic teaching, so that this problem - one of the most important social problems - will not be abandoned to the biased pens and deviant notions of those who err in the directions of deficiency and excess...a campaign against ostentation in dress and loose behavior; the instruction of women in what is proper, with particular strictness as regards female instructors, pupils, physicians, and students, and all those in similar categories...a review of the curricula offered to girls and the necessity of making them distinct from the boys' curricula in many stages of education...segregation of male and female students; private meetings between men and women, unless within the permitted degrees of relationship, to be counted as a crime for which both will be censured...the encouragement of marriage and procreation, by all possible means; promulgation of legislation to protect and give moral support to the family, and to solve the problems of marriage...the closure of morally undesirable ballrooms and dance-halls, and the prohibition of dancing and other such pastimes. [282]

Despite their failure to attract more female members to the Organization, the Muslim Brotherhood in Egypt rejected what they called the Western model for Muslim women. Their publications consistently emphasized the "exploitation" of women and female sexuality in the West as commodities in such fields as

---

[281] Shehadeh, 2007.

[282] Hasan Al-Banna. *Five Tracts of Hasan Al-Banna.* Translated by Charles Wendell. Berkeley, CA, 1978, 126.

advertisement, secretarial work, modeling, and sales to enhance profits.[283] However, while the Brothers encouraged women to seek education and forbade them no field of study as long as they were modest in their behavior and dress, they admitted that education for professionalism should not be the most desirable objective of women; their real mission was that of mothers and wives attending to their homes and families. Thus, Hasan al-Hudaybi, the successor of al-Banna as Supreme Guide, stated the Brotherhood's position on women in his declaration that "the women's natural place is home, but if she finds that after doing her duty in the home she has time, she can use part of it in the service of society, on condition that it is done within the legal limits which preserve her dignity and morality."[284]

Another Muslim Brotherhood ideologue who discussed the subject of women in Islam and Muslim societies is Sayyid Qutb. Qutb frequently argued that Islam gives women rights more than any other religion or secular system. In his book *Social Justice in Islam*, he writes:

> As for the relation between the sexes, Islam has guaranteed to women a complete equality with men with regard to their sex; it has permitted no discrimination except in some incidental matters connected with physical nature, with customary procedure, or with responsibility, in all of which the privileges of the two sexes are not in question. Wherever the physical endowments, the customs, and the responsibilities are identical, the sexes are equal; and wherever there is some difference in these respects, the discrimination follows that difference. [285]

Qutb further argued that "the strongest point in Islam is the equality which it guarantees to women in religion, as well as in their possessions and their gains. Also it gives them the assurance of marriage only with their own consent and at

---

[283] See for example the works of Lamia Rustum Shehadeh. *The Idea of Women in Fundamentalist Islam*. Jacksonville; FL: University of California Press, 2007., "Women in the Discourse of Sayyid Qutb." *Arab Studies Quarterly* 22, no. 3 (2000): 45-55. Valentine M. Moghadam. "Islamist Movements and Women's Responses in the Middle East." *Gender & History* 3, no. 3 (1991): 268-84.

[284] Shehadeh, 2007.

[285] Sayyid Qutb. *Social Justice in Islam* Translated by John B. & Hamid Algar Hardie. Revised edition. Baltimore, MD: Islamic Publications International, 2000, 49-53.

138

their own pleasure; they need not marry either through compulsion or through negligence; and they must get a dowry." [286]

In Sudan, the first women's organization emerged in June 1947 under the name of the League of Educated Young Women (LEYW). It was established during a meeting of women that was called by Fatima Talib (later, also a founding member of the Muslim Sisterhood). The organization's objectives were mainly social in the fields of welfare and education. They organized literacy and health classes for women and encouraged women who attended schools to further their education by attending colleges and becoming more active in society. Despite its progressive program, the LEYW lasted less than two years. As a result of political differences, the organization ceased to exist in 1949. A leading figure in the LEYW, 'Khalda Zahir' joined the Sudanese Communist Party (SCP) while Fatima Talib became the first women to join the Muslim Brotherhood organization in Sudan.[287]

In 1952 the Women's Union emerged as a united front for all women activists in Sudan. The establishment of the Women's Union was a political turning point in the women's movement in Sudan. Since its establishment, the Women's Union became active in Sudanese public life and the international arena and it was able to develop a close linkage with World's Women Movement, regionally and internationally.[288] These close relations with international women's movements, particularly from the Eastern Block, were clear indicators of the role that Communists in Sudan played in establishing this organization. Subsequently, the Muslim Brotherhood instructed their female members not to join the Women's Union despite the fact that Fatima Talib was chosen to lead the Union.[289]

---

[286] Ibid., 49-53.
[287] Nafisa al-Amin & Ahmed abdel-Magied. "A History of Sudanese Women Organizations and the Strive for Liberation and Empowerment." *Ahfad Journal* 18, no. 1 (2001): 2-23.
[288] Ibid.
[289] Ibid.

The early leadership of the Muslim Brotherhood in Sudan was also heavily influenced by the traditional views of some Muslim scholars who opposed political rights for women, such as voting rights and the rights to be elected and to hold offices. The new organization came under fierce attacks from some traditional Islamic scholars supported by the Brotherhood's leadership at that time, Babiker Karar and Merghani el-Nasri, who opposed any political rights for women.[290]

Women recruits were hard to bring into the Muslim Brotherhood in its early years. After Talib joined the organization in 1949, no other women joined until 1951, when Suad al-Fatih was recruited followed by Thoria Umbabi in 1952.[291] In 1954 all Islamist cells united under the name of the Muslim Brotherhood in Sudan. Following al-Banna's guidelines on the importance of women's role in the organization and in trying to address the issues surrounding women's recruitment, a women's bureau was established with its main mission to propagate the Muslim Brotherhood ideology among educated women and to increase their number in the organization. The new office consisted of nine members, three men and six women. Despite its limited resources and small size, the new office laid the fundamentals for the organization's work among educated women and published a weekly women's magazine called al-Manar (1956-1957, 1964-1969) edited by Suad al-Fatih.

Despite their modest view on the role of women in the Sudanese political life, the Muslim Brotherhood in Sudan was consistently put on the defensive with regard to their views on the role of women in public life. The Communists and other leftists groups frequently accused them of harboring reactionary views that devalued the status of women. As a result, the female students at the university (and the women's movement generally) became very hostile to the Islamists and very sympathetic to their communist adversaries who purported to support the rights of women.

---

[290] Haga Kashif Badri. *Women's Movement in the Sudan.* New Delhi: Asia News Agency, 1986.
[291] Ahmad, "*Harakat Al-Ikhwan Al-Muslimin Fi Al-Sudan, 1944 -1969,*"37.

In an attempt to enhance their position among women, especially those with education, the Muslim Brotherhood abandoned some of their early positions regarding women, and following the October Uprising in 1964, supported the move to give them the right to be elected. When this was granted, competition became very fierce for women support among political parties. This was reflected in the proliferation of party-affiliated women's groups. However, the largest and most influential organization in the field remained the communist-dominated Women's Union. The Muslim Brotherhood found itself squeezed out of the competition, beaten by communists, among educated women and frustrated by unshakable traditional allegiances among the uneducated.

In the 1956 and 1968 elections, educated women voted overwhelmingly against the Muslim Brotherhood. Because of the educated women's support, the Sudanese Communist Party (SCP) won 11 out of 15 parliamentary seats that were designated for high schools and college graduates only. One of these seats was won by Fatima Ahmed Ibrahim, who became the first Sudanese woman to be elected to the parliament. Also, the SCP affiliated students' organization dominated the student movements and the students' union associations in the country because of the support of the female students.

Despite their efforts to improve their image among women in general, the Muslim Brotherhood failed to give clear answers to most of the questions and challenges that faced Sudanese women in the 1960s, such as reformation of family law, under-age marriages, more liberal divorce laws, and participation of women in public and political life. This failure could be contributed to two major factors: the conservative nature of the MB leadership at that time, and its reliance on the intellectual contributions of the Egyptian Brotherhood, who clearly advocated a more conservative approach toward women. As al-Effendi observed in his introduction to al-Turabi's book *Women in Islam and Muslim Society*, "the Muslim Brotherhood's strategy toward women lacked coherence and clear theoretical foundations. The Islamists were moved mainly by reaction to communist and secularist successes and propaganda."[292]

The return of Hasan al-Turabi from France in the mid-1960, and his election as the leader of the Muslim Brotherhood in Sudan led to dramatic changes in the Muslim Brotherhood's positions toward women and women-related issues. Al-Turabi's position on women was a major shift in the Movement's views toward women. He gave more attention to the role of women, both in terms of the broader teachings of Islam and more specifically in terms of the Islamic Movement itself. The basic transformation, in al-Turabi's account, was that the Movement must reorient itself in order to be in accord with the standards of religion rather than only with the existing social norms.[293]

A critical turning point in the Movement's discourse on women was the publication in 1973 of al-Turabi's small book titled *Women in Islam and Muslim Society,* described by many as the most influential work ever written by him. As el-Affendi argued "it sparked a revolution that transformed the way in which the Islamic Movement in Sudan approached the role of women in society and within the Movement, and radically transformed the Movement itself." [294]

In that book al-Turabi convincingly argued that limitations on women's freedoms in traditional society had nothing to do with Islam. In fact they represented rare instances when the normally very conservative Muslim traditionalists decided to defy the clear injunction in the Quran and *Sunna* guaranteeing the rights of women. Additionally, he argued that defending these traditional restrictions was as un-Islamic as it is futile. Women's liberation was an inevitable consequence of the relentless material and technological progress sweeping through the Muslim world. So the question is not whether to oppose or endorse women's liberation, it was rather, do Islamists want women's liberation within the framework of Islam or outside it? For al-Turabi the answer was

---

[292] Hasan al-Turabi. *Women in Islam and Muslim Society.* London, U.K: Milestones Publishers 1991, 2.

[293] Esposito & Voll, 135.

[294] al-Turabi, " *Women in Islam,"*1-3.

obvious, and he argued that Sudanese Islamists should take the lead in the search for a solution of this issue within the context of Islam.[295]

In this book al-Turabi highlights the accomplishments of Muslim women during the lifetime of Prophet Mohammed and explains these within the context of the Quran and the *Sunna* (traditions) of the Prophet. He writes:

> In the religion of Islam, a woman is an independent entity, and thus a fully responsible human being. Islam addresses her directly and does not approach her through the agency of Muslim males. A woman assumes full capacity and liability once she attains maturity and receives the message of Islam.[296]

This means that women have the same obligation and rights as men:

> The verdict of Islamic jurisprudence is just the practical expression of the dictates of the faith. Women, according to Shari'a, are counterparts of men. And in Islamic jurisprudence, there is no separate order of regulations for them. There are, however, a few limited secondary regulations where a distinction is drawn between the two sexes. But these are intended purely to enable both of them to give a genuine expression of their faith in accordance with their respective human nature. But the Shari'a (or Islamic law) is essentially the same, and its general rules are common for both the sexes; it is addressed to both without any distinction. The underlying presumption in the Shari'a is that sex is immaterial, except where the text makes the distinction or where proof can be adduced to that effect.[297]

Al-Turabi further notes that in beginning, women converted to Islam as individuals, sometimes before the men of their households. They took an active role in public life, sometimes as warriors in battle, and occasionally participated in political affairs. Al-Turabi emphasizes the point that "public life is no stage where men alone can play. There is no segregation of sexes in public domains which call for joint efforts."[298] Al-Turabi places the blame squarely on Muslim males:

---

[295] Ibid., 3.
[296] Ibid., 5.
[297] Ibid., 11.
[298] Ibid., 11.

The Muslims in history have experienced a significant desertion from the general ideals of life as taught by Islam. It is, therefore, not at all surprising that their loss is equally great in the area of social guidance which Islam offered regarding women. Whenever weakness creeps into the faith of Muslim men they tend to treat women oppressively and seek to exploit them. This is natural and is amply demonstrated by the fact that most of the rulings of the Quran regarding women were sent down as restrictions on men with a view to preventing them from transgressing against women, as is their natural disposition and their actual practice in many societies. Only a few of the Quranic injunctions impose restrictions on women.[299]

The consequences of historical development, in al-Turabi's view, are that a "revolution against the condition of women in traditional Muslim societies is inevitable" and that it is the task of Islamists to "close the gap between the by-gone historical reality and the desired model for ideal Islam."[300] This task is made more complex by the circumstances of the modern world, where modern Western ideals for the role of women constitute "a serious temptation for the downtrodden Muslim women."[301] He strongly advocated that proper Islamic reform be undertaken before the alien trends became fully assimilated, and he opposed simple conservative opposition to Western influences. He wrote:

The Islamists should beware of an attitude that seeks refuge from the invading liberating western culture in the indigenous past as a lesser evil that should be preserved with some accommodation. Conservation is a wasted effort. The Islamists are worthy of the leadership of the movement of women's liberation from the traditional quagmire of historical Islam, and that of their resurgence towards the heights of ideal Islam. They should not leave their society at the mercy of the advocates of westernization who exploit the urgency of reform to deform society and lead it astray. The teachings of their own religion call upon Islamists to be the right-guided leaders for the salvation of men and women, emancipating them from the shackles of history and convention, and steering their life clear of the aberrations of mutative change.[302]

---

[299] Ibid., 38.
[300] Ibid., 46.
[301] Ibid., 46-47.
[302] Ibid., 47.

Al-Turabi's views on women's dress women and segregation in Islam are
also revolutionary and very liberal compared to other Islamic scholars; he argues:

> With respect to women, it is unfortunate that people just focus on
> women's dress. Men and women in public are both required to dress in a
> particular form. Segregation is definitely not part of Islam; this is just
> conventional historical Islam. Segregation of women, whether in classes,
> in the street or in the house, hareem quarters, this is a development
> which was totally unknown in the model of Islam, or in the text of Islam;
> it is unjustified. But dress, yes; in the Quran and the Sunna, there is
> definitely a prescription, not for the mode, but how much you should
> cover.[303]

In al-Turabi's views the final goal was not only to turn Islam into a vehicle
of liberation for women, but also to turn women into a dedicated corps in support
of Islamization. The result of this new emphasis on the role of women was that
the Muslim Brotherhood in Sudan became active in advocating women's rights
and in calling for comprehensive legal and social reforms to address women's
concerns. In the organization itself women came to play an increasingly important
part.

Women had already provided important leadership in the Sudanese
Communist Party (SCP) already in the 1960s, but by the 1980s the Brotherhood,
under al-Turabi's leadership, soon equaled and then surpassed the SCP as the
political group, receiving support from educated women. As Ismail and Hall
(1981) noticed, "the movement of the Muslim Brotherhood in Sudan was able to
attract many female supporters particularly among the student population." [304]
Even the most critical voices of the Islamic Movement in Sudan, such as Sondra
Hall, acknowledged the prominent role that women were playing in the
Movement. She wrote "Women are among the most active and visible organizers

---

[303] al-Turabi, Hasan & Lowrie Arthur L. *Islam, Democracy, the State and the West : A Round
Table with Dr. Hasan Turabi, May 10, 1992,* Wise Monograph Series ;; No. 1;. Tampa, Fla.,
U.S.A: World & Islam Studies Enterprise, 1993, 54-58.
[304] Bakhita Amin Ismail & Marjorie Hall. *Sisters under the Sun: The Story of Sudanese Women.*
London, U.K: Longman Group Limited, 1981, 25.

of the NIF and the NIF have considerable support at the university."[305] She also found that "women in the NIF are not only participating in but are central to the formation of NIF's 'modern Islamic woman'."[306] These female supporters played a significant role in reshaping the political map of Sudan, especially among the educated elite.

As a result of this new emphasis on the role of women within the organization and al-Turabi's liberal views on women's rights, the Muslim Brotherhood dominated the students' movement in Sudan for more than 25 years. For example, students' votes for the Muslim Brotherhood in the University of Khartoum students' union elections rose from 1172 votes in 1966 to 1589 in 1967 and again to 2026 in 1968. During the same period the Islamic Movement, for the first time in its history, started to regularly to list female candidates in students' unions elections. During the last democratic period, 1985-1989, the only two women that were elected to the People's Assembly were the Muslim Brotherhood candidates. Also, in this election the Islamic Movement in Sudan came third. The unprecedented support among educated female voters allowed the Islamic Movement to secure 23 graduate seats out of 28 in the graduate special constituencies, which were traditionally closed for SCP. The gain in the Graduates' Constituencies included all the 21 seats allocated for the Northern regions, plus two from the South.[307]

Al-Turabi's views on women and their role in the political and social life in Islam in general and in Sudan in particular, resulted in unprecedented growth in the numbers of female members of the Islamic Movement in Sudan. By the early 1970s with the rising numbers of female students in higher education and the establishment of several new higher education institutions in Sudan, such as Sudanese University for Science and Technology, Omdurman Islamic University

---

[305] Valentine M. Moghadam. "Islamist Movements and Women's Responses in the Middle East." *Gender & History* 3, no. 3 (1991): 268-84.
[306] Ibid.
[307] Osman, "The Political and Ideological Development,"305.

both for men and women, and El-Gezira University, and Juba University, the rising influence of the Movement became clear as it controlled all student unions in these institutions. Al-Turabi's views about women's segregation and Islamic dress literally revolutionized the works of the Islamists in these newly established higher education institutions.

The increase of Movement members among female students, coupled with the unprecedented expansion in Sudanese higher education institutions, allowed the Islamic Movement in Sudan to have more female graduate cadres in its ranks. As a result, the Islamic Movement in Sudan expanded its control to other professional associations which previously were dominated by leftists, particularly the Sudanese Communist Party.

With more graduates joining the ranks of the Islamic Movement, particularly female students, and with large numbers of Sudanese professionals leaving the country as a result of the country's economic crisis and the opening of better job opportunities in the Gulf countries, the candidates of the Islamic Movement were able to dominate the most influential professional associations in the country. Professional associations such as Sudanese Lawyers Association, Sudanese Physicians Association, and Sudanese Engineers Association came under total domination of the Islamists from the early 1970s to 1985 when other political parties led by communists started to run against the Islamists as a united front despite their deep differences.

Al-Turabi's views on women and their role in society also helped in expanding the role of women in the country beyond traditional roles. As a result of the establishing of Faisal Islamic Bank and other Islamic financial institutions and businesses, which were totally controlled by the Islamists, female members of the Movement were able to obtain employment in these newly created Islamic economic institutions. Islamic banks also created special branches for women. These special branches provided the female members of the Movement with loans, investment options, and other economic opportunities that resulted in the creation for the first time in the country's history of a class of "businesswomen." These new Islamist businesswomen were soon to expand the membership of the Movement for the first time among the uneducated and non-college graduate Sudanese women.

With the help of Islamic banks in Sudan the Islamist businesswomen were able to control the market of women-related products. As a result, large numbers of "Islamic" small and medium businesses started to dominate the Sudanese economy. Businesses such as clothing boutiques and stores, hair shops, Islamic wedding dresses, manicure and pedicure products and stores, women's and children's boutiques and small manufactures were owned and managed by the female members of the Islamic Movement and their close allies and friends. Islamic clothing stores were given particular attention by the Movement leadership, as they gave the Movement the needed exposure among Sudanese women and among the general public. The real mission of these stores was not only profit gains, but also shaping the way that women dressed in Sudan. As result, by the mid-1980s the Islamic dress became the standard in Sudan, not only because it was favored by the Islamists or Sudanese women, but also because of its affordability compared to traditional Sudanese women's clothes.

The female members of the Movement also helped in expanding the Movement's nonprofit organizations. Newly graduated female members were recruited in the Movement's nonprofit organizations to work in education, women's health, and child welfare. Islamic clinics provided unlimited employment opportunities for the Movement's female members. Hundreds of small clinics were established in poor neighborhoods to deliver services for women and children. Also, hundreds of Islamic private schools and childcare centers were built in these neighborhoods and in different parts of the country. As a result, the Islamic Movement expanded its female base to many different parts of the country and increasingly also among non-college graduate women and sometimes even among illiterate women.

148

In his assessment of the role of women in the Islamic Movement in Sudan in 1992, al-Turabi states:

> In Islamic Movement, I would say that women have played a more important role of late than men. They came with vengeance because they had been deprived, and so when we allowed them in the movement, more women voted for us than men because we were the ones who gave them more recognition and a message and place in society. They were definitely more active in our election campaigns than men. Most of our social work and charitable work was done by women.[308]

While many will disagree with the optimistic tone of this assessment, it is clear that the impetus given by al-Turabi's ideas about women in Islam has had an important influence on political life in Sudan.

Al-Turabi's views on the role of women in public life were met with little or no resistance within the ranks of the Movement because the Movement leadership clearly understood the important role that educated women played in the public life of the country. Unlike their counterparts in neighboring countries, the list of accomplishments by Sudanese women by the early 1970s included: the achievement of women's suffrage in 1952; the first parliament member in 1965; increased participation by women in local, regional, and national political bodies, particularly under the Nemeri regime (1969-1985); extension of government pensions to female workers; and confirmation of a commitment to equality of treatment at the workplace after Sudan became signatory to two International Labour Organization (I.L.O.) Conventions -- No. 100, guaranteeing equal remuneration for men and women in similar jobs, and No. 111, against sex discrimination in employment and promotion.[309]

Students

The rise of the Islamic Movement in Sudan is also directly linked to the rapid expansion of education in Sudan since World War II. As in many other

---

[308] Esposito & Voll, 46-47.

[309] For full details on Sudanese women accomplishments compared to women in neighboring countries see William J. House. "The Status of Women in the Sudan." *The Journal of Modern African Studies* 26, no. 2 (1988): 277-302.

newly independent countries, the mass education system of Sudan has been a catalyst for social change and mobility. The role of established educational institutions in Sudan was also similar to their roles in other underdeveloped countries. Universities in underdeveloped countries play a significant role in shaping countries' future because the elite of the modern sector of society are drawn very largely from the reservoir of persons with university training.[310] Universities' roles in these countries is especially important as Lipset (1966) argued "because there is no class of indigenous business enterprisers who, without university training, have taken or are likely to be allowed to take the main responsibility for economic development –as they did in Europe and America in the nineteenth century."[311] Understanding their task as vanguard in their country, and the important role that they play in determining the country's future, university students in Sudan have significantly shaped the country's political future.

The history of Sudanese students' movement and its role in shaping the country's political past and future starts with the establishment of the modern education system in the country during the British administration (1898-1956). Before 1898, during the Turco-Egyptian rule (1821-1885) and al-Mahdia's period (1885-1898), there was no regular education in the country. The education process was mainly conducted by small religious schools known as *Khalwa*. In these *Khalwas* Sudanese children learned how to recite Quran and other Islamic studies. A few of these students who came from notable backgrounds were able to continue their education in Egypt.

The history of modern education in Sudan started with the establishment of Gordon Memorial College in 1899 which was named in honor of General Charles George Gordon of the British army, who was killed during the al-Mahdi's revolution in 1885. The purpose of the college at the time was to prepare

---

[310] Seymour Martin Lipset. "University Students and Politics in Underdeveloped Countries" *Comparative Education Review* 10, no. 2 (1966): 132-62.
[311] Ibid.

Sudanese cadres to support the British administration in Sudan. Many Sudanese boycotted Gordon College at the beginning as they saw the establishment of it as an attempt by the British administration to westernize their children. The ultimate result of this boycott was that those few individuals who were privileged from western education were mainly descended from the houses of the notables and tribal chiefs who were closely allied with the British administration.[312] As a result, the intelligentsia that emerged at the turn of the 19th century was less enthusiastic about becoming involved in opposition politics as they were the main beneficiaries of the colonial system in the country.

After the World War II the need for more trained and educated Sudanese citizens to administer the country resulted in expanding the educational opportunities for Sudanese nationals not associated with tribal leaders or the two major religious sects in the country – al-Ansar led by al-Mahdi's son, and al-Al-Khatmiyya led by Ali al-Mirghani. With the increasing numbers of Sudanese students, more and more students started to organize around social and cultural clubs and associations. The culmination of these activities was a meeting in 1940 at Omdurman Graduates Club that established a union for high school and college graduates. The British administration accepted the idea of the union with the condition that it should limit its activities to sport and cultural issues.[313] In February 1941 the first executive committee was elected and Ahmed Kheir was elected president.[314]

Following World War II the activities of the Union started to shift toward political demands and finally in 1948 the Union became clearly involved in politics when it voiced its objection to the idea of creating a legislative assembly by the British administration, which the Union considered an attempt by the administration to jeopardize Sudanese calls for self-determination and independence.

---

[312] Yahia Hussin Babiker. *KUSU Political Role During 1969-1979*. Khartoum: Sudan: Khartoum University Students Union, Foreign Affairs Secretariat, 1980, 4.

[313] Bashier, *"Al-Harakah Al-Wataniyah,"*258.

[314] Ibid., 258.

In 1949 the Sudanese Communist Party (SCP) established the Students' Congress – an organization that united students at Khartoum University College, formerly known as Gordon Memorial College. The Communists and leftists were able to dominate the Students' Congress during its first years. Unable to compete with Communists and leftists in the College, the Islamists, who at that time were weakly organized and divided, concentrated their efforts among high schools students. By the mid-1950s large numbers of high school "Islamists" entered Khartoum College; this was coupled with a rift within the Communists in Sudan that resulted in creation of several Communist student groups and organizations at the university. As a result, in 1954 the Islamists were able for the first time to capture the Students' Congress which, at that time was renamed to the Students' Union. [315]

These Islamists who worked under the name of the Islamic Groups (IG), according to Ahmed, remained largely a clandestine students' movement due to colonial surveillance. Entrance was only possible through a special oath. The IG movement up to that point neither had a constitution nor possessed a clear ideology beside its anti-Communist stands.[316] In 1956 following the country's independence, the College name was changed to the University of Khartoum and the Students Union became the Khartoum University Students Union (KUSU).

By 1946 large numbers of Sudanese students started to arrive in Egypt. The Muslim Brotherhood and the Communist activists in Egypt were able to establish contact with a number of these students. Some of these students frequently visited the Brotherhood headquarters, especially to attend al-Banna's popular Tuesday lectures. This practice, according to el-Affendi, was not a significant departure from what Sudanese used to do at home, where religious speeches by popular preachers were important attractions. Despite the fact that many of these newly arrived students were not members of the Sudanese Muslim Brotherhood and were mainly supporters of Nile Valley Unity, which was the

---

[315] Ahmad, "*Harakat Al-Ikhwan Al-Muslimin Fi Al-Sudan, 1944 -1969*,"33.
[316] Ibid., 32.

political slogan for those who called for a political union between Sudan and Egypt, they were closely attached to the Brotherhood in Egypt which also advocated the call for the a unity between Egypt and Sudan.[317]

As a result of the rising numbers of Sudanese students in Egypt, the Sudanese Students Union (SSU) was established. Since its establishment, SSU was dominated by Sudanese Communists who were the majority among the Sudanese student body in Egypt. Unlike their counterparts, the Unionists and the Brotherhood, Sudanese Communists advocated self-determination for the Sudanese people and called for creation of an independent Sudanese state with close ties to Egypt.

In 1947 a group of Sudanese students, who were anti-Marxist Unionists closely allied with the Brotherhood, created a parallel student organization to the SSU and named it the League of Sudanese Students (LSS).[318] LSS was mainly dominated by students who advocated unity between Egypt and Sudan. With the rising influence of the left among Sudanese students and declining support among the Sudanese people in general, and the Sudanese intelligentsia in particular for the call for unity between Sudan and Egypt, the LSS students started to search for new political organizations and found their needs in the ideology of the Muslim Brotherhood.[319] A leading figure of the LSS was Sadiq Abdallah Abdel Magid who had come to Egypt in 1940. In 1943 he initiated contacts with Sayyid Qutb and Hasan al-Banna. He appealed to the Muslim Brotherhood for help in fighting the rising influence of Communism in Sudan, particularly among educated Sudanese.[320]

With the rapid expansion of higher education institutions in Sudan, the numbers of Sudanese students in Egypt rapidly declined. The struggle between the Muslim Brotherhood and SCP to control the student movement shifted to

---

[317] Ibid., 27.
[318] El-Affendi, *"Turabi's Revolution,"*47.
[319] Ibid., 47.
[320] Ahmad, *"Harakat Al-Ikhwan Al-Muslimin Fi Al-Sudan, 1944 -1969,"*26.

Sudan, particularly to the University of Khartoum, which is considered by many Sudanese as the most prestigious and influential educational institution in the country. The Brotherhood dominated the KUSU for more than three decades from 1955 to 1989 with the exception of five years 1956, 1969, 1979, 1984, and 1988. The Brotherhood also dominated the student unions at Sudanese Polytechnic Institute, Omdurman Islamic University, Cairo University-Khartoum Branch, Juba University, and El-Gezeria University.

The Brotherhood's domination of the student movement in Sudan could be attributed to several factors: the first factor was the declining influence of the Sudanese Communist Party. As a result of a failed coup in 1971, the SCP leadership was executed and thousands of its active members were imprisoned or forced out of the country. Nemeri's campaign against the SCP greatly weakened its position, especially among students. Also, as a result of the Soviet Union's invasion of Afghanistan in 1979, the image of the USSR as a major supporter for Arab and developing nations' causes was greatly diminished. Due to the change in Sudanese public opinion about the positive role of USSR, coupled with the troubling news that was coming from Communist-oriented countries in the region such as Ethiopia and Southern Yemen, the general mood among Sudanese intellectuals was becoming increasingly hostile toward Communists and their ideology.

In addition, following the 1967 war with Israel, the influence of Nasser's sympathizers and other Arab Nationalist groups among Sudanese students declined. The failure of Nasser's regime, coupled by Anwar al-Sadat's new orientation toward closer relations with the West, particularly the United States, resulted in alienating Nasser's sympathizers both in Egypt and Sudan. In Sudan, following the failed Communist coup in 1971, Nemeri released large numbers of the Brotherhood members in an attempt to counter the SCP influence among students. The same strategy was used successfully by al-Sadat in Egypt when he released the Brotherhood from prisons to counter the Nasserists and Communists in Egyptian universities and professional associations. This strategy achieved great success in Sudan.

Furthermore, al-Turabi's liberal views on women and their role in public life literally revolutionized the way that the Movement functioned and operated in universities. Al-Turabi's views on the segregation of women resulted in expanding the joint works between the male and female members of the Movement who previously functioned separately. His views also resulted in a rapid increase among female students who joined the Movement. Al-Turabi's liberal views on issues such as art and music also expanded the Movement's membership to new frontiers. For the first time, the Movement started to recruit students in the Sudanese College of Fine Arts and the High Institute of Music; both institutions were previously dominated by Communists and independents.

Moreover, the National Reconciliation Accord of 1977 between the Movement and Nemeri's regime, which guaranteed the Movement freedom of operation in exchange for its political support of the regime, resulted in unprecedented growth among the Movement's student membership. The Movement's students, in their attempts to convince the regime that they were its true allies and defenders, took the task of silencing all opposition in high schools and on university campuses. Supporters of other parties and members of opposition parties were routinely muzzled, not only by Nemeri's security apparatus, but also by the violent tactics of the Movement's students.[321]

The new political alliance between Nemeri's military regime and the Movement had a great effect on the student movement in the country. For the first time the military regime of Nemeri was able to infiltrate universities and other higher education institutions through the Movement's membership. According to several anti-government student-activists, following the 1977 accord, the Movement's members in higher education institutions regularly supplied

---

[321] Ali Abdalla Abbas. "The National Islamic Front and the Politics of Education." *Middle East Report*, no. 172 (1991): 22-25.

Nemeri's security apparatus with lists of names of students' and political organizations' leaders who opposed the regime.[322]

Also, following its strategy of grand expansion as a result of the 1977 Accord, the Movement encouraged many of its members to join the teaching profession in middle and high schools and to propagate the Movement's ideology among their students. Members of the Movement were able to infiltrate the Ministry of Education during the 1970s; this gave them access to the development of curricula and the appointment of teachers. Teachers who were members or who were sympathetic to the Movement played a major role in mobilizing student support for the Movement. Many senior members of the Islamic Movement today were exposed to the Movement at primary or secondary school in the 1940s, 1950s, and 1960s. Teachers at elementary levels were able to attract support for the Movement by encouraging students to join social and religious organizations. While their work did not necessarily bring new members to the Movement, it still helped in creating a large pool of potential recruits.

Movement members were also able to effectively use the regime's ban on political activities in high schools to build their cells under the pretext of religious and cultural societies, prayers and Quranic groups. When these students later joined the universities, they became full members of the Movement.[323] By recruiting students in their early years in high schools, the Movement avoided the fierce competition with other political groups at the university level. This was very important for the Movement as it started to lose its grip on the student movement after 1977 because of its unconditional support to Nemeri's regime, which was becoming increasingly unpopular, particularly among university students.

Furthermore, al-Turabi's views on the future of the membership helped the Movement in increasing its members among students. Unlike some leading figures in the Movement who wanted the membership to be restricted and

---

[322] Ibid., 22-25.
[323] Ibid., 22-25.

intensive indoctrination administered, al-Turabi advocated a creation of an open organization accessible for all. Al-Turabi successfully argued, "Islam could not be served by exclusive groups, but by an open organization accessible for all. Political activism does not need to be preceded by indoctrination or "education" since the service of the people in politics, the trade unions, was in itself the best education."[324] As a result of al-Turabi's arguments, the Movement became more open to the public.

In addition, the organizational structure and mobilization techniques of the Movement inside universities and high schools helped it to expand. The Movement mobilized through a variety of activities on the campuses such as trips, picnics, camps, public exhibits and fairs, public debates, and discussion groups. These activities were attended by both sexes. In addition, the Movement organized direct recruits and future members into a series of cells, called *usar* (families. singular: *usrah*). *Usar* on university campuses and high schools functioned independently from the *usarh* of their geographic region.

For example, despite the fact that the University of Khartoum was located in the city of Khartoum and was supposed to function under the direction of the Movement organization in Khartoum, the Movement branch at the University functioned as an independent unit within the national organization. The leadership of the Movement in that university answered directly to the national organization rather than to the Movement's leadership in the city of Khartoum. Students and faculty members belonged to a network of *usrah* on the campus. The activities of these cells focused on the affairs of the Movement at the university, their political agenda, distribution of pamphlets and other publications by the Movement. The university students and high school members of the Movement simultaneously belonged to other *usrah* in the area of their residence. The university and high school branches of the Movement were politically very significant because in the

---

[324] El-Affendi, *"Turabi's Revolution,"*87.

period of military rule they were the only forum in which the Movement could speak openly.

The other major factor that played a crucial role in strengthening the position of the Movement, not only among students but also in the country, was its growing control over the country's economic and financial institutions. The latter was viewed by the Movement's leadership as the most important key to political power. The return of some the Movement's members from exile in Saudi Arabia and other Gulf countries (1969-1976) and the establishment of Faisal Islamic Bank in 1978 and other Islamic banks and financial institutions in the following years, resulted in unprecedented growth among the Movement's student members.[325] The establishment of these Islamic economic institutions helped the Movement's activities among students in two ways:

First, like many other ideological parties in developing countries, the Movement was unable to keep its student members after their graduation. This was due in large part to the fact that the civil service in Sudan, like in many other developing countries, favored less those actively engaged in any political activities. This is especially true in those countries with military rulers. Students who were members of the Movement following their graduation tended to sever their relationships in order to be able to secure government jobs. Also, in Sudan, starting from mid-1970s, and as a result of the economic crisis in the country and the rising needs for professionals in Gulf countries, large numbers of Sudanese professionals left to work in these countries.

The control of newly established Islamic banks and institutions provided the Movement with a needed tool to solve its membership dilemma. The Movement's university members following their graduation were easily able to find jobs in these Islamic enterprises; those who decided to leave the country were offered job opportunities in other Islamic enterprises in the Gulf region. Also, the

---

[325] Kursany, Ibrahim. "The Politics of the National Islamic Front (NIF) of the Sudan: Old Wine in New Bottle." In *Third International Sudan Studies Conference*. Boston U.S.A: Sudan Studies Conference, 1994.

investment patterns of these banks, which encouraged the growth of small and medium-size businesses, played a major role in expanding economic opportunities for the Movement's newly graduated university students. Over 90 percent of their investments were allocated to the export-import trade and only four percent to agriculture.[326] The Movement encouraged its members to establish their own businesses in order to end the domination of the other two traditional parties al-Umma, led by Sadiq al-Mahdi and the Democratic Unionist Party -- (DUP), led by Mohammed Osman al-Mirghani over Sudanese economy.

The second way in which the creation of Islamic banks enhanced the position of the Islamic Movement in Sudan among students was the ability of the Movement to use the funds obtained from these banks in the form of *zakah* (religious tax) and donations to send its members to study in other countries. With the rising numbers of students in Sudan and the limited numbers of seats available for them in Sudanese higher education institutions, large numbers of Sudanese students started to leave the country for the purpose of education. With the SCP offering scholarships for its supporters to study in the USSR and Eastern Block countries, including Cuba and Southern Yemen, the Islamic Movement started to offer its members and supporters scholarships to study in Egypt, Morocco, India, Pakistan, and Malaysia. Those who were deemed by the Movement as bright and loyal were sent for graduate studies in leading Western countries and the United States to study in programs such as media, technology-related professions, journalism, sociology, and psychology that were thought to be crucial by the Movement's leadership.

The Movement also benefited from its relationship with the Nemeri regime to enhance its position among students. Nemeri was determined to follow the footsteps of the Egyptian president Sadat in his successful policy which called for the unleashing of Islamists against leftist forces in Egypt to eradicate or limit

---

[326]Abbashar Jamal. "Funding Fundamentalism: The Political Economy of an Islamist State." *Middle East Report*, no. 172 (1991): 14-38.

leftist influence in universities. Following the 1977 Accord, and unlike other student political groups who constantly suffered harassment, arrest and detention because of their opposition to the Nemeri regime, student Movement members who allied with the regime were freely allowed to move about and recruit in high schools and universities.[327]

While emphasis has been placed upon university student political organizations, it should not be concluded that they monopolized the field. Others existed; traditionally, university students, gathered from all parts of Sudan, organized themselves into social-welfare groups based upon their hometown, region, or ethnic background. These groups engaged in welfare work during holidays and intercession; they provided literacy classes for the illiterate and organized health and educational campaigns (such as campaigns against female circumcision). While most of the time students in these groups worked together despite their political differences, increasingly, as a result of political tensions between their members, these social-welfare groups started to reorganize around member political ideology. The establishment of Islamic banks and other financial institutions in the country resulted in enhancing the position of the Movement's members in these groups. Islamic banks provided those groups that were dominated by the Movement's members with all needed resources for their campaigns.

The combined effect of these factors was a total domination of the Sudanese student movement and, subsequently, professional associations (such as physicians, engineers, teachers, lawyers etc) by the Islamic Movement. This domination became clear in the 1986 election when the National Islamic Front (the new name for the Islamic Movement) won 51 out of 236 seats contested in the newly elected parliament.[328] The NIF made most of its gains in urban areas and in special Graduate Constituencies. The NIF won 28 seats in the geographical

---

[327] For details on the Movement works and strategy in the area of education see Abbas, 22-25.
[328] Osman, "The Political and Ideological Development,"305.

constituencies out of 236 contested.[329] The biggest gain of the NIF was among the educated elite. The NIF captured all 21 seats that were allocated to the Northern regions in the special Graduate Constituencies, plus two seats in the South. The NIF gains in geographical constituencies came mainly from urban areas. It won 13 seats in Khartoum region, four seats in the Central and Northern regions, three in Kordofan, two in Darfur, and one in Eastern region.[330] The progress achieved by the NIF in the 1986 elections was undeniable.

The group moved from a tiny pressure group, concentrated among the educated elite that controlled only five seats and enjoyed the support of 2.48% of the vote in the 1965 elections, to a powerful third party in 1986, with 51 seats and 18.46% of the popular vote.[331] Following the 1986 elections the NIF leaders argued that their gains, which occurred mainly within urban areas and among the educated elite, meant that they had become the "party of the future."[332]

Islamic Financial Institutions

As a result of Nasser's prosecutions in Egypt in the 1950s and the 1960s, many members of the Muslim Brotherhood fled the country to Saudi Arabia and other Gulf countries. These members were predominately highly qualified college graduates who played major roles in administering new modernization projects which started to take place in these countries at that time. The Muslim Brotherhood members who went to the Gulf region successfully accumulated large amounts of wealth that allowed them to support their organization back in Egypt.[333] The same process happened in the Sudan. After the Communist-sponsored military coup of Nemeri in 1969, large numbers of the Movement's well-qualified members in Sudan fled the country to Saudi Arabia and other Gulf countries.

---

[329]Ibid., 305.

[330] Ibid., 306-307.

[331] Ibid., 307.

[332] Ibid., 308

[333] al-Saed Yousif. *Al-Ikhwan Al-Mouslimoun Wa Guzur Al-Tataraf Al-Dinni Wa Al-Irhab Fi Misr*, Egyptians' History. Cairo, Egypt: Egyptian General Establishment for Books, 1999.

Those individuals who became wealthy through their work as professionals contributed to the Movement's work back in Sudan, while helping newly graduated members of the Movement in securing work opportunities in the Gulf countries. At the same time, during their stay in Saudi Arabia, Sudanese Islamists established contact with members of the Saudi royal family who showed sympathy to their cause. They also obtained needed support from the Saudi conservative religious establishment, as well as from the Saudi government, which at that time was in opposition to Nasser and other regimes in the region that followed his steps, such as Sudan and Libya. One of those who showed a great deal of sympathy to the Islamists in Sudan and Egypt was the Saudi Prince Mohammed Ibn al-Faisal Al Saud, the son of King Faisal and founder of Faisal Islamic Bank (FIB).[334]

Sudan inherited his traditional banking system from the Anglo-Egyptian Condominium (1899-1955) when the National Bank of Egypt was opened in Khartoum in 1901 and the value of the currency used in Sudan (Sudanese Pound) was tied to the Egyptian Pound. This situation became unsatisfactory to Sudanese nationalists following the country's independence in 1956. In 1957 the Bank of Sudan was established as the central bank of Sudan.[335] Following its establishment, five Sudanese commercial banks were established: Bank of Khartoum, al-Nelien Bank, Sudan Commercial Bank, the People's Cooperative Bank, and the Unity Bank.[336]

Following his successful military coup, Nemeri decreed the 1970 Nationalization of Banks Act; all domestic banks were then controlled by Bank of Sudan. In 1974 as a result of Nemeri's disillusion with the left after the unsuccessful Communist coup of 1971, and following al-Sadat's "open door" policy which called for the liberalization of the Egyptian economy and the encouragement of private investment, the Sudanese government began to relax its

---

[334] Ahmad, "*Al-Harakah Al-Islamiyah Fi Al-Sudan, 1969-198*," 40.
[335] Kursany, 1994.
[336] Ibid.

controls over the economy to encourage private sector and foreign capital investment. Particularly, foreign banks were urged to establish branches or joint ventures (JV) with Sudanese capital. Several banks took advantage of the opportunity, most notably Citibank, Chase Manhattan Bank, the Faisal Islamic Bank (FIB), and the Arab Authority for Agriculture Investment and Development.[337]

The relationship of the Islamic Movement of Sudan with Prince Mohammed Ibn al-Faisal Al Saud, the founder of the FIB was not new. Members of the Islamic Movement in Sudan were active members of his financial empire during their exile in Saudi Arabia. Unlike their counterparts, the Egyptian Islamists who mainly trained in Egypt and thus spoke only Arabic with limited English, Sudanese Islamists were fluent in English and most of them received their education or graduate study in British leading schools. Following the 1973 oil crisis, which resulted in unprecedented oil-revenues for Saudi Arabia and other oil producing countries, Prince Mohammed Ibn al-Faisal Al Saud was eager to establish contact with foreign suppliers, particularly British and American, and, because of their training and language skills, he relied heavily on the Sudanese-Islamists in establishing needed contact. Prince Mohammed Ibn al-Faisal Al Saud also played a major role in brokering the National Reconciliation Accord of 1977 between the armed Sudanese opposition that included the Islamists and Nemeri's military regime.[338]

The decision to establish FIB by the Saudis was in large part due to the fact that, following the 1973 War and the unprecedented rise in oil prices, many oil-producing countries, particularly Saudi Arabia, accumulated a large monetary surplus. Egypt and Sudan were selected to open the new FIB mainly because both countries were coming out of state-controlled economies and were eager to attract foreign investors by offering many incentives and guarantees to them. Also, the

---

[337] Ibid.

[338] Zakaria Bashier. *The National Reconciliation in the Sudan and Its Aftermath*, Seminar Papers 12. Leicester, England: Islamic Foundation, 1981.

Saudis wanted to help both countries in their transitions from socialist-oriented economies and political orientations to liberal economies that would eventually strengthen their relation with the West and thus eradicate any future ideological threat for their regime. By infiltrating the economies of both countries, the Saudis reasoned, they would be able to influence of both the internal and foreign policies of both countries.

The FIB was established in 1977 by a special presidential executive order called The Faisal Islamic Bank Act. In his attempt to develop a close relationship with Saudi Arabia and to encourage more Saudi investments in the country, Nemeri granted the FIB many privileges that were denied to other commercial banks; full tax exemption on assets, profits, wages, pensions, and the right of transferring all their profits abroad, as well as guarantees against confiscation or nationalization.[339] Moreover, these privileges came under Nemeri's protection from 1983 onward as he became committed to applying Islamic doctrine to all aspects of Sudanese life.

The theory of Islamic banking is derived from the Quran teachings, which clearly prohibited interest or usury, and from Prophet Mohammed's exhortations against exploitation and the unjust acquisition of wealth defined as *riba* or, interest or usury. Profit and trade are encouraged and provide the foundation for Islamic banking. The prohibitions against interest are founded in the Islamic concept of property that results from an individual's creative labor or from exchange of goods or property. Interest on loaned money falls within neither of these concepts and is thus unjustified. In the Quran one reads:

> Those who live on usury shall rise up before Allah like men whom Satan has demented by his touch, for they claim that usury is like trading. But Allah has permitted trading and forbidden usury (Quran, The Cow: 2:175)

Also:

---

[339] Elfatih Shaaeldin & Richard Brown. "Towards an Understanding of Islamic Banking in Sudan: The Case of the Faisal Islamic Bank." In *Sudan: State, Capital and Transformation*, edited by Tony & Abdelkarim Barnett, Abbas. New York, NY: Croom Helm, 1988.

Believers, have fear of Allah and waive what is still due to you from usury, if your faith be true; or war shall be declared against you by Allah and his apostle. If you repent, you may retain your principal, suffering no loss and causing no loss to anyone (Quran, The Cow: 2:276).

Despite the fact that FIB shares were divided between Saudis, Sudanese, and other Muslims in a ratio of 4:4:2 respectively, the Sudanese, represented by the members of the Movement, played a dominant role in managing, staffing, and directing the bank.[340] The first FIB board of trustees consisted of 18 members and had seven Sudanese members who were active members of the Movement in Sudan including Mousa Hussein Dirar, Mohammed Yousif Mohammed, and Nasser el-Haj Ali. Members of the Movement in Sudan have continued to dominate the FIB board of trustees from 1977 until the present.[341] The Movement's members also dominated the bank's cadres since its establishment as the employment policies of the bank clearly favored "religious" people and it was controlled by the Movement leadership.

Traditional businessmen in Sudan were wary of the new "Islamic" venture, which they thought would not succeed. This gave the Movement's members and supporters the needed opportunity and all bank activities and investments were exclusively reserved for the Movement's members and their loyal supporters. To benefit from bank services a person had to provide a letter of recommendation of "good character" from a well-known person. The recommendation letters were usually written by the Movement's leadership.

The investment patterns of FIB and later other Islamic banks which encouraged the growth of small and medium-sized business (over 90 percent of their investments were allocated to export/import trade and only four percent to agriculture), played a major role in the emergence of a new class of "Islamist" businessmen who became rich almost over night.[342] The success of the FIB also

---

[340] Shaaeldin & Brown, 1988.
[341] Faisal Islamic Bank Board of Trustees members. Available at:
http://www.fibsudan.com/old_council.php. Accessed 11/26/2006.
[342] Kursany, 1994.

had a deep impact on the balance of power within Sudanese society. The FIB revolutionized access to credit, and wrested the virtual monopoly of this vital sector from privileged groups, many of whom were foreign nationals such as Greeks, Armenians, Indians, Copts, and Syrians, who alone had the knowledge and influence to enable them to make full use of bank credit.

Another important impact that FIB had on the Movement was its success for the first time in achieving diversification in membership. Before 1977 the Movement was able to attract few members from outside the modern-educated sector, or even preserve their non-student membership. With the establishment of FIB and other Islamic enterprises, the Movement was able to attract large numbers of businessmen, wealthy farmers, and merchants who traditionally supported the two traditional parties in Sudan.

The emergence of Islamic enterprises helped the Movement in keeping its members following their graduation. During the early 1970s membership outside the universities contracted even further reaching its lowest ebb during 1976-1977. Some of the Movement's membership was recruited in high schools and continued with active roles during university years, but upon graduation this membership tended to sever its relationship with the Movement as they faced a predominately hostile environment in their attempt to secure employment, since the Sudanese government would not employ persons who were politically active against the regime during their student years. Also, opportunities for employment in the private sector, which was dominated by anti-Movement groups such as foreign investors, Christian groups and individuals, al-Khatmiyya, and al-Ansar business owners, were scarce.[343]

The pressure to prosper financially tended to cause members to drift away. This was coupled with the opening up of opportunities to migrate to the Gulf which further caused members' attrition. Three waves of migration; after the Nemeri coup of 1969, after the collapse of the Shaaban Uprising in 1973, and

---

[343] Abbas, 22-25.

after the failure of the 1976 military operation against Nemeri's regime, almost decimated the Movement. With the signing of the National Reconciliation Accord in 1977 and the access to the power and to the newly created Islamic economic institutions, the Movement began to overcome the problems of membership and finance that almost paralyzed its activities.[344]

The rising of Islamic financial institutions eased the financial problems of the Movement significantly. The maintenance of full-time cadres, especially at the leadership level became possible. The National Reconciliation Accord, which granted to the Movement ministerial and other high-ranking positions in the central government, coupled with the rising influence of Islamic Bank Institutions, especially FIB, gave the Movement power to apportion favors to supporters who no longer needed to compromise their membership under economic pressure.

The process of Islamization of the Sudanese economy that began in 1977 and reached its peak in 1983 with the declaration of Shari'a laws by Nemeri's regime substantially strengthened the Movement cumulative social, political, and economic clout as its supporters became strategically placed to influence key decisions in state and society. Also, following the declaration of the 1983 Islamic laws, several Islamic banks and Islamic investment institutions were founded, such as; al-Baraka Finance House and al-Baraka bank, the Sudanese Islamic Bank, the Sudanese-Saudi Bank, and the Islamic Bank for Western Sudan.

By the end of 1979 hundreds of small businesses that were mainly owned by Movement members emerged as major economic and political powers in the country. The FIB expanded rapidly as tens of branches were opened around the country. During the period between 1979 and 1982, total deposits with the FIB increased almost 14 times and FIB's share of total commercial bank deposits increased from four percent in 1979 to 15 percent in 1982.[345]

---

[344] Haydar Ibrahim Ali. *Suqut Al-Mashru Al-Hadari* Khartoum-Sudan: Markaz al-Dirasat al-Sudaniyah, 2004.
[345] Shaaeldin & Brown, 1988.

Following its unprecedented expansion, FIB leadership decided to open "specialized" branches that were designed to serve specific segments of the society such as women, workers, farmers, and exporters. The FIB, which concentrated its work in import and export operations which guaranteed a quick return of revenues to the bank and its investors, became a dominant power in the country's economy. Besides financial services in its "specialized" branches, the FIB started to offer goods to their clients such as appliances, electronics, clothes, equipment, sewing machines, electric generators, cars, and water pumps. As a result, the Movement's members were able to infiltrate all the segments of Sudanese society and heavily influence trade unions, women, and professional associations. Movement membership became the key for a prosperous economic future for Sudanese youth, women, and professionals.

The creation of Islamic economic institutions also helped the Movement in creating a network of non-governmental organizations that covered all aspects of the country's life. Large numbers of Islamic non-profit groups emerged in the late 1970s and early 1980s, such as the *Munazzamat Al-Dawa Al-Islamiyyah* (Organization of Islamic Propagation), with the main function of spreading Islam in Sudan and Africa. These INGOs were created in an effort by the Movement and its supporters in Sudan to solve basic socio-economic problems within an Islamic framework.[346] Although legal conditions and government oversight prohibited direct political activities through INGOs, Movement members were able to utilize these institutions to expand the support of the public and to combat the work of European humanitarian and missionary NGOs that had historically dominated the welfare and humanitarian work in the country.

The deteriorated economic situation in the country in the early 1980s coupled with the government's acceptance of the International Monetary Fund (IMF) and the World Bank (WB), recommendations to privatize state-owned

---

[346] Quintan Wiktorowicz and Suha Taji Farouki. "Islamic NGO's and Muslim Politics: A Case from Jordan." *Third World Quarterly* 21, no. 4 (2000): 685-99.

enterprises and to adopt "structural adjustment programs" (SAP) and other economic measures recommended by the IMF and WB, resulted further in enhancing the position of the Movement sponsored INGOs . Following the IMF and the WB recommendations, the government eliminated subsidies on basic services such as education and health. As result, hundreds of thousands of people became largely dependent on these INGOs to obtain these services.

The education and health services were provided to the public by the INGOs with nominal or no fees. Members of the Movement were actively involved in running these organizations and promoting their programs and ideology. These INGOs allowed the Movement's membership to expand into many areas that were previously considered closed to its influence as they were dominated by the two major religious sects in the country; al-Khatmiyya and al-Ansar. Movement expansion in Darfur, for example, was a major success to the Movement as the region was previously considered the most loyal part in the country for the al-Ansar sect. Thousands of Darfurians, particularly, the educated, joined the Movement.

The Islamic Movement's membership in Darfur expanded to the level that a decision was made by the Movement's leadership in Khartoum to extend its Darfur branch full autonomy. These INGOs also allowed the Movement to find new allies among tribal chiefs who were traditionally loyal to al-Khatmiyya and al-Ansar sects. With these two sects in opposition, and Nemeri's government unable to provide needed services for their regions, tribal chiefs turned to the Movement and its economic power as represented in Islamic banks and INGOs. Tens of Islamic banks branches were opened in small and obscure places in all regions in order to gain the support of these chiefs. Hundreds of small projects were initiated by the Movement's closely linked economic institutions and INGOs in these regions, such as building schools, mosques, hospitals, small clinics, and drinking-water systems. Major projects were also implemented such as building roads to connect villages and major cities.[347]

The greatest attention in the Movement's philanthropic works was given to education, as hundreds of schools for boys and girls were built. The Movement's leadership strongly believed that the expansion of education in Sudan could greatly enhance its influence among the public, while eradicating or limiting the influence of both traditional sects among the public, which until that time was strong, particularly among non-educated citizens.

The Sudanese government was reluctant in cracking down on these Islamic financial institutions and INGOs despite their close ties with Islamists in Sudan for several reasons. First, in the early 1980s as a result of drought, corruption, and failed negotiations with the IMF and other international financial lenders, the economic situation in Sudan began to deteriorate rapidly. The Sudanese government was unable to provide needed educational, social, and health services for people in the regions, particularly in Darfour. The INGOs started to provide these services which relieved the government from facing massive protest or demonstrations that could jeopardize its future. Second, most of the established Islamic banks and investment companies were partially owned by foreign entities, particularly the Saudis and Kuwaitis. Any attempts to eradicate or limit Islamist influence within these enterprises could anger shareholders who were mainly members of the royal families in Kuwait and Saudi Arabia. Finally, most of these Islamic enterprises were launched following the declaration of the "Open Door Policy" which was initiated by the Sudanese government in an attempt to attract foreign capital and investment. Any interference in the work of these enterprises could be interpreted by foreign investors and international financial institutions as a shift in the government position away from the creation of a liberal market economy in the country.

---

[347] Osman, "The Political and Ideological Development,"308.

The emergence of Islamic bank systems and other Islamic investment institutions in general, played a major role in transforming the Islamic Movement in Sudan into a massive political organization with members all over the country. It also helped the Movement in diversifying its membership, which previously was concentrated among only the educated elite. The building of these economic institutions also helped the Movement in infiltrating the traditional bases of its political opponents. For example, its "specialized" Islamic banks for workers and women, both groups who were considered strong supporters for the SCP, helped in shifting the balance of power to its favor among these two groups. Also, the Movement work during the 1980s in more regions, particularly the western region of Sudan, helped in rallying support for the Movement and its programs among tribal leaders while undermining the bases of the traditional parties of al-Umma and the DUP that had historically had dominated these regions.

Organizational Structure

Since its establishment under the name of the Muslim Brotherhood in 1954, the Islamic Movement in Sudan was structured after the classical organizational system that was inherited from the Egyptian organization. The system included the *usrah* usually comprised of five members acting as a unit for indoctrination and education of new members.[348] In Sudan, the *usrah* had been the primary agent of recruitment. It had been effective in developing the Movement's support base by functioning within social (especially educational) institutions. Members of the *usrah* were encouraged to recruit individuals at a highly individualized level. The idea was to create a bond of close relationship as a means of drawing an individual into the *usrah*. During the Movement's early years, *usrah* members sought out recruits mostly in mosques or educational institutions.[349]

---

[348] Ahmad, "*Al-Harakah Al-Islamiyah Fi Al-Sudan, 1969-1985*,"158-164.
[349] Ibid., 158-164.

An *usrah* member would start by gradually developing his/her acquaintance with a potential recruit who would be presented with Islamic books and engaged in discussions about "Islamic" issues. If he/she was found responsive, more materials about the Movement's ideology would be provided and discussed. Finally, the potential recruit's opinion on the Movement would be sought and, if he/she was still responsive, then he/she would be invited to a discussion circle at a pre-*usrah* level. At this level, discussions were led by a "responsible individual" whose duty was to assess the suitability of recruits and make certain that the new recruit was a good Muslim.[350]

Considerable time was spent in the study groups and discussion circles led by the *usrah* leader (*ameer*). The *ameer* was responsible for the spiritual and moral education of *usrah* members. Particular emphasis is usually placed on reading and understanding of the Quran and *Sunna* and on the member's personal and social behavior. Members of the *usrah* were encouraged to develop a close relationship by attending weekly *usrah* meetings and attending prayers together in specific mosques.[351] Leaders of *usrah* were encouraged to identify their members with special talents and skills. Good speakers, for example, were chosen to attend special "schools" within the Movement that prepared them to become spokespersons for the Movement at universities or mosques. Those with high organizational skills usually moved to the different specialized *usrah*, such as finance, communication, recruitment, and propaganda.

The *usrah* was the basic unit in a complex hierarchal organization. Each group of five to ten *usrah* formed a *shu'ba* (branch) headed also by an *ameer*. The *ameer* of the *shu'ba* was responsible to the regional branch office which was elected by *shu'ba ammers*.[352] Branches existed in all major urban centers, high schools and universities. The branch executive office, elected by the leaders of *usrah* in the region, was responsible for all administrative duties of the Movement

---

[350] Ibid., 158-164.
[351] Ibid., 158-164.
[352] Ibid., 158-164.

in the region. Its members coordinated the region's activities with the executive office, monitored financial operations, and organized "specialized schools" for talented members.

The Movement's regional branches enjoyed little administrative autonomy and absolutely no political authority. They mainly served to execute the policy agenda of the center. However, regional branches had an indirect say in formulating the Movement's policies as they elected the members of the *majlis al-Shura* (Consultative Council) which was considered the highest authority in the Movement. *Majlis al-Shura* members elected the Movement General Secretary and the executive office of the Movement.[353]

Following his election as General Secretary for the Movement, al-Turabi suggested wide reforms in the Movement's organizational structure. He suggested increasing the numbers of the *usrah* members to allow new members to interact freely with each other. He also suggested a less rigid approach in teaching and education of the new members. Following the SCP organizational structure, al-Turabi also advocated creation of separate *shu'ba* for universities, trade unions, women's organizations, and professional associations. Upon their return to their area of residence, members of these groups worked with the Movement's organization there. Students in high schools were allowed to have a limited autonomy, but mainly functioned under the guidance of the closest university branch.

Al-Turabi's new organizational structure also suggested creation of "satellite" youth, women, student, and professional organizations. The idea of setting up these satellite organizations reflected al-Turabi's admiration for the recruitment strategy of the SCP, which successfully used satellite organizations in enhancing its position among these groups thus giving the SCP needed exposure. The SCP created numerous satellite organizations, such as The Democratic Front, which was established as an alliance between Communist-students and

---

[353] Ibid., 158-164.

democratic-students, and the League of Socialist Teachers, an alliance between Communist-teachers and democratic-teachers. Similar organizations were created as alliances between Communists and women, youth, lawyers, physicians, engineers, etc. Al-Turabi's plan called for satellite organizations that included the Movement's members and other "Islamists" who were not members of the Movement, yet consistently showed sympathy and support for its programs. The plan approved by the Movement's leadership and the newly created satellite organizations became part of the Movement grand strategy for expansion.

In the following years, the newly-created satellite organizations played a major role in enhancing the Movement's position among women, youth, students, labor unions, and professional associations. The satellite organizations, which usually had the word "Islamist" in their name, such as The Islamists Teachers, The Islamists Physicians, or The Islamists Workers, gave the Movement needed exposure among more segments of the public and thus helped in driving new recruits to the Movement.

In the period from 1969 to 1985, the Movement created a decentralized organization.[354] This change was finally formalized in the Movement's constitution of 1982. The new constitution called for nine regional offices and a central office to coordinate their activities. The regional offices were divided according to the country's administrative units (nine provinces) and each province office consisted of *usrah*, *shu'ba*, and a regional executive office answering directly to the central office. The central office consisted of the Constituent Assembly, the *Shura* Council, the General Secretary, and the Executive Office.

The Constituent Assembly, which met every four years, consisted of representatives of the provinces, who elected the members of the *Shura* Council and the General Secretary. The General Secretary nominated the members of the Executive Office to the *Shura* Council, who either approved or disapproved them. The nomination of the Executive Office members by the General Secretary was

---

[354] Ahmad, "*Al-Harakah Al-Islamiyah Fi Al-Sudan, 1969-1985*," 107.

very important to al-Turabi who wanted to surround himself with those who clearly advocated his views and shared his political ambitions.[355]

The new decentralized internal arrangements were followed by a new organizational approach toward the Movement's relation with the International Organization of the Muslim Brotherhood, which was dominated by the Egyptian Brotherhood. The Islamic Movement in Sudan, which had its indigenous roots in Sudanese nationalism and student politics of the 1940s, had fought against the hegemonic tendencies of the Egyptian Brotherhood to turn it into a satellite of the metropolitan Brotherhood in Egypt.[356] Having won independence from a condominium colonialism (Anglo-Egyptian rule of Sudan 1899-1956) in which Egypt had been implicated, the nationalistic Sudanese movement militated against this Egyptian haughtiness from the very beginning. However, the Movement in Sudan quieted their negative response to Egyptian hegemony because of the hard times the founding Brotherhood experienced under President Nasser in the 1960s. During those years, the Movement in Sudan voluntarily joined other Arab Brotherhood organizations in forming the executive office to coordinate the activities of the pan-Arab brotherhood called the International Organization.[357]

However, a conflict ensued when the Egyptian movement proposed that the Sudanese activists integrate themselves into this international brotherhood led by the Egyptian organization. Realizing that their movement would be reduced to a branch of the Egyptian Brotherhood, the Movement in Sudan turned the offer down. Instead, it proposed a plan of coordination reconciling local autonomy with international and pan-Arab commitments.[358] The Egyptian organization insisted on integration, and only a small faction of the Movement in Sudan, which was angered by al-Turabi's innovative approaches to *ijmaa*, *ijtihad*, and *tajdid*, decided to join the International Organization. This small faction was led by Sadiq Abdallah Abdel-Magid, Burat Abdallah, and al-Hibir Nour al-Daiem.

---

[355] Osman, "The Political and Ideological Development,"318-322.
[356] Ibrahim, "A Theology of Modernity,"194-222.
[357] Ibid
[358] Ibid.

In rejecting the Egyptian organization's offer, al-Turabi, who kept a close eye on how international communist movements were functioning, cited the failure of the Comintern experiment (Communist International) in the U.S.S.R. which was established to claim Communist leadership of the world socialist movement and to coordinate the work of communist parties around the globe. He argued that Muslim Brotherhood organizations must accept the nation-state as a framework for their political action.[359] By accepting the nation-state as their political framework, Islamic movements would have greater flexibility in dealing with their own internal problems and challenges. Giving local organizations their autonomy also greatly enhanced their ability to maneuver, make alliances, and to quickly respond to the social, political, and economic changes in their societies.

Military

In spite of the fact that most African and Middle Eastern nations have come out of colonialism with small armed forces, the latter quickly became involved in the politics of these nations, particularly, during the period between the 1960s and the 1980s. Military coups, countercoups, and cycles of military-civilian rule have dominated the political scene of the African and Middle Eastern nations for a long period of time. On the African continent between 1960 and 1982, almost 90 percent of the 45 independent African countries experienced a military coup, an attempted coup, or a plot. During the course of some 115 legal governmental changes, there were 52 successful coups, 56 attempted coups, and 102 plots. In the late 1980s, the central executive of 25 of these 45 countries was in military hands and the military remained a powerful force in most other countries.[360]

In the Middle East, with the exception of the Gulf countries, the situation is not different. The Middle East has provided fertile ground for coups. Between March 1949 (the first coup after World War II) and the end of 1989, fifty-five

---

[359] El-Affendi, *"Turabi's Revolution,"*177-178.
[360] Craig J. Jenkins & Augustine J. Kposowa. "Explaining Military Coups D'etat: Black Africa, 1957-1984." *American Sociological Review* 55, no. 6 (1990): 861-75.

coups were attempted in Arab States, half of them successful. These military coups brought down the old ruling elite, based on great landowners, and installed new regimes in which military officers and senior bureaucrats predominated. These new political orders embraced radical ideologies, notably pan-Arabism and socialism, and implemented populist programs such as land reform. Although Iran is not an Arab State, the United States sponsored overthrow of the government of Mohammed Mosadaq in 1954 contributed to the coup fascination in the region.[361]

Sudan is not an exception. Military interference has dominated the country's political life for more than 41 years following the country's independence in 1956. The first military coup to occur was on November 17, 1958. It was a bloodless army coup led by General Ibrahim Abboud to topple the government of Abdullah Khalil. On assuming power, General Abboud declared that he would rule through a thirteen-member army junta and that democracy was being suspended in the Sudan in the name of "honesty and integrity." Abboud's regime was toppled in 1964 when massive public demonstrations that were supported by junior officers of the Sudanese army forced him out of power.

The new democratic regime lasted for only five years when a group of Arab Nationalists and Communist officers in the Sudanese army, who were inspired by Nasser's experiment in Egypt and led by Colonel Nemeri, overthrew the democratic regime and established a new republic, based on the ideas of Arab Socialism and close relationships with Egypt.[362] In early 1985 discontent with Nemeri's regime had been growing and in April, while away on a visit to the United States, he was deposed in a military coup led by Lt. Gen. Swar al-Dahab, who after a period, passed the reigns of government to civilian rule, headed by Sadiq al-Mahdi. Again, following further discontent in the country and within the military, another bloodless coup d'etat, that was planned by the Islamic Movement and led by Colonel Omar Hassan 'Ahmed el-Bashir took place on June 30, 1989.

---

[361] James T. Quinlivan. "Coup-Proofing: Its Practice and Consequences in the Middle East." *International Security* 24, no. 2 (1999): 131-65.
[362] Kamal Osman Salih. "The Sudan, 1985- 1989: The Fading Democracy." *The Journal of Modern African Studies* 28, no. 2 (1990): 199-224.

He quickly dismantled civilian rule, suspended constitution, and dissolved the National Assembly and all political institutions.[363]

Like many ideological parties in the Middle East, the Islamic Movement in Sudan clearly understood the important role of the military in the politics of the region. This is particularly true in the case of Sudan where the army is the only "national" institution that represents all the tribes and regions of the country. Following Nasser's successful coup in 1952, other leftist groups in Sudan started to pay more attention to the role that the military could play in shaping the country's political future. Communists and Arab Nationalists were able quickly to organize their secret cells inside the Sudanese army.[364] In 1964 the members of these cells played a crucial role in overthrowing Abboud's military regime after they refused to obey his orders on crushing demonstrators. Led by Communists and Arab Nationalists, these army officers went further by declaring their unconditional support for the demands of political parties in ending the military regime and finding a peaceful solution to the Southern problem.[365]

Although the Islamic Movement clearly understood the vital role of the military in the country's politics, the early leadership of the Movement was very hesitant in trying to build "Islamic" cells in the army. This was due to the experience of the Egyptian Muslim Brotherhood in Egypt with Nasser's military regime. Despite their support for Nasser's regime in his early years, the rising competition between the Brotherhood and Nasser's regime resulted in unprecedented persecution of the Brotherhood's members. As a result of this experience the Islamic Movement in Sudan in its early days rarely recruited members of the Sudanese military.[366] Furthermore, the leadership of the Movement looked to the officers of the Sudanese army with suspicion because

---

[363] Ibid.

[364] Mohammed Nuri El-Amin. "The Role of the Egyptian Communists in Introducing the Sudanese to Communism in the 1940s." *International Journal of Middle East Studies* 19, no. 4 (1987): 433-54.

[365] Yusuf Fadl Hasan. "The Sudanese Revolution of October 1964." *The Journal of Modern African Studies* 5, no. 4 (1967): 491-509.

[366] Ahmad, *"Harakat Al-Ikhwan Al-Muslimin Fi Al-Sudan, 1944 -1969,"*

many of them served under the British administration in the period before the country's independence. Also, following the country's independence, many of these officers started to receive their military training in Western countries and later in Egypt following the Egyptian Revolution of 1952. In short, the Islamic Movement in Sudan in its early years viewed the Sudanese military as an anti-Islamic institution that was dominated by secularists and leftists.

In 1955 when he was giving a speech at Al-Manshiya in Alexandria, Egypt, an attempt was made on Nasser's life, allegedly by a member of the Muslim Brotherhood. As a result the group was declared illegal. Six members of the Brotherhood were executed. Thousands of the Brothers were also arrested. Thousands fled from Egypt to Syria, Saudi Arabia, Jordan, Lebanon, and Sudan. Among those who fled to Sudan was Abu al-Makarim Abdel Hai - an Egyptian army officer who was also a member of the Muslim Brotherhood. Abdel Hai was an important figure within the organization's paramilitary wing *(al-Jihaz al-Khas)*. He was the person responsible for *al-Jihaz al-Khas* – the Brother's secret organization that directed its membership in the Egyptian military and police forces. Abdel Hai convinced the leadership of the Sudanese Movement of the importance of working within the army and helped the Movement in Sudan in its early years in developing needed tactics and recruitment strategies to infiltrate the army and the police forces in Sudan.[367]

The first attempt by the Islamic Movement to infiltrate the Sudanese army was in 1955. The Movement recruited a few members among the students of the Sudanese Military College, such as Bashier Mohammed Ali, Abdallah al-Tahir, Abdelrahman Farah, and Abdelrahman Swar al-Dahab. While these students accepted the Movement's membership during their study at the Military College, the majority of them lost their contacts and active roles within the Movement following graduation. The rising influence of Arab Nationalists and Communists in the military played a major role in limiting the Islamic Movement's ability to

---

[367] Ahmad, *"Harakat Al-Ikhwan Al-Muslimin Fi Al-Sudan, 1944 -1969,"* 93.

further recruit new members among the military or even continue the work with those who accepted the allegiance of the Movement while they were in the Military College.[368]

In 1959, and despite the objection of the Movement's leadership, al-Rasheed al-Tahir, who at that time was the General Secretary of the Movement in Sudan, decided to commit the Movement's resources to a military coup aimed at overthrowing the military regime of General Abboud (1957-1964). Al-Tahir, who at that time was working as a judge in Eastern Sudan, started to contact some of the military officers stationed in the East of Sudan. The Sudanese intelligence uncovered the coup before it started and all the officers who agreed to join the coup were arrested including al-Tahir. Six of these officers were sentenced to death and al-Tahir was sentenced to five years in prison. The failed military attempt had disastrous results on the Movement. First, the Movement lost its General Secretary; second, the Movement lost all of its secrets cells in the army; and finally, the failed attempt revealed the serious problems in the Movement's internal structure, which allowed its General Secretary to commit the Movement to a military coup despite the objection of its leadership. [369]

After the failed 1959 military coup, the Islamic Movement decided to change its recruitment strategies among the military. Instead of waiting to recruit new members after they joined the Military College or after graduation, the Movement started to concentrate its recruitment activities among high school students and then directed those who showed unconditional loyalty to the Movement to apply to the Military College. During the 1960s and 1970s large numbers of high school students who became committed Movement members joined the Sudanese military.[370]

As a result of the leftist-led military coup in 1969, the Islamic Movement joined the military opposition against the new regime that was established in

---

[368] Ibid., 93.
[369] Ibid., 94.
[370] Mirghani, 223.

Libya by Sadiq al-Mahdi and al-Sherif al-Hendi. Many Movement members, particularly university students, decided to enroll at military training campuses that were established in Libya to train the opposition forces. On July 2, 1976 the opposition's forces attacked Khartoum, the capital of Sudan, and after more than four days of street fights they were defeated.

The unsuccessful military attempt to overthrow Nemeri's regime, coupled with the Movement leadership's concerns about the rising influence of the "secular" regime of al-Qadafi over the Movement's allies, particularly al-Sadiq al-Mahdi, and as a result of a meditation between Saudi Arabia and the opposition, the Movement's leadership endorsed the National Reconciliation Accord (NRA) with Nemeri in 1977. The newly signed NRA guaranteed full amnesty to all opposition members and release of political prisoners, plus the freedom of operation for the opposition members in exchange for the political support of the regime. Among those who were released from prison as a result of this accord was Hasan al-Turabi.

Following the 1977 Accord, the recruitment work of the Movement among the military intensified. Several factors played major roles in enhancing the Movement's recruitment efforts with the Sudanese military following the 1977 Accord: first, the declining influence of the Sudanese Communist Party among Sudanese intellectuals in general, and among military officers in particular, following the party massacre in 1971; second, the declining influence of Arab Nationalists and Nasser's sympathizers among the Sudanese intellectuals and military officers following the 1967 war with Israel and the death of Nasser in 1970; third, as a result of its support for the regime, the Islamic Movement had the freedom of operation needed to intensify its works among high school students without fear of persecution by Nemeri's security forces. Finally, following the new course of "Islamization" that was initiated by Nemeri in 1983, the Movement intensified its recruitment campaigns among military personnel as they were positioned as teachers and heads of newly established Islamic programs within the Sudanese military.[371]

The Islamic Movement divided its military recruitment strategies into three approaches. The first approach was the building of a secret military organization of the most loyal members of the Movement. Members of this organization, who answered directly to the Supreme leader of the Movement Hasan al-Turabi, were selected from those Brothers who attended military training camps in Libya during the early days of opposition to Nemeri's regime. Also, following the Soviet invasion of Afghanistan in 1979 and with the start of the phenomenon of the "Arab Afghans," the Islamic Movement in Sudan sent large numbers of its most loyal members to attend military training camps that were established in Pakistan. Also, following Israel's invasion of Lebanon in 1982, large numbers of the Islamic Movement members were sent to receive their military training in the camps of Islamic Resistance Movement in Lebanon. The training of these members was also conducted inside Sudan in secret areas but on a limited scale.[372]

The second approach, which was the most important in the Movement military strategy, was to penetrate the Sudanese military establishment. After the 1977 reconciliation accord, a directive was issued by the Movement leadership to its members to apply to the Military College. By directing its student-members to join the Military College from high school, the Movement infiltrated the military with large numbers of recruits who raised no concerns among the army intelligence services who were more concerned with the activities of ranking military officers. Also, the Movement directed its less known university graduate members to join the army as engineers, physicians, lawyers, economists, accountants etc.[373]

---

[371] Ibid., 238.
[372] Ibid., 229.
[373] Ibid., 230.

The third approach was to contact all those army officers who were members of the Movement but had discontinued their relations with the Movement following Nemeri's coup. Part of this approach also was to contact those officers with family members in the Movement, particularly, those who regularly attended prayers and did not smoke or drink alcohol, which at that time was a wide-spread phenomenon among the officers of the Sudanese army.[374]

The Islamic Movement also gave special attention to the intelligence services within the military responsible for the screening of new applicants' backgrounds and political affiliation. They directed their members in the army to get into these services. By infiltrating these services the Movement increased the numbers of its members inside the military. Like its civilian secret organization, the Movement's activities within the military were directed by the Movement's leader Hasan al-Turabi.[375]

Nemeri's declaration of "Islamic" laws in 1983 and the beginning of the implementation of the Shari'a laws gave the Islamic Movement the needed opportunities to expand its work within the army. As a result of the new "Islamic orientation," of the country, drinking alcohol was outlawed in the country, this included the military barracks and hundreds of small mosques built inside these barracks, and finally, all medium and top-ranked military officers were ordered to attend Islamic studies courses in the African Islamic Center in Khartoum, which was mainly established, supported, and maintained by Movement cadres.

The curriculum of these courses, which was mainly taught by the members of the Movement, was designed to teach and discuss issues such as implementation of *Shari'a*, *Jihad* in Islam, and the history of Islam with emphasis on the role of Islamists throughout history in leading Muslims and others to a more prosperous life. After the end of these courses, officers were given an opportunity to apply to visit Saudi Arabia for *Haj* (Pilgrim) or *umra* (Visiting the Holy Places in Saudi Arabia). Also, if the attending officer showed potential for

---

[374] Ibid.237-239.
[375] Ibid., 239.

recruitment or some enthusiasm he was usually directed to open bank accounts with one of the Islamic banks, particularly Faisal Bank where loans and investments were available according to "Islamic" teachings that prohibited *riba* (interest). These Islamic courses gave the Movement the opportunity to have access to all ranking officers in the military. The Movement was able to build a comprehensive database of officers' social lives and political orientations. These Islamic courses also allowed the Movement to greatly expand its members among ranking officers for the first time.[376]

The political situation in the country in early 1983 also played a major role in enhancing the Movement's presence in the military. On June 5, 1983, Nemeri sought to counter the south's growing political power by re-dividing the Southern Region into the three old provinces of Bahr al Ghazal, al-Istiwaya, and Aali al-Nil; he had suspended the Southern Regional Assembly almost two years earlier. As a result, a mutiny started among southern army officers stationed in the south. A few months later, in September 1983, Nemeri declared the *Shari'a* as the basis of the Sudanese legal system. The Southerners denounced the declaration of *Shari'a* laws. Meanwhile, the security situation in the south had deteriorated so much that by the end of 1983 the situation in the south amounted to a resumption of the civil war. By early 1985 discontent with Nemeri's regime had been growing and in April, while on a visit to the United States, he was deposed in a military coup led by Lt. Gen. Swar al-Dahab, who after a year passed the reigns of government to civilian rule, headed by al-Sadiq al-Mahdi the newly elected Prime Minister.[377]

The renewal of the civil war in the south coupled with the al-Mahdi's inability to supply the military with needed equipment or to find a peaceful political solution for the problem in the south, resulted in unprecedented growth among Movement members within the Sudanese military. As a result, the

---

[376] Ibid., 238-239.
[377] Francis Mading Deng. "War of Visions for the Nations." *Middle East Journal* 44, no. 4 (1990): 596.

Movement's leadership decided to reorganize its structure within the military. The Movement's members within the military were divided into three groups. The first group consisted of officers loyal to the Movement, particularly those officers who were instructed by the Movement to join the military; this group joined the military from high schools or as professional specialists following their graduation from university. They were considered to be the heart of the Movement cells in the Sudanese military establishment.[378]

The second group was the "Islamists" officers. Members of this group were classified as Islamists during the Islamic courses that were mandated by the military for its ranking officers after the declaration of Islamic laws in 1983. Members of this group were mainly unorganized Islamists who supported the Movement or who had close ties with its members and officers who belonged to Sufi groups and were in favor of establishing an Islamic state in Sudan.[379] The third group included those officers important to the future of any military coup. Members of this group included the leading military officers in the capital, those who held key positions in the military intelligence, police forces, Forces Command, and the Commander in-Chief office.[380]

The civilian military organization, consisted mainly of the Movement's most loyal members who were trained in Libya, Lebanon, and Pakistan, remained secret. The idea behind this secrecy, as was later explained by the Movement's leadership after its successful 1989 coup, was that this secret organization would be able to function as a parallel to the Sudanese military in case the Movement decided to launch a military coup. The organization would also act as a separate unit in supporting any coup carried out by the military wing of the Movement while helping to suppress any other attempted coups. The secret organization would also play a role similar to the role of the Islamic Revolutionary Guards in

---

[378] Mirghani, 228.
[379] Ibid., 236-237.
[380] Ibid., 265-271.

Iran which helped the Islamic Revolution in its early days against any counter coups. [381]

As a result of its detailed plans and dedicated work among the Sudanese military establishment, the Islamic Movement in Sudan had infiltrated and held control of the Sudanese military and security establishments. Nemeri, who constantly directed security forces to follow Movement activities, was not aware of its presence in the army and security forces. In March 1985 when Nemeri finally decided to crack down on the Islamists, their security contacts tipped them off, which gave them enough time to go underground.[382] As el-Affendi accurately observed, "Nemeri's diligent efforts to Islamize the military establishment made the army as a whole a more favorable organ so far as Ikhwan [Islamists] were concerned." [383]

In June 1989 when the Movement decided to stage the coup and take control of the country, all three groups plus the secret civilian organization were able to control all of the important posts and the military barracks. The Movement's secret paramilitary organization's role was crucial during the early hours of the coup. Its members secured bridges, operated the country's main radio station, and arrested leading political figures and top military officers in the country. After the coup, and as a result of an unprecedented purge among Sudanese military officers, members of the Movement's secret organization were appointed to key positions in the military; other members became the backbone of the Popular Defense, a separate armed militia created by the Movement to play a role that is similar to the role of the Islamic Revolutionary Guards in Iran, which is to suppress any counter-coup attempts by the regular army.

---

[381] Haydar Ibrahim Ali. *Al-Ikhwan Wa Al-Askar*. Cairo, Egypt: Markaz al-Hadarah al-Arabiyah, 1993.
[382] El-Affendi, *"Turabi's Revolution,"* 129.
[383] Ibid., 129.

Trade Unions and Labor Movement

The trade union movement has played a central role in Sudan's national politics since its emergence after World War II. In 1946 the British government proposed the formation of works councils, or joint consultative advisory committees, in government departments and private industry as the basis on which trade unions could subsequently be formed on a solid foundation. About the same time a Workers' Affairs Association (WAA) was established by artisans in the Mechanical Department of the Sudan Railways and it demanded recognition and the development of trade unionism. The WAA, which became the spearhead of the trade-union movement, was hostile to the works council proposal, regarding it as a device by management to obstruct the growth of trade unions. The WAA became increasingly aggressive and anti-colonialist, and in 1947 succeeded in winning recognition through strike.[384]

After the enactment of trade-union legislation in 1949, the WAA was changed into the Sudan Railway Workers' Union and unions were rapidly formed in other government departments and in private industry. More than 130 unions were established with a total membership of 100,000, or more by the late 1940s. Paramount among these was the Sudan Railway Workers' Union (SRWU) with about 25,000. Membership of other unions fell between 1,000 and 1,500 members with an average of about 600. Many were unions of workers in government departments such as irrigation, education, and transportation, while in private industry they were often organizations of workers employed by individual companies. Trade unionism during that time was insignificant outside the urban centers and played little role in Southern Sudan and other non-urban areas in the country.[385]

Most of the unions became affiliated with the Sudan Workers' Trade Union Federation (SWTUF), which was formed in 1950 under the leadership of

---

[384] Saad Ed Din Fawzi. *The Labour Movement in the Sudan, 1946-1955.* London: Oxford University Press for the Royal Institute of International Affairs, 1957, 77.

[385] Ibid., 96.

the railway workers. It started in a militant mood, brought the trade unions into the nationalist movement, claiming that the colonial government was the main obstacle to the workers' efforts to improve their condition. The SWTUF organized a series of general strikes mainly to secure wage increases and improve working conditions. The SWTUF, which was controlled by pro-Egyptian unionists, became more involved in national politics when it opposed the Anglo-Egyptian Agreement of February 1953 by which the Sudan could achieve early self-determination within a period of three years. The SWTUF remained militant after Sudan gained independence and continued to function as a major political force in the country.[386]

Unlike their counterparts in Egypt, the Islamic Movement in Sudan in its early days had a weak presence among Sudanese workers for two main reasons. The first reason was the elitist nature of the Sudanese Movement in its early days. Unlike the Egyptian movement, which started with a group of workers who accepted al-Banna's call for establishing the Muslim Brotherhood, the Movement in Sudan started mainly among the educated elite. These elite classes paid little or no attention to spreading the Movement's ideology among workers; they concentrated their recruitment efforts among the educated elite only.

The second reason that greatly limited the influence of the Movement among Sudanese workers and trade unions was the dominant presence of the Sudanese Communist Party (SCP) among Sudanese workers. The SCP was active in the trade union movement. It was highly successful in organizing the railway workers at Atbara, the center of the Sudanese railways. In 1950 the Sudan Workers' Trade Union Federation (SWTUF) was established under the control of the SCP; later the union became one of the strongest trade union movements in Africa and the Middle East. The SCP also exerted strong influence on the al-Gezeria Farmers' Association, the main cotton growers' trade union.[387]

---

[386] Ibid., 116.
[387] Bashier, "*Al-Harakah Al-Wataniyah*," 246.

The earliest activities by the Movement among trade unions was in 1952 when Yassin Omer al-Imam, one of the Movement's founders who had recently returned from Egypt, traveled to Atbara, the heart of the workers' movement in Sudan, where he obtained a job as an accountant. Upon his arrival in Atbara, al-Imam proceeded with other Movement members to spread the Movement's ideology among the workers and to counter the rapid influence of SCP. During his stay in Atbara, al-Imam convinced the Atbara branch of the Movement to pay more attention to the workers and he also directed the Movement's students from the Khartoum College School of Engineering who regularly traveled to Atbara for training, to spread the Movement's ideology and programs among workers. A few months later, al-Imam was dismissed from his work as a result of his involvement in a strike that was organized by trade unions in Atbara. His isolated attempts to make inroads into the trade unions collapsed after his departure.[388]

In 1957 fresh attempts were made to organize the activities of the Movement among the trade unions in Khartoum when the Workers' Bureau (WB) was established by Movement member Muawia Abdelaziz, who at the time was a mechanical engineer in the capital.[389] Abdelaziz divided the works of the WB into three branches to represent the three parts of the capital; Omdurman, Khartoum, and Khartoum North. Abu-Algasim Abdelgadir was selected to represent the Omdurman branch of the Movement's workers, Ahmed Sadig to represent the Khartoum branch, and Mohammed al-Hasan to represent Khartoum North.[390]

The newly established WB met regularly in the Movement's headquarters in Omdurman and discussed trade union organization and strategies to end the monopoly of Communists over the trade union movement. It was proposed in these meetings that the break up of the Sudan Workers' Trade Union Federation could be a step toward this end, and that could be accomplished by introducing three specialized union federations, one for public sector workers, a second for

---

[388] Ahmad, "*Harakat Al-Ikhwan Al-Muslimin Fi Al-Sudan, 1944 -1969,*"83.
[389] Ibid., 83.
[390] Ibid., 83-84.

private sector workers, and a third for artisans. The general aim of the Movement at that time was not so much the control of the unions but rather the removal of the Communists from their leadership.[391] The Movement also encouraged more cooperative relations with the two main traditional religious sects in the country the al-Ansar and the al-Khatmiyya, who were deeply concerned about the rising Communist influence among trade unions.[392]

The WB functioned for a limited time and by 1958 it collapsed as a result of the departure of Muawia Abdelaziz to the United States for further education and the transfer of Algasim Abdelgadir from Khartoum to Atbara. As a result of Abboud's military coup in 1958, most of the Movement's activities among trade unions were spontaneous and reflected personal attempts by Movement members rather than an approved plan by the Movement. In 1958 Movement members who acted independently were unable to rally any significant support among the workers against the Communists in SWTUF.[393]

The WB was revived again in December 1961 with new leadership that consisted of three elected members. Its first success came in August 1963 with the election of Movement member Abdel-Rahman al-Bakheit to the executive committee of the SWTUF. This partial success resulted in more attention by the Movement's leadership to the trade union movements.[394] In August 1964 a new WB was established and al-Imam was elected as its head. The new WB executives consisted of Jaafar Sheikh Idris, Abdel-Rahim Hamdi, Abddallah Ahmed Bilal, and Abdel-Rahman al-Bakheit.[395] The presence of college graduates and highly organized individuals such as Jaafar Sheikh Idris and Abdel-Rahim Hamdi reflected the Movement's dramatic shift toward working among trade unions. For the first time in the history of the Movement, those who were previously in charge of successful recruitment strategies in universities were put

---

[391] Osman, "The Political and Ideological Development,"200-201.
[392] Ibid., 84.
[393] Ahmad, "Harakat Al-Ikhwan Al-Muslimin Fi Al-Sudan, 1944 -1969,"84.
[394] Ibid., 84.
[395] Ibid., 85.

in charge of expanding the Movement's ideological and political programs among trade unions. It also signified the final departure of the Movement from an elite-centered organization to a massive social movement. The revival of the WB in 1964 was in large due to al- Turabi's general drive to revitalize the Movement.

In 1965 the Movement's leadership proceeded with its early plan against the Communist-dominated SWTUF by establishing the Patriotic Trade Unionists' Congress (PTUC) to rival SWTUF. The declared aim of the PTUC was to create an independent labor movement. According to the PTUC leadership, the SWTUF became a Communist organization. The leaders of the PTUC presented their organization as an organization independent from any influence by particular political groups or ideologies. The newly created PTUC largely consisted of the Movement's members, independent workers, anti-Communist workers, and workers with allegiance to the traditional religious sects, particularly al-Khatmiyya. The newly created organization was greatly welcomed and supported by government officials and business owners who saw PTUC as an important tool to undermine SCP's influence in the trade unions.[396]

The Movement's attempts to limit or eradicate communist influence among trade unions achieved limited success, as the SCP maintained its grip on the trade unions due in large part to its extensive recruitment among workers. Unlike the Movement's WB, which consisted mainly of college graduates, the SCP created an effective working organization within the party of workers and trade unions representatives. Al-Shafia Ahmed el-Sheikh and Qasim Ameen, who were prominent leaders in the Sudanese trade unions in the period from 1940 to 1971, were also members of the Central Committee of the Sudanese Communist Party.

In 1971 as a result of a failed coup attempt, the SCP lost most of its leadership. Thousands of party activists were imprisoned or forced into the exile, Al-Shafia Ahmed el-Sheikh was executed and Qasim Ameen was briefly put in

---

[396] Osman, "The Political and Ideological Development,"202.

prison before he was sent into exile. The SCP lost most of its influence among trade unions. After the 1976 reconciliation accord between Nemeri and the Movement, the Movement was allowed to resume its activities among the workers. Nemeri's regime supported the Movement's efforts among the trade unions as a way to counter the remaining influence of the SCP. The old plan of dividing the SWTUF into three groups was put again in action and with the support of Nemeri's regime, it was approved. In the period from 1976 to 1985, the Movement campaign among trade unions was marked with great success. The Movement established strong presence among workers as it was the only political power that was freely allowed to move among them. The newly established Islamic banks and investment institutions, particularly the Faisal Islamic Bank, opened specialized branches which provided members of the trade unions with interest-free loans and allowed them to buy "expensive" needed items such as home appliances and electronic products at reasonable prices and in installments.

After the collapse of Nemeri's regime in 1985 the SWTUF returned to one united structure. The Movement lost its grip on the trade unions, as opposition parties allied against it. Despite their loss, the Movement's leadership achieved its main goal of limiting or eradicating Communist influence in the trade unions. In order to remove the Movement's members from the SWTUF leadership, the SCP was forced to work with other political parties, such as al-Umma (The Nation) and the Democratic Unionist Party (DUP); historically both were SCP opponents and did not support the rights of workers while in government. Despite the fact that it was removed from the SWTUF's leadership, the Movement still remained the single most influential group within the Sudanese trade union movement; only through the formation of a united front with other political parties was the SCP able to keep the Movement's members from winning the trade union elections.

Despite success in ousting the SCP from the leadership of most trade union and worker organizations, the Movement was unable to fully control them because of the strong presence of the other two traditional parties; al-Umma and the DUP. Also, because of its weak position financially, especially compared to that of the Movement, the SCP leadership decided to cooperatively work with representatives of al-Umma and the DUP in the trade unions in order to overpower the Movement's representatives.

CHAPTER VII

Conclusion

During the past decades political Islam has become a major topic of scholarship in international relations, particularly in the regard to Middle Eastern politics. The interest on political Islam began with the military coup of Dia-alhag in Pakistan in 1977, but more importantly with the Islamic Revolution in Iran in 1979. Other early incidents that brought political Islam to the attention of academia were the assassination in December 1948 of Egyptian Prime Minister Naqrashi Pasha, who disbanded the Society of Muslim Brotherhood, and in retaliation, the Egyptian Secret Police assassinated of Hassan al-Banna, the Brotherhood's supreme leader in February 1949; the conflicts between former Egyptian president Nasser and the Muslim Brotherhood in Egypt in 1954 and 1966 that resulted in the hanging of Sayyid Qutb and five other Muslim Brotherhood leaders; the seizure of the Grand Mosque in Mecca in 1979; the assassination of President Anwar Sadat in Egypt in 1981; the bloody battles of 1982 between the Muslim Brotherhood and the Syrian government in Hama, Syria; and the Islamists' successful military coup in Sudan in 1989. Following the tragic events of 9/11/2001 political Islam surfaced again and became a dominant issue in the western literature. The rise of Islamic movements in the Islamic world in general, and in the Middle East in particular, has led to widespread debate in the West regarding the causes, values and goals of these movements.

Two general schools of thought have emerged on the subject: the cultural-religious school and the socio-economic and political school. Members of the first school explain the emergence of Islamic movements as a reaction against the political, moral and technological incursions of the West into Muslim societies. They also view these movements as monolithic across the Muslim world, representing a politico-religious "civilization" that would ultimately come into direct confrontation with the West. The socio-economic school, on the other hand, views the emergence of Islamic movements as a product of complex internal and external factors. They include the ideological vacuum in the Arab world in the wake of the Arab defeat in the 1967 War, and the collapse of Nasser's "Arab Nationalist" ideology; the failure of post-independence governments in the Middle East to achieve economic prosperity; the undemocratic nature of political regimes in Muslim countries; the secularization of Muslim societies; and the alienation of Islam from public life.

Using a wider theoretical framework and recognizing the gaps that exist in studying political Islam, this study utilized Social Movement Theory (SMT) in examining the rise of the Islamic Movement in Sudan (1945-1989). Social Movement Theory (SMT) provides a more comprehensive framework for understanding the Islamic movement in Sudan. The theory permits the exploration of the Movement's understudied mechanisms of contention and successful expansion, including liberal ideology toward adapting Islam to contemporary life; progressive views on the role of women in public life; organizational structure; recruitment among students, women, workers, military personnel and merchants; development of economic institutions; media utilization; and tactical consideration in the use of violence and accommodation.

The increasing strength and influence of the Islamic Movement in Sudan is traceable to the liberal views of its leadership, particularly Hasan al-Turabi. Al-Turabi's personality, charisma and liberal and anti-elite views played a major role in moving the Movement from elite-centered to a more popular political movement willing to ally itself with other political parties and groups for achieving strategic goals. His anti-*effendis* views also helped in expanding the Movement's social base beyond its traditional base (university students) to unionized workers, Sufi groups, military personnel, and regionally marginalized ethnic groups in East, West, and North Sudan. Al-Turabi's views on issues such as *ijtihad, ijmaa, tajdid* in Islam, women, law, and democracy helped the Movement to expand to new territories previously considered impenetrable.

The Movement's changing stand on women's role in public life was also significant in enhancing its position among educated women in Sudan. The Movement leadership consistently argued in favor of a greater role for women in the Movement and in society in general. They advocated greater opportunities for women in work and education and also called for their full participation in the Movement's activities and in the country's political process. The Movement's progressive views on women revolutionized its work among women and heavily influenced the outcome of the Sudanese student union elections as more women started to vote regularly for the Movement's members, thus enhancing their position in higher education institutions.

The Movement also benefited from the flow of foreign investments in Sudan after the declaration of an open-door policy by Nemeri that encouraged foreign investment in Sudan. The emergence of Islamic economic institutions, such as Faisal Islamic Bank (FIB), helped change the political landscape in the country in favor of the Movement as it facilitated the Movement's control of these financial institutions and utilized them in building a solid economic base in the country, particularly in the foreign trade area which traditionally was controlled by foreigners and supporters of DUP. The newly created financial institutions enhanced Movement presence among students, women, trade unions, and professional associations because they provided needed services and products for these groups. Newly created Islamic institutions also helped the Movement in the creation of a large network of Islamic Non-Government Organizations (INGOs), which also enhanced the presence and the visibility of the Movement, particularly in the regions where these INGOs were able to provide much needed services, such as educational and health services.

The Movement's innovative organizational structure and recruitment strategies among students, military personnel, and trade union members greatly enhanced the Movement's presence among these groups. After al-Turabi's election as leader, the Movement rejected the Egyptian recruitment style that called for a long period of indoctrination for new members before they were accepted as full members. The movement in Sudan adopted an open and flexible recruitment strategy that eventually netted a dramatic increase in members. The Movement also rejected the centralized model that was inherited from the Egyptian Brotherhood in favor of a flexible structure that gave the regions, students, and trade unions more freedom and flexibility in handling local issues.

Under the leadership of al-Turabi, the Movement intensified its recruitment campaigns among students by directing its members to work as high school and middle school teachers in order to start recruiting new members earlier than its rivals, who with the exception of the SCP, tended to wait until students entered universities and colleges. The Movement also crafted a detailed recruitment strategy to infiltrate the Sudanese military establishment that resulted in strengthening the Movement presence among military officers. The Islamization of the army that followed the declaration of *Shari'a* laws in Sudan in 1983 also gave the Movement momentum within the army. All army officers were ordered to attend special Islamic courses that were mainly administered by the Movement's members and sympathizers at the African Islamic Center, currently International University of Africa.

In general, this study has questioned a number of traditional views that have dominated the western literature about Islamic movements. In particular it has questioned the widely held belief that Islamic movements were products of deplorable societal conditions or negative reactions to modernization. The conception of Islamism as a "major threat" "is widespread and deeply embedded in Western minds."[397] This study demonstrates clearly the strong belief among many observers of political Islam in the ability of small groups not only to force the ruling establishment to meet their political and social demands but also, under

---

[397] Brynjar,1998.

proper leadership, to transform themselves into a forceful and effective political-religious mass movement.

The findings of this study point to the need to look closely at the mechanisms of grassroots mobilization of different Islamic movements. There exists no comprehensive study of the social, educational, and economic welfare projects of the Islamic Movement in Sudan in the pre-1989 period, not even in Arabic. Discussions and comparative analysis should be encouraged on the differences between *Jihadi* and *Salafiyya* groups, on one hand, and the mainstream Islamic political movements such as the Islamic Movement in Sudan and the Muslim Brotherhood in Egypt, on the other hand. More importantly, scholars and researchers should give more attention to the process by which Islamists interpret Islamic traditional teachings and integrate modern principles and ideas with their ideological framework. This process of interpretation of Islamic traditional teachings and the integration of modern ideas is what differentiates mainstream Islamic political movements like the Islamic Movement in Sudan from other *Jihadi* and *Salafiyya* groups in the Islamic world.

Islamic revivalism incorporates a much wider movement than anti-Western militant groups. As summarized by Esposito

> . . . Islamic revivalism has ceased to be restricted to small, marginal organization on the periphery of society and instead has become part of mainstream Muslim society, producing a new class of modern-educated but Islamically oriented elites who work alongside, and at times in coalitions with, their secular counterparts. Revivalism continues to grow as a broad-based socio-religious movement, functioning today in virtually every Muslim country and transnationality. It is a vibrant, multifaceted movement that will embody the major impact of Islamic revivalism for the foreseeable future. Its goal is the transformation of society through the Islamic formation of individuals at the grass-roots level. *Dawa* (call) societies work in social services (hospitals, clinics, legal-aid societies), in economic projects (Islamic banks, investment houses, insurance companies), in education (schools, child-care centers, youth camps), and in religious publishing and broadcasting.[398]

---

[398] Esposito. The Islamic Threat, 23.

Bibliography

Abbas, Ali Abdalla. "The National Islamic Front and the Politics of Education." *Middle East Report*, no. 172 (1991): 22-25.

Abbott, Freeland. *Islam and Pakistan*. Ithaca: Cornell University Press, 1968.

Abd al-Jabbar, Falih. *Al-Dawlah, Al-Mujtama` Al-Madani Wa-Al-Tahawwul Al-Dimuqrati Fi Al-`Iraq*, Silsilat Dirasat Mashru` Al-Mujtama` Al-Madani Wa-Al-Tahawwul Al-Dimuqrati Fi Al-Watan Al-`Arabi;. al-Qahirah: Markaz Ibn Khaldun bi-al-ishtirak ma`a Dar al-Amin lil-Nashr wa-al-Tawzi`, 1995.

———. "Ayatollahs, Sufis and Ideologues: State, Religion and Social Movements in Iraq." London, UK: Dar al-Saqi, 2002.

———. *Ma`Alim Al-`Aqlaniyah Wa-Al-Khurafah Fi Al-Fikr Al-Siyasi Al-`Arabi*, Buhuth Ijtima`Iyah ;; 16;. London, UK: Dar al-Saqi, 1992.

Abd al-Jabbar, Falih & Benedict Anderson R. *Al-Qawmiyah: Marad Al-`Asr Am Khulasah?* Beirut, Lebanon: Dar al-Saqi, 1995.

Abdelgader, Mohammed al-Khier. *Nashat Al-Harakah Al-Islamiyah Al-Hadisa Fi Al-Sudan.* Khartoum, Sudan: Sudanese House For Books, 1999.

Abdelmagied, Ahmed, Wifag Salah, Nayla ElTahir, Tamadur NurEldin, and Sahar Shareef. "Perception and Attitudes of Religious Groups toward Female Genital Mutilation." *Ahfad Journal* 22, no. 2 (2005): 53-63.

Abed-Kotob, Sana. "The Accommodationists Speak: Goals and Strategies of the Muslim Brotherhood of Egypt." *International Journal of Middle East Studies* 27, no. 3 (1995): 321-39.

Abootalebi, Ali R. "Islam, Islamists, and Democracy." *Middle East Review of International Affairs* 3, no. 1 (1999): 14-24.

Aboul-Enein, Youssef H. "Al-Ikhwan Al-Muslimeen: The Muslim Brotherhood" *Military Review* 83, no. 4 (2003): 26-31.

Abu-Rabi, Ibrahim M. "Arabism, Islamism, and the Future of Arab World." *Arab Studies Quarterly* 22, no. 1 (2000): 91-101.

———. *Contemporary Arab Thought: Studies in Post-1967 Arab Intellectual History*: Sterling, Virginia: Pluto Press, 2004.

———. *Intellectual Origins of Islamic Resurgence in the Modern Arab World.*, SUNY Series in near Eastern Studies; Albany, NY: State University of New York Press, 1996.

Adar, Korwa G. "Ethno-Religious Nationalism in Sudan: The Enduring Constraint on the Policy of National Identity " In *Shifting African Identities*, edited by Bekker, Simon B., Dodds, Martine & Khosa, Meshack M. Pretoria, South Africa: Human Sciences Research Council, 2001.

Ahmad, Anis. "Mawdudi's Concept of Shari'ah." *Muslim World* 93, no. 3/4 (2003): 533-545.

Ahmad, Dallal. "Appropriating the Past: Twentieth-Century Reconstruction of Pre-Modern Islamic Thought." *Islamic Law & Society* 7, no. 3 (2000): 325-58.

Ahmad, Hasan Makki Muhammad. *Al-Harakah Al-Islamiyah Fi Al-Sudan, 1969-1985 M: Tarikhuha Wa-Khatabuha Al-Siyasi.* Khartoum-Sudan: Ma'had al-Buhuth wa-al-Dirasat al-Ijtima'iyah: Bayt al-Ma'rifah lil-Intaj al-Thaqafi, 1990.

———. *Al-Harakah Al-Tullabiyah Al-Sudaniyah Bayna Al-Ams Wa-Al-Yawm.* Khartoum-Sudan: Dar al-Fikr, 1987.

———. *Harakat Al-Ikhwan Al-Muslimin Fi Al-Sudan, 1944 M-1969* Silsilat Al-Kurrasat Ghayr Al-Dawriyah ; Raqm 16;. Khartoum, Sudan: Ma'had al-Dirasat al-Afriqiyah wa-al-Asiyawiyah, Jami'at al-Khartum, 1982.

Ahmad, Khurshid. "Islam and Democracy: Some Conceptual and Contemporary Dimensions." *Muslim World* 90, no. 1/2 (2000): 1-21.

Akhavi, Shahrough. "The Dialectic in Contemporary Egyptian Social Thought: The Scripturalist and Modernist Discourses of Sayyid Qutb and Hasan Hanafi." *International Journal of Middle East Studies* 29, no. 3 (1997): 377-401.

Al-Amin, Nafisa & abdel-Magied, Ahmed. "A History of Sudanese Women Organizations and the Strive for Liberation and Empowerment." *Ahfad Journal* 18, no. 1 (2001): 2-23.

Al-Banna, Hasan. *Five Tracts of Hasan Al-Bannd' (1906-1949): A Selection from the Majmuat Rasil al-Imam al-Shahid Hasan al-Banna.* Translated by Charles Wendell. Berkeley, CA: University of California Press, 1978.

Al-Banna, Hasan. "The Message of the Teachings." Available at http://www.youngmuslims.ca/online_library/books/tmott/. Accessed 09/31/2006.

Al-Faruql, Maysam "Engaging Political Islam " *Policy Briefs*, no. 11/14/2006, http://www.mideasti.org/articles/doc588.html Accessed 08/12/2007

Al-Ghannoushi, Rashid, and Linda G. Jones. "Rashid Al-Ghannoushi: "Deficiencies in the Islamic Movement." *Middle East Report*, no. 153 (1988): 23-24.

Al-Ghannoushi, Rashid & al-Turabi, Hasan. *Al-Harakah Al-Islamiyah Wa-Al-Tahdith.* Beirut, Lebanon: Dar al-Jeel, 1980

Ali, Haydar Ibrahim. *Al-Ikhwan Wa Al-Askar.* Cairo, Egypt: Markaz al-Hadarah al-Arabiyah, 1993.

―――. *Al-Tayyarat Al-Islamiyah Wa Qadiyat Al-Dimuqratiyah.* Beirut: Lebanon: Markaz Dirasat al-Wahdah al-`Arabiyah, 1996.

―――. *Azmat Al-Islam Al-Siyasi: Al-Jabhah Al-Islamiyah Al- Qawmiyah Fi Al-Sudan Namudhajan.* Alexandria, Egypt: Markaz al-Dirasat al-Sudaniyah, 1992.

―――. *Lahut Al-Tahrir: Al-Din Wa-Al-Thawrah Fi Al-`Alam Al- Thalith.* Alexandria: Egypt: Dar al-Nil, 1993.

―――. *Suqut Al-Mashru Al-Hadari.* Khartoum, Sudan: Markaz al-Dirasat al-Sudaniyah, 2004.

Al-Mawdudi, Abul A'la. *Toward Understanding Islam.* Lahore, Pakistan: Medeena Books, 1967.

Al-Mawdudi, Abul A'la. *Come Let Us Change the World.* Translated by Kaukab Siddique. Washington: The Islamic Party of North America, 1972.

Almquist, Kate, Voll, John & Rone, Jemera. "Western Perspectives on Religion and Politics in Sudan." In *Religion and Peacemaking* Washington, D.C: U.S. Institute of Peace, 1997.

Al-Qaradawi, Yusuf. *Islamic Awakening between Rejection and Extremism.* 2nd ed. Herndon, VA: The Institute of Islamic Thought, 1991.

———. *Priorities of the Islamic Movement in the Coming Phase.* Doha, Qatar: al-Dar, 1992.

Al-Qawmiyah, Jabhah al-Islamiyah. *Mithaq Al-Sudan.* Khartoum, Sudan: al-Jabhah, 1987.

Alrasheed, Nayel Amina. "Sudanese Women in Exile: Islam, Politics, and the State." *Respect* 1, no. 4 (2006): 1-23.

Al-Sa'id, Rif'at *Hasan Al-Banna: Mata... Kayfa... Wa-Limadha?* Cairo, Egypt: Maktabat Madbuli, 1977.

———. *History of the Socialist Movement in Egypt (1900-1925).* Leipzig, Germany: Karl Marx University, 1978.

Al-Turabi, Hasan. *Al-Harakah Al-Islamiyah Fi Al-Sudan,* Afaq Al-Ghad 8. Kuwait: Dar al-Qalam, 1988.

———. *Al-Harakah Al-Islamiyah Fi Al-Sudan: Al-Tatawwur Wa-Al-Kasb Wa-Al-Manhaj.* Cairo, Egypt: al-Qari al-ʿArabi, 1991.

———. *Al-Iman: Atharuhu Fi Hayat Al-Insan.* Kuwait: Dar al-Qalam, 1974.

———. *Al-Islamiyun Wa-Al-Masalah Al-Siyasiyah,* Silsilat Kutub Al-Mustaqbal Al-ʿArabi 26. Beirut, Lebanon: Markaz Dirasat al-Wahdah al-Arabiyah, 2003.

———. *Al-Ittijah Al-Islami Yuqaddimu Al-Marah Bayna Taalim Al-Din Wa-Taqalid Al-Mujtama.* Jeddah, KSA: al-Dar al-Saʿudiyah lil-Nashr wa-al-Tawziʿ, 1984.

———. *Al-Marah Bayna Al-Usul Wa-Al-Taqalid.* Khartoum, Sudan: Markaz Dirasat al-Marah, 2000.

———. *Al-Mashrue Al-Islami Al-Sudani: Qiraat Fi Al-Fikr Wa-Al-Mumaasah.* Khartoum, Sudan: Maʿhad al-Buhuth wa-al-Dirasat al-Ijtimaʿiyah, 1995.

―――. *Al-Musalahat Al-Siyasiyah Fi Al-Islam.* Beirut, Lebanon: Dar al-Saqi, 2000.

―――. *Al-Salah Eimad Al-Din.* Jeddah, KSA: al-Dar al-Sa'udiyah lil-Nashr wa-al-Tawzi', 1984.

―――. *Al-Shura Wa-Al-Dimuqraiyah.* Khartoum, Sudan: Alam al-Alaniyah, 2000.

―――. *Al-Siyasah Wa-Al-Hukm: Al-Nuzum Al-Sultaniyah Bayna Al-Usul Wa-Sunan Al-Waqi».* Al-Tab'ah 1. Beirut, Lebanon: Dar al-Saqi, 2003.

―――. *Islam, Democracy, the State and the West: A Round Table with Dr. Hasan Turabi, May 10, 1992.* Beirut, Lebanon: al-Dar al-Jadid, 1995.

―――. "Islamic Fundamentalism in the Sunni and Shia Worlds." Available at http://www.islamfortoday.com/turabi02.htm. Accessed 02/12/2006.

―――. *Tajdid Al-Fikr Al-Islami.* Al-Rabat, Morocco: Dar al-Qarafi lil-Nashr wa-al-Tawzi, 1993.

―――. *Tajdid Usul Al-Fiqh Al-Islami.* Beirut, Lebanon: Dar al-Jil, 1980.

―――. *Women in Islam and Muslim Society.* London, U.K: Milestones Publishers, 1991.

―――. *Manhajiyat Al-Tashri Al-Islami* Edited by al-Tayib Zein al-Abdin, Islammiyat Al-Marifa. Washington, DC: International Institute of Islamic Thought, 1992.

―――."Principles of Governance, Freedom, and Responsibility in Islam." *The American Journal of Islamic Sciences* 4, no. 1 (1987): 1-11.

Al-Turabi, Hasan & Lowrie, Arthur L. *Islam, Democracy, the State and the West : A Round Table with Dr. Hasan Turabi, May 10, 1992*, Wise Monograph Series ;; No. 1. Tampa, FL: U.S.A: World & Islam Studies Enterprise, 1993.

Al-Turabi, Hasan, Sardar, Ziauddin, Jamal, Mahmood & Zuber, Marc. *The Islamic State.* Princeton, N.J.: Films for the Humanities & Sciences, 1994. Videorecording (VHS) tape.

Anderson, Lisa. "Political Decay in the Arab World." In *Middle Eastern Lectures. 4*. The Moshe Dayan Centre for Middle Eastern and African Studies. Tel Aviv, Israel: Tel Aviv University, 1999.

An-Na`im, Abdullahi Ahmed. *Islamic Fundamentalism and Social Change: Neither The "End of History" Nor A "Clash of Civilizations"*. Edited by Busuttil, James & Haar, James J. The Freedom to Do God's Will: Religious Fundamentalism and Social Change. New York: Routledge, 2002.

———. "The Islamic Law of Apostasy and Its Modern Applicability: A Case from Sudan." *Religion, State & Society*, no. 16 (1986): 197-224.

———. "Religious Minorities under Islamic Law and the Limits of Cultural Relativism." *Human Rights Quarterly* 9, no. 1 (1987): 1-18.

An-Na`im, Abdullahi A. & Francis M. Deng "Self-Determination and Unity: The Case of Sudan." *Law & Policy* 19, no. 3 (1997): 199-223.

Arjomand, Said A. *The Political Dimensions of Religion*. Albany, New York: State University of New York Press, 1993.

———. *The Shadow of God and the Hidden Imam: Religion, Political Order, and Societal Change in Shi'ite Iran from the Beginning to 1890*. Chicago: University of Chicago Press, 1987.

———. *The Turban for the Crown: The Islamic Revolution in Iran*. New York: Oxford University Press, 1989.

Ashford, Douglas E. "The Political Usage of 'Islam' And 'Arab Culture'." *The Public Opinion Quarterly* 25, no. 1 (1961): 106-14.

Ayoob, Mohammed. "Political Islam: Image and Reality." *World Policy Journal* 21, no. 3 (2004): 1-14.

Ayubi, Nazih N. M. "The Political Revival of Islam: The Case of Egypt." *International Journal of Middle East Studies* 12, no. 4 (1980): 481-99.

———. "The Politics of Militant Islamic Movements in the Middle East." *Journal of International Affairs* 36, no. 2 (1983): 271-283.

Babiker, Yahia Hussin. *KUSU Political Role During 1969-1979*. Khartoum: Sudan: Khartoum University Students Union, Foreign Affairs Secretariat, 1980.

Badri, Haga Kashif. *Women's Movement in the Sudan*. New Delhi, India: Asia News Agency, 1986.

Badri, Malik B. "A Tribute to Mawlana Mawdudi from an Autobiographical Point of View." *Muslim World* 93, no. 3/4 (2003): 487-502.

Bahramitash, Roksana. "Myths and Realities of the Impact of Political Islam on Women: Female Employment in Indonesia and Iran." *Development in Practice* 14, no. 4 (2004): 508-20.

Barsalou, Judy. "Islamic Extremists: How Do They Mobilize Support?" Washington, D.C: United States Institute of Peace, 2002.

Bashier, Zakaria. *Islamic Movement in the Sudan: Issues and Challenges*, Seminar Papers 6. Leicester, England: Islamic Foundation, 1987.

————. *The National Reconciliation in the Sudan and Its Aftermath*, Seminar Papers 12. Leicester, England: Islamic Foundation, 1981.

Bayat, Asef. "Islamism and Social Movement Theory." *Third World Quarterly* 26, no. 6 (2005): 891-908.

————. "Revolution without Movement, Movement without Revolution: Comparing Islamic Activism in Iran and Egypt." *Comparative Studies in Society and History* 40, no. 1 (1998): 136-69.

Baylouny, Anne Marie. "Emotions, Poverty or Politics: Misconceptions About Islamic Movements." *Strategic Insights* 3, no. 1 (2004): 1-6.

Beinin, Joel. "Political Islam and the New Global Economy: The Political Economy of Islamist Social Movements in Egypt and Turkey." In *French and US Approaches to Understanding Islam*. France-Stanford Center for Interdisciplinary Studies, 2004.

Beinin, Joel & Stork, Joe. *Political Islam: Essays from Middle East Report*. Berkeley, CA: University of California Press, 1997.

Bellucci, Stefano. "Islam and Democracy: The 1989 Palace Coup in Sudan." *Middle East Policy* 7, no. 3 (2000): 168-175.

Bernal, Victoria. "Migration, Modernity and Islam in Rural Sudan." *Middle East Report*, no. 211 (1999): 26-28.

Beshir, Mohamed Omer. *Al-Harakah Al-Wataniyah Fi Al-Sudan 1990-1969.* Translated by Riad, Henry., Omer, Aljneed A., & Riad, William. Khartoum, Sudan: Sudanese House For Books, 1977.

Bogaards, Matthijs. "Electoral Choices for Divided Societies: Multi-Ethnic Parties and Constituency Pooling in Africa." *Commonwealth & Comparative Politics* 41, no. 3 (2003): 59-80.

Bokhari, Kamran A. "Islamist Attitudes toward Democracy." In *Islam, Democracy and the Secularist State in the Post-Modern Era.* Washington, D.C: Georgetown University, 2001.

Bola, Abdalla. "Shajarat Nasab Al-Ghul Fi Mushkil Al-Huwiya Al-Sudaniyah." *Assahifa* 5 (1998): 12-15.

Bremmer, Ian. "The Saudi Paradox." *World Policy Journal* 21, no. 3 (2004): 23-30.

Brown, Cameron S. "Waiting for the Other To Shoe to Drop: How Inevitable Is an Islamist Future?" *Middle East Review of International Affairs* 10, no. 2 (2006): 108-20.

Brown, Leon Carl. "The Islamic Reformist Movement in North Africa." *The Journal of Modern African Studies* 2, no. 1 (1964): 55-63.

Brynjar, Lia. *The Society of the Muslim Brothers in Egypt: The Rise of an Islamic Mass Movement 1928-1942.* Dryden, NY: Ithaca Press, 2006.

Bulliet, Richard W. "The Future of the Islamic Movement." *Foreign Affairs* 72, no. 5 (1993): 38-44.

Burgat, François. *The Islamic Movement in North Africa.* Austin: TX: Center for Middle Eastern Studies, University of Texas at Austin, 1993.

Butko, Thomas J. "Revelation or Revolution: A Gramscian Approach to the Rise of Political Islam." *British Journal of Middle Eastern Studies* 31, no. 1 (2004): 41-62.

Campagna, Joel. "From Accomodation to Confrontation: The Muslim Brotherhood in the Mubarak Years." *Journal of International Affairs* 50, no. 1 (1996): 278-304.

Choueiri, Y. M. "Theoretical Paradigms of Islamic Movements." *Political Studies* 41, no. 1 (1993): 108-16.

Claes-John, Lampi Sorensen. "The Islamic Movement in Sudan: External Relations and Internal Power Struggle after 1989." Master's Thesis, American University Beirut, 2002.

Committee on Foreign Affairs. *Islamic Fundamentalism in Africa and Implications for U.S. Policy*, 102nd Congress, 2nd Session, May 20 1992. Washington, DC: US GPO, 1993.

Connell, Dan. "Political Islam under Attack in Sudan." *Middle East Report*, no. 202 (1996): 34-36.

Cowell, Alan. "Military Coup in Sudan Ousts Civilian Regime" *The New York Times. Late Edition (East Coast)* July 1, 1989.

Cox, James L. "The Freedom to Do God's Will. Religious Fundamentalism and Social Change." *Studies in World Christianity* 8, no. 2 (2002): 317-19.

Dangor, Suleman. "Shura, Democracy and the Muslim World." *The American Muslim* (2003), http://theamericanmuslim.org/tam.php/features/articles/shura_democracy_the_muslim_world/. Accessed 01/18/2006.

De Waal, Alexander, ed. *Islamism and Its Enemies in the Horn of Africa.* Bloomington, IN: Indiana University Press, 2004.

Dekmejian, Hrair R. *Egypt under Nasir: A Study in Political Dynamics.* Albany, New York: State University of New York Press, 1971.

———. *Islam in Revolution: Fundamentalism in the Arab World.* Syracuse, NY: Syracuse University Press, 1985.

Della Porta, Donatella & Diani, Mario. *Social Movements: An Introduction.* 2nd ed., Ames, IA: Blackwell Publishing Limited, 2006.

Deng, Francis M. "Identity in Africa's Internal Conflicts." *American Behavioral Scientist* 40, no. 1 (1996): 46-65.

———. "Sudan--Civil War and Genocide." *Middle East Quarterly* 8, no. 1 (2001): 13-21.

———. "War of Visions for the Nations." *Middle East Journal* 44, no. 4 (1990): 596-609.

Denoeux, Guilain. "The Forgotten Swamp: Navigating Political Islam." *Middle East Policy* 9, no. 2 (2002): 56-81.

Dessouki, Ali E, ed. *Islamic Resurgence in the Arab World.* New York: Praeger Publishers, 1982.

Elaesh, Abdelmagid. *Hadas Fi Al-Sudan: Yawmiyat Al-Dawlah Al-Islamiyah.* Khartoum, Sudan: Azza For Publishing and Distribution, 2005.

El-Affendi, Abdelwahab. "Eclipse of Reason: The Media in the Muslim World." *Journal of International Affairs* 47, no. 1 (1993): 163-193.

―――. "The Long March from Lahore to Khartoum: Beyond the 'Muslim Reformation'." *Bulletin (British Society for Middle Eastern Studies)* 17, no. 2 (1990): 137-51.

―――. *Turabi's Revolution: Islam and Power in Sudan.* London: UK: Grey Seal Books 1991.

El-Amin, Mohammed Nuri. "The Role of the Egyptian Communists in Introducing the Sudanese to Communism in the 1940s." *International Journal of Middle East Studies* 19, no. 4 (1987): 433-54.

El-Solh, Raghid. "Islamist Attitudes Towards Democracy: A Review of the Ideas of Al-Ghazali, Al-Turabi and 'Amara." *British Journal of Middle Eastern Studies* 20, no. 1 (1993): 57-63.

El-Tayeb, Salah El Din El Zein. *The Students' Movement in the Sudan: 1940-1970.* Khartoum, Sudan: Khartoum University Press, 1971.

Emirates Center for Strategic Studies and Research. *Islamic Movements: Impact on Political Stability in the Arab World.* Abu Dhabi, UAE: Emirates Center for Strategic Studies and Research, 2003.

Esposito, John L. *Political Islam: Revolution, Radicalism, or Reform?* Boulder, Colorado: Lynne Rienner Publishers, 1997.

―――. "Sudan's Islamic Experiment." *The Muslim World* 76, no. 3-4 (1986): 181-202.

―――. *Voices of Resurgent Islam.* New York: Oxford University Press, 1983.

Esposito, John L. & Haddad, Yvonne Y. *Islam, Gender, and Social Change.* Oxford, New York: Oxford University Press, 1997.

Esposito, John L. & Voll, John Obert. *Makers of Contemporary Islam*. New York: Oxford University Press, 2001.

Fawzi, Saad Ed Din. *The Labour Movement in the Sudan, 1946-1955*. London: Oxford University Press for the Royal Institute of International Affairs, 1957.

Filali-Ansary, Abdou. "Islam and Liberal Democracy: The Challenge of Secularization." *Journal of Democracy* 7, no. 2 (1996): 76-80.

Flores, Alexander. "Secularism, Integralism and Political Islam: The Egyptian Debate." *Middle East Report*, no. 183 (1993): 32-38.

Fluehr-Lobban, Carolyn. "Challenging Some Myths: Women in Shari'a Law in the Sudan." *Expedition* (Spring, 1983): 33-34.

———. "Women in the Political Arena in the Sudan." In *7th Annual Middle East Studies Association Meeting*. Milwaukee, WI, 1973.

Fluehr-Lobban, Carolyn & Richard Lobban. "The Sudan since 1989: National Islamic Front Rule." *Arab Studies Quarterly* 23, no. 2 (2001): 1-9.

Fukuyama, Francis & Samin, Nadav. "Can Any Good Come of Radical Islam? A Modernization Force? Maybe." *Commentary Magazine* 114, no.2 (September, 2002): 34-38.

Gallab, Abdullahi A. "The Insecure Rendezvous between Islam and Totalitarianism: The Failure of the Islamist State in the Sudan." *Arab Studies Quarterly* 23, no. 2 (2001): 87-108.

Gambill, Gary C. "Democratization, the Peace Process, and Islamic Extremism." *Middle East Intelligence Bulletin* 6, no. 6/7 (2004): 16-22.

Gerges, Fawaz. *The Far Enemy: Why Jihad Went Global*. New York: Cambridge University Press, 2005.

Giddens, Anthony. *Sociology*. 4th ed. Cambridge, U.K: Polity Press, 2001.

Giugni, Marco, McAdam, Doug & Tilly, Charles, ed. *How Social Movements Matter* Minneapolis, MN: University of Minnesota Press, 1999.

Glenn, David. "Who Owns Islamic Law?" *Chronicle of Higher Education* 51, no. 25 (2005): A14-A16.

Goddard, Hugh. "Islam and Democracy." *Political Quarterly* 73, no. 1 (2002): 3-9.

Gramsci, Antonio. *The Antonio Gramsci Reader: Selected Writings, 1916-1935.* Edited by Forgacs, Davis & Hobsbawm, Eric. New York: New York University Press, 2000.

Gresh, Alain. "The Free Officers and the Comrades: The Sudanese Communist Party and Nimeiri Face-to-Face, 1969-1971." *International Journal of Middle East Studies* 21, no. 3 (1989): 393-409.

Gruenbaum, Ellen. "Feminist Activism for the Abolition of Fig in Sudan." *Journal of Middle East Women's Studies* 1, no. 2 (2005): 89-112.

Haddad, Mahmoud. "Arab Religious Nationalism in the Colonial Era: Rereading Rashid Rida's Ideas on the Caliphate." *Journal of the American Oriental Society* 117, no. 2 (1997): 253-277.

Haddad, Yazbeck Yvonne. "The Quranic Justification for an Islamic Revolution: The View of Sayyid Qutb." *The Middle East Journal* 37, no. 1 (1983): 14-29.

Hale, Sondra. "Activating the Gender Local: Transnational Ideologies and 'Women's Culture' In Northern Sudan." *Journal of Middle East Women's Studies* 1, no. 1 (2005): 29-52.

———. "Gender Politics and Islamization in Sudan." Women Living Under Muslim Laws 1997. Available at: http://www.wluml.org/english/pubsfulltxt.shtml?cmd%5B87%5D=i-87-2670. Accessed 08/25/2006.

———. "Mothers and Militias: Islamic State Construction of the Women Citizens of Northern Sudan." *Citizenship Studies* 3, no. 3 (1999): 373-386.

———. "Sudanese Women and Revolutionary Parties: The Wing of the Patriarch." *Middle East Report*, no. 138 (1986): 25-30.

Halliday, Fred. "The Politics of the Umma: States and Community in Islamic Movements." *Mediterranean Politics* 7, no. 3 (2002): 20-41.

Hamidi, Muhammad al-Hashimi. "Islam and Liberal Democracy: The Limits of the Western Model." *Journal of Democracy* 7, no. 2 (1996): 81-85.

Hamidi, Muhammad al-Hashimi & al-Turabi, Hasan. *The Making of an Islamic Political Leader: Conversations with Hasan Al-Turabi / Uniform Title: Hasan Al-Turabi.* Boulder, Colo.: Westview Press, 1998.

Hasan, Yusuf Fadl. "The Sudanese Revolution of October 1964." *The Journal of Modern African Studies* 5, no. 4 (1967): 491-509.

Hassan, Yousif. *Al-Deen Wal Al-Siyasa Fi Al-Sudan.* Cairo-Egypt: Dar al-Ameen, 2001.

Hassouna, Hussein A. "Arab Democracy: The Hope." *World Policy Journal* 18, no. 3 (2001): 49-52.

Haynes, Jeffrey. *Religion in Global Politics.* London, U.K: Longman, 1998.

———. "Understanding Religion and Political Change in Africa" (2005), http://www.law.emory.edu/IHR/worddocs/haynes6.doc.   Accessed 03/25/2006.

Hirschkind, Charles. "What Is Political Islam?" *Middle East Report,* no. 205 (1997): 12-14.

Holt, P. M. "Funj Origins: A Critique and New Evidence." *The Journal of African History* 4, no. 1 (1963): 39-55.

———. *A History of the Sudan: From the Coming of Islam to the Present Day.* 5th edition. London, UK: Longman, 2000.

———. *The Sudan of the Three Niles: The Funj Chronicle, 910-1288/1504-1871.* Boston, MA: Brill Academic Publishers, 1999.

———. "A Sudanese Historical Legend: The Funj Conquest of Suba." *Bulletin of the School of Oriental and African Studies, University of London* 23, no. 1 (1960): 1-12.

Hopkins, Nick & Vered Kahani-Hopkins. "Identity Construction and British Muslims' Political Activity: Beyond Rational Actor Theory." *British Journal of Social Psychology* 43, no. 3 (2004): 339-56.

House, William J. "The Status of Women in the Sudan." *The Journal of Modern African Studies* 26, no. 2 (1988): 277-302.

Hovsepian, Nubar. "Competing Identities in the Arab World." *Journal of International Affairs* 49, no. 1 (1995): 1-24.

Howard-Hassmann, Rhoda, An-Na`im, Abdullahi Ahmed, and Deng, Francis. *Group Versus Individual Identity in the African Debate on Human Rights*, Human Rights in Africa: Cross-Cultural Perspectives, 1990.

Hunter, Shireen. *The Politics of Islamic Revivalism: Diversity and Unity.* Bloomington, IN: Indiana University Press, 1988.

Huntington, Samuel P. "the Clash of Civilization?" "Foreign *Affairs* 72, no. 3 (1993): 22-49.

———. *The Clash of Civilizations: Remaking of World Order.* New York: Simon & Schuster, 1997.

———. *The Soldier and the State: The Theory and Politics of Civil-Military Relations.* 12th ed. Cambridge: Harvard University Press, 1995.

Ibrahim, Abdullahi Ali. "The Root Causes of Sudan's Civil Wars." *International Journal of African Historical Studies* 37, no. 3 (2004): 561-62.

———. "A Theology of Modernity: Hasan Al-Turabi and Islamic Renewal in Sudan." *Africa Today* 46, no. 3/4 (1999): 195-222.

Ibrahim, Saad Eddin. "Anatomy of Egypt's Militant Islamic Groups: Methodological Note and Preliminary Findings." *International Journal of Middle East Studies* 12, no. 4 (1980): 423-53.

Idris, Amir H. *Conflict and Politics of Identity in Sudan.* New York: Palgrave Macmillan, 2005.

Idris, Jaafar Sheikh. *Contemporary Islamic Movement: Reflections on Methodology.* Washington DC: IANA, 1999.

———. "The Islamic Fundamentalism of Wahhabi Movement." 1995. Available at: http://www.jaafaridris.com/English/Books/Wahabism.htm. Accessed 05/25/2006.

———. "The Process of Islamization." 1983 Available at: http://www.jaafaridris.com/English/Books/procisla.htm. Accessed 05/25/2006.

————. "Shoora and Democracy: A Conceptual Analysis." Available at: http://www.jaafaridris.com/English/Articles/shoora.htm. Accessed 05/25/2006.

Idris, Sajjad. "Reflections on Mawdudi and Human Rights." *Muslim World* 93, no. 3/4 (2003): 547-561.

Ismail, Bakhita Amin & Hall, Marjorie. *Sisters under the Sun: The Story of Sudanese Women.* London, U.K: Longman Group Limited, 1981.

Ismail, Salwa. "Being Muslim: Islam, Islamism and Identity Politics." *Government & Opposition* 39, no. 4 (2004): 614-31.

Jamal, Abbashar. "Funding Fundamentalism: The Political Economy of an Islamist State." *Middle East Report*, no. 172 (1991): 14-38.

Jang, Ji-Hyang. "The Politics of Islamic Bank in Turkey: Taming Political Islamists by Islamic Capital." In *Annual Meeting of the Midwest Political Science Association.* Chicago, IL: Midwest Political Science Association, 2003.

Jenkins, Craig J. & Kposowa, Augustine J. "Explaining Military Coups D'etat: Black Africa, 1957-1984." *American Sociological Review* 55, no. 6 (1990): 861-75.

Jones, Linda G. "Portrait of Rashid Al-Ghannoushi." *Middle East Report*, no. 153 (1988): 19-22.

Kameir, El-Wathig & Kursany, Ibrahim. *Corruption as A "Fifth" Factor of Production in the Sudan.* Uppsala, Sweden: The Scandinavian Institute of African Studies, 1985.

Kamil, Nafisa. *Al-Marah Al-Sudaniyah Bayna Al-Madi Wa-Al-Hadir.* Khartoum-Sudan: Abd al-Majid Hasan 'Ali Karar, 1997.

Kamrava, Mehran. "Military Professionalization and Civil-Military Relations in the Middle East." *Political Science Quarterly* 115, no. 1 (2000): 67-92.

Karagiannis, Emmanuel. "Political Islam and Social Movement Theory: The Case of Hizb Ut-Tahrir in Kyrgyzstan." *Religion, State & Society* 33, no. 2 (2005): 137-49.

Karakir, Irem Askar. "Rising Political Islam: Is It a Matter of Ideology or Pragmatism?" *Turkish Policy Quarterly* 5, no. 4 (2006): 1-9.

Karrar, Ali Salih. *The Sufi Brotherhoods in the Sudan*. London, UK: Munster, 1992.

Keddie, Nikki R. *An Islamic Response to Imperialism: Political and Religious Writings of Sayyid Jamal Ad-Din "Al-Afghani."* Berkeley, CA: University of California Press, 1968.

Kepel, Gilles. "Islamism Reconsidered." *Harvard International Review* 22, no. 2 (2000): 22-27.

———. *Jihad: The Trail of Political Islam* Translated by Anthony F. Roberts. New Edition. Cambridge, MA: Belknap Press, 2003.

Khatab, Sayed. "Arabism and Islamism in Sayyid Qutb's Thought on Nationalism." *Muslim World* 94, no. 2 (2004): 217-44.

———. "Hakimiyyah and Jahiliyyah in the Thought of Sayyid Qutb." *Middle Eastern Studies* 38, no. 3 (2002): 145-170.

Kheris, Talal. "Hasan Turabi: Interview to Al-Shira." *Al-Shira* 1994, 26-27.

Kok, Peter Nyot. "Hasan Abdulla Al-Turabi." *Orient* 33, no. 2 (1992): 185-92.

Kok, Peter Nyot, Abdelmmoula, Adam & Mayer, Ann. "Religious Pluralism, Constitutional Issues and Reconciliation." In *Religion and Peacemaking*. Washington, D.C: U.S. Institute of Peace, 1997.

Kposowa, Augustine J., and J. Craig Jenkins. "The Structural Sources of Military Coups in Postcolonial Africa, 1957-1984." *American Journal of Sociology* 99, no. 1 (1993): 126-163.

Kursany, Ibrahim. "The Politics of the National Islamic Front (NIF) of the Sudan: Old Wine in New Bottle." In *Third International Sudan Studies Conference*. Boston U.S.A: Sudan Studies Conference, 1994.

Kyle, Keith. "The Sudan Today." *African Affairs* 65, no. 260 (1966): 233-44.

Lambton, Ann, ed. *The Clash of Civilizations: Authority, Legitimacy and Perfectibility*. In Islamic Fundamentalism. Edited by R.M. Burrell. London: UK: Royal Asiatic Society of Great Britain and Ireland, 1988.

Lane, Ruth. *The Art of Comparative Politics*. Needham Heights, MA: Allyn & Bacon, 1997.

Langewiesche, William. "Turabi's Law." *Atlantic Monthly* 274, no. 2 (1994): 26-33.

Laremont, Richardo R, ed. *Borders, Nationalism, and the African State.* Boulder, CO: Lynne Rienner Publishers, 2003.

Lawrence, Bruce ed. *Islamic Fundamentalist Movements.* Edited by Barbara Stowasser, The Islamic Impulse. London: UK: Croom Helm, 1987.

Lesch, Ann Mosely *The Sudan - Contested National Identities.* Bloomington, IN: Indiana University Press 1998.

Lewis, Bernard. *The Crisis of Islam: Holy War and Unholy Terror.* New York, NY: Modern Library 2003.

―――. "Islam and Liberal Democracy." *Atlantic Monthly* 271, no. 2 (1993): 89-98.

―――. *Islam and the West.* New York, NY: Oxford University Press, 1993.

―――. *The Political Language of Islam.* Chicago, IL: University Of Chicago Press 1990.

―――. "The Roots of Muslim Rage." *The Atlantic Monthly* 266, no. 3 (1990): 47-60.

―――. *What Went Wrong? The Clash between Islam and Modernity in the Middle East.* New York: HarperCollins Publisher, 2002.

Lia, Brynjar. *The Society of the Muslim Brothers in Egypt: The Rise of an Islamic Mass Movement, 1928-1942.* Reading, England: Ithaca Press, 1998.

Lim, Timothy C. *Doing Comparative Politics: An Introduction to Approaches and Issues.* Boulder, CO: Lynne Rienner Publishers, 2006.

Lipset, Seymour Martin "University Students and Politics in Underdeveloped Countries." *Comparative Education Review* 10, no. 2 (1966): 132-62.

Lobban, Richard Jr. A, Kramer, Robert S., Lobban-Flueher, Carolyn. *Historical Dictionary of the Sudan.* Lanham, MD: The Scarecrow Press, Inc., 2002.

Louay, Safi M. "Islam and the Secular State: Explicating the Universal in Formative Islamic Political Norms " *American Journal of Islamic Social*

216

Sciences (2005), Available at: http://www.islamawareness.net/Secularism/secular.html. Accessed 01/25/2006.

Luckham, Robin. "The Military, Militarization and Democratization in Africa: A Survey of Literature and Issues." *African Studies Review* 37, no. 2 (1994): 13-75.

Macionis, John J. *Sociology*. 7th ed. New Jersey: Prentice Hall, 1999.

Maghen, Ze'ev. "Theme Issue: The Interaction between Islamic Law and Non-Muslims: Lakum Dinukum Wa-Li-Dinin." *Islamic Law and Society* 10, no. 3 (2003): 267-75.

Mahjoub, Abdelkhalig. *Araa Wa Afkar Hawl Falsafat Al-Ikhwan Al-Muslimeen.* Khartoum: Sudan: Azza For Publishing and Distribution, 2001.

Mahjoub, Mohammed Ahmed. *Al-Dimuqratiyah Fi Al-Mizan.* New Edition ed. Khartoum, Sudan: Mutbat al-Umlah, 2004.

Mahmoud, Fatima Babiker. "Democratic Transformation and the Participation of Women in Political Institutions in the Sudan." *Respect* 1, no. 1 (2005): 1-7.

Mahmoud, Mohamed. "Islam and Islamization in Sudan: The Islamic National Front." In *Religion and Peacemaking*. Washington, DC: U.S Institute of Peace, 1997.

Mamdani, Mahmood. "America and Political Islam." *Z Magazine* 18, no. 1 (2005). Available at http://www.zmag.org/content/showarticle.cfm?ItemID=7131 Accessed 03/25/2006.

Mazrui, Ali A. "Islam, Political Leadership and Economic Radicalism in Africa." *Comparative Studies in Society and History* 9, no. 3 (1967): 274-91.

McCarthy, John D & Zald, Mayer N. "Resource Mobilization and Social Movements: A Partial Theory." *The American Journal of Sociology* 82, no. 6 (1977): 1212-41.

Menkhaus, Ken. "Political Islam in Somalia." *Middle East Policy* 9, no. 1 (2002): 109-123.

Meyer, Katherine, Helen Rizzo, and Yousef, Ali. "Islam and the Extension of Citizenship Rights to Women in Kuwait." *Journal for the Scientific Study of Religion* 37, no. 1 (1998): 131-44.

Miller, Judith. "The Challenge of Radical Islam." *Foreign Affairs* 72, no. 2 (1993): 43-56.

———. "Faces of Fundamentalism. Hassan Al-Turabi and Muhammed Fadlallah." *Foreign Affairs* 73, no. 6 (1994): 123-42.

Mirghani, Isam al-Deen. *Al-Geash Al-Sudani Wa Al-Siyasa.* Cairo: Egypt: Afrongi For Printing, 2002.

Mirza, M. & Baydoun, N. "Accounting Policy Choice in Riba-Free Environment." *Accounting, Commerce and Finance: The Islamic Perspective Journal* 4, no. 1 (2000): 30-47.

Mitchell, Richard P. *The Society of the Muslim Brothers.* New York: Oxford University Press, 1993.

Moghadam, Valentine M. "Islamist Movements and Women's Responses in the Middle East." *Gender & History* 3, no. 3 (1991): 268-84.

Mohammed, al-Daw. *Al-Sudan Suqut Al-Agniaa: Sanawat Al-Khiaba Wa Al-Amal.* Cairo, Egypt: Sutair Company, 2006.

Mohi Eldeen, Abdelrahim Omer. *Al-Turabi Wa Al-Ingaz Siraa Al-Hawia Wal Al-Hawa: Fitnat Al-Islameen Fi Al-Sultah Mein Muzakirat Al-Ashrah Ela Muzakirat Al-Tafahum Maa Garang.* 3rd ed. Khartoum, Sudan: Marawi Bookshop, 2006.

Morris, Aldon. "Reflections on Social Movement Theory: Criticisms and Proposals." *Contemporary Sociology* 29, no. 3 (2000): 445-54.

Morrison, Scott. "The Political Thought of Hasan Al-Turabi of Sudan." *Islam & Christian-Muslim Relations* 12, no. 2 (2001): 153-60.

Morsy, Soheir A. "Islamic Clinics in Egypt: The Cultural Elaboration of Biomedical Hegemony." *Medical Anthropology Quarterly* 2, no. 4 (1988): 355-69.

Moten, Abdul Rashid. "Mawdudi and the Transformation of Jama'at-E-Islami in Pakistan." *Muslim World* 93, no. 3/4 (2003): 391-413.

Moussalli, Ahmad S. "Hassan Al-Turabi's Islamist Discourse on Democracy and Shura." *Middle Eastern Studies* 30, no. 1 (1994): 52-63.

———. *Moderate and Radical Islamic Fundamentalism.* Jacksonville, FL: University of Florida Press, 1999.

Munson, Ziad. "Islamic Mobilization: Social Movement Theory and the Egyptian Muslim Brotherhood. " *The Sociological Quarterly* 42, no. 4 (2001): 487–510.

Nandy, Ashis. *The Intimate Enemy: Loss and Recovery of Self under Colonialism.* New Delhi, India: Oxford University Press, 1983.

Narli, Nilufer. "The Rise of the Islamist Movement in Turkey." *Middle East Review of International Affairs* 3, no. 3 (1999): 34-48.

Nettler, Ronald L. "Guidelines for the Islamic Community: Sayyid Qutb's." *Journal of Political Ideologies* 1, no. 2 (1996): 183-196.

Niezen, R. W. & Barbro Bankson. "Women of the Jama'at Ansar Al-Sunna: Female Participation in a West African Islamic Reform Movement." *Canadian Journal of African Studies / Revue Canadienne des Etudes Africaines* 29, no. 3 (1995): 403-28.

Niblock, Tim. *Class and Power in Sudan: The Dynamics of Sudanese Politics, 1898-1985.* Albany, NY: State University of New York Press, 1987.

Nicholls, Walter J. "The Geographies of Social Movements" *Geography Compass* 1, no. 3 (2007): 607-22.

Nikkel, Marc, Deng, Francis & Malwal, Bona. "Religion and Identity in the South." In *Religion and Peacemaking.* Washington, D.C: U.S. Institute of Peace, 1997.

Novati, Giampaolo Calchi & Stefano Belucci. "Islamic Governance in Algeria and Sudan: A Fading Quest for a Model?" *Mediterranean Quarterly* 12, no. 1 (2001): 100-114.

O'Fahey, R. S. "Islam and Ethnicity in the Sudan." *Journal of Religion in Africa* 26, no. 3 (1996): 258-67.

Onians, Charles. "Supply and Demand Democracy in Egypt." *World Policy Journal* 21, no. 2 (2004): 78-84.

Osaghae, Eghosa E. "Political Transitions and Ethnic Conflict in Africa." *Journal of Third World Studies* 21, no. 1 (2004): 221-40.

Osman, Abdelwahab A M. "The Political and Ideological Development of the Muslim Brotherhood in Sudan 1945-1989." Ph.D. Dissertation, University of Reading: UK 1989.

Osman, Fathi. "Mawdudi's Contribution to the Development of Modern Islamic Thinking in the Arabic-Speaking World." *Muslim World* 93, no. 3/4 (2003): 465-485.

Perry, Glenn E. "Huntington and His Critics: The West and Islam." *Arab Studies Quarterly* 24, no. 1 (2002): 31-48.

Pipes, Daniel. *In the Path of God: Islam and Political Power*. New edition ed. Edison, NJ: Transaction Publishers, 2002.

———. *The Long Shadow: Culture and Politics in the Middle East* Edison, NJ: Transaction Publishers, 1999.

———. *Militant Islam Reaches America* New York: W. W. Norton & Company, 2003.

———. *Miniatures: Views of Islamic and Middle Eastern Politics*. Edison, NJ: Transaction Publishers, 2003.

———. "The Muslims Are Coming! The Muslims Are Coming!" *National Review* 42, no. 22 (1990): 28-31.

Piscatori, James. *Accounting for Fundamentalisms: The Dynamic Character of Movements*. Chicago: University Of Chicago Press, 2004.

———. *Islam in the Political Process*. Cambridge: Cambridge University Press, 1983.

Piscatori, James & Eickelman, Dale F. *Muslim Politics*. New Edition, Princeton, NJ: Princeton University Press, 2004.

Quinlivan, James T. "Coup-Proofing: Its Practice and Consequences in the Middle East." *International Security* 24, no. 2 (1999): 131-65.

Qutb, Sayyid. *Milestone*. Cedar Rapids, IA: The Mother Mosque Foundation, 1981.

Qutb, Sayyid. *Social Justice in Islam.* Translated by John B. & Algar Hardie, Hamid. Revised edition. Baltimore, MD: Islamic Publications International, 2000.

Rabasa, Angel, Benard, Cheryl, Schwartz, Lowell H. & Sickle, Peter. "Building Moderate Muslim Network." Washington, D.C.: RAND - Center For Middle East Public Policy, 2007.

Rahman, Fazlur. *Islam.* Chicago, IL: University of Chicago Press, 1979.

Ramadan, Abdelazeem. *Al-Ikhwan Al-Muslimeen Wa Al-Tanzeem Al-Siri.* 2nd ed. Cairo: Egypt: Egyptian General Establishment For Books, 1993.

Randall, Vicky & Theobald, Robin. *Political Change and Underdevelopment: A Critical Introduction to Third World Politics.* 2nd ed. Durham, NC: Duke University Press, 1998.

Reinhart, Kevin A. "Islamic Law as Islamic Ethics." *Journal of Religious Ethics* 11, no. 2 (1983): 186-203.

Republicans' Brothers. *Adwa Ala Al-Mushkila Al-Dasturiyah.* 2nd ed. Khartoum: Sudan: Republicans' Brothers Press, 1968.

———. *Faisal Islamic Bank.* 1st ed. Khartoum, Sudan: Republicans' Brothers Publishing, 1983.

Ricks, Irelene P. "Islamic Crusades in North Africa and Their Impact on Female Human Capital Development in Egypt and Sudan." *Mediterranean Quarterly* 10, no. 1 (1999): 116-131.

Rosander, Eva E. & Westerlund, David. *African Islam and Islam in Africa: Encounters between Sufis and Islamists.* Athens, OH: Ohio University Press, 1997.

Roy, Olivier. "Radical Islam: A Middle East Phenomenon or a Consequence of the Globalization of Islam?" In *Press Freedom in Afghanistan.* New York: Open Society Institute, 2003.

Sabet, Amr G. E. "The End of Fundamentalism?" *Third World Quarterly* 21, no. 5 (2000): 891-902.

Said, Edward W. *Covering Islam: How the Media and the Experts Determine How We See the Rest of the World.* Revised edition. London: UK: Vintage, 1997.

————."A Devil Theory of Islam." *New York Times*, no. 08/12/1996 (1996), http://www.thenation.com/doc/19960812/said

————. *Orientalism*. London: UK: Vintage, 1979.

Salem, Paul. "The Rise and Fall of Secularism in the Arab World." *Middle East Policy* 4, no. 3 (1996): 147-160.

Salih, Kamal Osman. "The Sudan, 1985-1989: The Fading Democracy." *The Journal of Modern African Studies* 28, no. 2 (1990): 199-224.

Sayyid Ahmad, Warraq. *Harakat Al-Turabi: Uslub Al-Khitab Wa-Ittijahat Al-Mumarasah*. al-Tab`ah 1. Ed, Silsilat Al-Alf Qadiyah; Al-Kitab 2; Cairo-Egypt: al-Sharikah al-I`lamiyah, 1997.

Servin-Gonzalez, Mariana, and Oscar Torres-Reyna. "Trends: Religion and Politics." *The Public Opinion Quarterly* 63, no. 4 (1999): 592-621.

Shaaeldin, Elfatih & Brown, Richard. "Towards an Understanding of Islamic Banking in Sudan: The Case of the Faisal Islamic Bank." In *Sudan: State, Capital and Transformation*, edited by Tony & Abdelkarim Barnett, Abbas. New York, NY: Croom Helm, 1988.

Shahin, Emad Eldin. *Political Ascent: Contemporary Islamic Movements in North Africa*. Boulder, Colo.: Westview Press, 1997.

Sharkansky, Ira. "The Utility of Elazar's Political Culture: A Research Note." *Polity* 2, no. 1 (1969): 66-83.

Shehadeh, Lamia Rustum. *The Idea of Women in Fundamentalist Islam*. Jacksonville; FL: University of California Press, 2007.

————. "Women in the Discourse of Sayyid Qutb." *Arab Studies Quarterly* 22, no. 3 (2000): 45-55.

Shitu-Agbetola, Ade. "The Equality of Man and Woman in Islam: Sayyid Qutb's View Examined." *Islamic Studies* 28, no. 2 (1989): 131-37.

Shukrallah, Hala. "The Impact of the Islamic Movement in Egypt." *Feminist Review*, no. 47 (1994): 15-32.

Sidahmed, Abel Salam. *Politics and Islam in Contemporary Sudan*. New York: Palgrave Macmillan 1997.

Sidahmed, Abel Salam & Sidahmed, Alsir. *Sudan*. London, UK: RoutledgeCurzon, 2005.

Siegle, Joseph T., Michael M. Weinstein, and Morton H. Halperin. "Why Democracies Excel." *Foreign Affairs* 83, no. 5 (2004): 57-71.

Sinanovic, Ermin. "The Majority Principle in Islamic Legal and Political Thought and Its Application in Decision-Making Processes." M.A. Thesis, International Islamic University-Malaysia, 2002.

Spaulding, Jay. "The Funj: A Reconsideration." *The Journal of African History* 13, no. 1 (1972): 39-53.

Takeyh, Ray. "The Lineaments of Islamic Democracy." *World Policy Journal* 18, no. 4 (2001): 59-67.

Tamimi, Azzam. "The Obstacles Facing Transition to Democracy in the Contemporary Arab World." In *International Symposium on Islam and Democracy*. Istanbul, Turkey, 1998.

Taraki, Lisa. "Islam Is the Solution: Jordanian Islamists and the Dilemma of the Modern Women." *British Journal of Sociology* 46, no. 4 (1995): 643-61.

Tarrow, Sidney. *Power in Movement: Social Movements and Contentious Politics*. 2nd ed. Cambridge: UK: Cambridge University Press, 1998.

Taylor, Peter J. *Modernities: A Geohistorical Interpretation*. Minneapolis, MN: University of Minnesota Press, 1999.

The National Commission on Terrorist Attacks Upon the United States. "The 9/11 Commission Report: Final Report of the National Commission on Terrorist Attacks Upon the United States." edited by Kean, Thomas H. & Hamilton, Lee H. Washington DC: Government Printing Office, 2004.

Thompson, Edward P. *The Making of the English Working Class*. London: Penguin, 1963.

Tibi, Bassam. "Islamism, Peace, and Maghrib." In *Middle Eastern Lectures*. The Moshe Dayan Centre for Middle Eastern and African Studies. Tel Aviv, Israel: Tel Aviv University, 2000.

Tilly, Charles. *Social Movements, 1768 - 2004*. Boulder, CO: Paradigm Publishers, 2004.

Toprak, Binnaz. "Religion and State in Turkey." In *Middle Eastern Lectures. 4.* The Moshe Dayan Centre for Middle Eastern and African Studies. Tel Aviv, Israel: Tel Aviv University, 1999.

United Nations High Commissioner for Refugees (UNHCR). "Identity Crisis and the Weak State: The Making of the Sudanese Civil War." edited by United Nations High Commissioner for Refugees (UNHCR). Geneva, Switzerland: UNHCR, 1996.

Usenmez, Ozgur. "A Neo-Gramscian Approach to the Rise of Political Islam." In *Annual Meeting of the International Studies Association.* Honolulu, Hawaii, 2005.

Vatikiotis, P. J. *Islam and the State.* London, UK: Croom Helm, 1987.

Viorst, Milton. "Sudan's Islamic Experiment." *Foreign Affairs* 74, no. 3 (1995): 45-58.

Voll, John O. "The British, the 'Ulama', and Popular Islam in the Early Anglo-Egyptian Sudan." *International Journal of Middle East Studies* 2, no. 3 (1971): 212-18.

Volpi, Frederic. "Understanding the Rationale of the Islamic Fundamentalists' Political Strategies: A Pragmatic Reading of Their Conceptual Schemes During the Modern Era." *Totalitarian Movements & Political Religions* 1, no. 3 (2000): 72-96.

Walsh, John. "Egypt's Muslim Brotherhood." *Harvard International Review* 24, no. 4 (2003): 32-36.

Walton, Jeremy F. "Contradictions and Convergences in Coexistence: Islam, Secularism, Political Ideology and Public Practice in Contemporary Turkey." In *19th Middle East History and Theory Conference.* University of Chicago: University of Chicago, 2004.

Warburg, Gabriel & Kupferschmidt, Uri M. *Islam, Nationalism, and Radicalism in Egypt and the Sudan.* Westport, CT: Praeger, 1983.

Warburg, Gabriel R. "Islam and State in Numayri's Sudan." *Africa: Journal of the International African Institute* 55, no. 4 (1985): 400-13.

———. "Mahdism and Islamism in Sudan." *International Journal of Middle East Studies* 27, no. 2 (1995): 219-36.

Watt, Montgomery M. *Islamic Fundamentalism and Modernity*. New York: Routledge, 1988.

————. "The Political Relevance of Islam in East Africa." *International Affairs (Royal Institute of International Affairs)*. 42, no. 1 (1966): 35-44.

Wenger, Martha. "Sudan: Politics and Society." *Middle East Report*, no. 172 (1991): 3-7.

Wiktorowicz, Quintan. "Islamic Activism and Social Movement Theory: A New Direction for Research." *Mediterranean Politics* 7, no. 3 (2002): 187-211.

————, ed. *Islamic Activism: A Social Movement Theory*. Bloomington, IN: Indiana University Press, 2003.

————. "Islamists, the State, and Cooperation in Jordan." *Arab Studies Quarterly* 21, no. 4 (1999): 1-17.

Wiktorowicz, Quintan & Karl Kaltenthaler. "The Rationality of Radical Islam." *Political Science Quarterly* 121, no. 2 (2006): 295-319.

Wiktorowicz, Quintan & Farouki, Suha Taji. "Islamic NGOs and Muslim Politics: A Case from Jordan." *Third World Quarterly* 21, no. 4 (2000): 685-99.

Wilson, John. *Introduction to Social Movements*. New York: Basic Books, 1972.

Wright, Robin. "Islam and Liberal Democracy: Two Visions of Reformation." *Journal of Democracy* 7, no. 2 (1996): 64-75.

Yakan, Fathi. *Islamic Movement: Problems and Prospective*. Indianapolis, IN: American Trust Publications, 1984.

Yousif, al-Saed. *Al-Ikhwan Al-Muslimeen Wa Guzur Al-Tataraf Al-Dinni Wa Al-Irhab Fi Misr*, Egyptians' History. Cairo, Egypt: Egyptian General Establishment For Books, 1999.

Zakaria, Fouad. *Myth and Reality in the Contemporary Islamist Movement*. London, UK: Pluto Press, 2005.

Zeidan, David. "Radical Islam in Egypt: A Comparison of Two Groups." *Middle East Review of International Affairs* 3, no. 3 (1999): 1-10.

Zin al-Abdeen, Eltayeb. *Magalat an Al-Harakah Al-Islamiyah Fi Al-Sudan.* Khartoum, Sudan: Sudanese House For Books, 2003.

Index

Abboud, 91-92, 113, 115, 124, 177-178, 180, 190

Abdelgader, Mohammed al-Kheir, 33, 87

Accommodationist, 34

Abdelmagid, Sadiq Abdallah, 82, 89-90, 92, 102, 153, 176

Abduh, Mohammed, 69-71, 79

al-Afghani, 69-71, 79, 127, 145, 182

Alawa, 58-59

al-Banna, 5, 7, 14, 69, 71-74, 76, 79, 82, 84, 136-137, 139, 152-153, 189, 195

al-Fatih, Suad, 139

al-Ghannoushi, 5, 21

al-Mahdi, Mohammed Ahmed, 63-64, 82

al-Mahdi, Sadiq, 1, 3, 96-100, 106-109, 158, 181, 185

al-Manar, 71, 139

al-Mawdudi, 8, 12, 70-71, 74-75, 79, 120, 123-124

al-Tahir al-Rashid, 86-88, 90-92, 180

al-Turabi, 5-9, 17, 21, 30, 32-34, 36, 44, 49, 79, 86, 92-102, 105-108, 111, 112, 114-132, 141-148, 154, 156, 173, 174, 176, 182, 184, 196, 198

anti-colonial, 38

al-Umma Party, 3, 7, 10, 34, 82, 91, 95, 98-99, 106, 111, 158, 171, 193

Arab world, 19-20, 27, 33-34, 46, 134, 196

Arab-Israeli conflict, 3, 30

Arab-nationalism, 6

Badri, Malik, 92, 120

Brotherhood, 3, 5-11, 14, 22, 31-33, 35, 40, 62, 66, 69, 71, 73-74, 76-77, 81-83, 86-87, 89-90, 93, 102, 115, 131-132, 135-141, 144-145, 152-154, 161, 171, 175-176, 179, 144-145, 152-154, 161, 171, 175, 176, 179-180, 189, 195, 198-199

Brynjar, Lia, 10

cadres, 2, 6, 9, 90, 103-104, 106, 112, 146, 150, 165, 167, 184

charisma, 98, 120, 132, 196

charismatic, 36, 63, 71, 82, 132

Christianity, 21-22, 42, 58, 75, 127

civil war, 1, 36-37, 39, 57, 91, 98, 103, 108, 185

civilization, 5, 16, 21, 23, 25-27, 42, 67, 69, 72, 75, 76, 195

Communism, 6-7, 44, 153

cultural-religious school, 18, 21, 25-27, 40, 195

Darfur, 1, 10, 59-61, 101, 103, 113, 160, 169

Dekmejian, Hrair, 20, 24

Democratic Unionist Party (DUP) 1, 3, 7, 10, 34, 82, 91, 95, 98-100, 106-108, 111-112, 119, 158, 171, 193, 197

effendis, 121-121, 197

Egypt, 2, 3, 5, 7-8, 10-11, 14, 20, 22-23, 30, 32-33, 35, 38-39, 41, 57-58, 61-63, 65-66, 68-70, 72-74, 76-77, 79, 81-88, 90, 113, 131-132, 134-137, 141, 150, 152-154, 159, 161-163, 175, 178-179, 189, 195, 199

El-Affendi, Abdelwahab, 33-34, 45, 69, 152, 186

election, 9-10, 22, 38, 88-90, 93-96, 101, 105-107, 115, 119, 141, 145, 148, 160, 173, 191, 198
elite, 7, 9, 11, 32-33, 36, 47, 6869, 76, 111, 118-121, 125, 132, 145, 149, 160-161, 171, 177, 189, 191, 196
Esposito, John, 19-21, 24, 134

Faisal Islamic Bank (FIB), 100, 102, 112, 162-163, 165-168, 197
financial institutions, 6, 9, 11, 36, 112, 147, 157, 160-161, 167, 170, 171
fiqh, 122, 126-129
Fluehr-Lobban, Carolyn, 134
Fuller, Graham, 14
fundamentalism, 13, 15-17, 20, 27, 38, 41-42, 48, 116
Funj, 59-62

Gordon, 65, 85, 150-151
Graduate Congress (GC), 66, 82, 83
Graduate Constituencies (GC), 10, 38, 94, 106, 115, 119, 160
Gramscian approach, 41, 47
Gulf, 31, 73, 103, 146, 157, 158, 161, 167, 177

Haddad, Yvonne, 20, 134
hakimiyya, 75
hijab, 133
Huntington, Samuel, 4, 25-27, 29

ibtila, 117-118
ideology, 2, 6-7, 9, 12, 17, 19-20, 22, 26, 28, 32-34, 36, 38, 40-42, 45-49, 55, 70, 73-74, 83-85, 89, 102, 110, 112, 116, 120, 123, 125, 139, 152-155, 160, 169, 172, 189, 196
ijmaa, 7-8, 111, 122, 125, 127, 132, 176, 196
ijtihad, 6-8, 102, 111, 122, 125-127, 176, 196

Islamic activism, 4, 48, 53
Islamic Charter Front (ICF), 81, 93-98, 119-120, 124
Islamic law, 20, 23, 107-108, 124, 143, 167, 187
Islamic Liberation Movement (ILM), 85-87
Islamic non-profit organizations (INGOs), 102, 104, 113, 168-170, 197
Islamic State, 8, 13-14, 71, 73, 75, 78, 94, 108, 111, 119, 122, 124, 186
Islamists, 2-3, 10-11, 15, 17-119, 22, 24, 31, 34-35, 37, 39-40, 47, 76, 79, 87-88, 101, 105, 115, 121-123, 131, 140-144, 146-148, 151, 159, 161, 163, 170, 174, 184-187, 195, 199
Islamization, 3, 35-36, 61, 78, 104, 108, 124, 144, 167, 182, 198

Jahilliyya, 75, 77-79, 124
Jihad, 22-23, 77-79, 184
Jihadists, 22-23, 76

Karar, Babiker, 84-88, 139
Kepel, Gilles, 22-23
Khartoum University Students Union (KUSU), 91-93, 98, 115, 152-153
Khatmiyya, 7, 44, 62-63, 65-66, 82, 150, 167, 169-170, 190, 192

Lambton, Ann, 16, 42-43
leadership, 2, 9, 31-32, 36, 60, 66, 72, 78, 81, 83-94, 96-105, 107-109, 111, 119-121, 124, 132, 139, 141, 144-145, 147-148, 153, 157, 159, 165-170, 174, 176, 179-181, 183. 185-186, 188, 190-193, 196-198
Lewis, Bernard, 4, 25
liberal views, 112, 145, 154, 196

Mahadia, 63-65, 150

Marxism, 16, 32, 73
media, 28, 35, 49, 55, 159, 196
membership, 9, 90, 97, 101-103, 105, 106, 111-112, 119-120, 131, 136, 147, 154-156, 158, 166-169, 171, 180, 188
Middle East, 3, 5, 18-20, 30, 45, 47, 69-71, 113, 176-178, 189, 195-196
military, 1-2, 6, 9, 11, 14, 24, 31-36, 47, 49, 65, 67-68, 81, 91-93, 95-99, 107-108, 111, 113, 115-116, 124, 155, 157-158, 161-163, 167, 176-187, 190, 195-196, 198
mobilization, 4, 49, 51, 53-54, 116, 156, 199
modernity, 8, 41-45, 76, 111, 116-118, 121, 132
modernization, 5, 41-45, 55, 61, 69-70, 74, 161, 198

National Islamic Front (NIF), 2, 81, 105-109, 145, 160-161
National Reconciliation Accord (NRA), 9, 100-102, 108, 124, 181
Nationalism, 5, 22, 39, 74, 121-122, 175
Nemeri, 2, 9, 32, 34-35, 81, 97-108, 113, 124, 149, 153-156, 159, 161-164, 167, 170, 178, 181-186, 192-193, 197

October Uprising, 81, 93, 94, 115-116, 140
Open Door Policy, 162, 171
organizational structure, 6, 21, 33, 49, 55, 72-73, 84-85, 89, 96, 105, 113, 116, 156, 171, 173-174, 196-197
orientalists, 4, 28

parliament, 95, 101, 115, 140, 149, 160
personality, 133, 196
Piscatori, James, 20-21, 24

political Islam, 1, 5, 11, 13-16, 18-20, 22, 24-25, 27-30, 37-38, 41, 45-449, 52, 67, 195-196
pragmatic, 6, 9, 65, 105
professional associations, 1, 10-11, 93, 103-104, 107, 113, 115-116, 146, 154, 160, 168, 173, 173-174, 197

Qutb, 5-6, 8, 12, 14, 23, 70-71, 75-79, 96, 123-124, 132, 137138, 153, 195

rational, 46, 49, 53, 55
recruitment, 6, 9, 32-33, 35-36, 49, 55, 92-93, 101, 113-114, 116, 119, 121, 139, 155, 157, 171-172, 174, 180-182, 189, 191, 196-198
renewal, 6, 8, 17, 21, 67-69, 111, 122, 125-128, 185
revival, 16, 18, 26, 67, 71, 78, 85, 127, 131, 191
riba, 89, 164, 184
Rida, Rashid, 69-71, 79

Said, Edward, 26-29
salafiyya, 22, 128, 130, 199
Saudi Arabia, 30, 62, 98, 100, 131, 157, 161-163, 171, 179, 181, 184
secular, 7, 11, 16, 21, 23, 25-26, 34, 71, 75, 78, 102, 111, 114, 118, 121-124, 133, 137, 181
shura, 6, 31, 51, 69, 71, 92, 102, 105, 106, 122, 125, 132, 173, 175
Social Movement Theory (SMT), 49, 52, 196
social movements, 7, 49-55, 116
socio-economic, 5, 18-19, 21, 24, 40-41, 43, 45-47, 168, 195-196
strategy, 35, 41, 92, 102, 112-114, 119, 141, 154-155, 174, 183, 198
Sudanese Communist Party (SCP), 2, 7, 9, 38, 66, 89-91, 94-98, 105-107, 109, 111, 114, 119, 124, 138,

140, 145-146, 151, 153-154, 159, 171, 173-174, 189, 192-193, 198
Sudanese People Liberation Movement (SPLM), 104, 107-108
Sudanese Socialist Union (SSU), 101, 104, 106, 124, 152
Sufism, 114, 130

Talb Allah, Ali, 83-87
tawhid, 78, 121, 123, 130
trade unions, 10-11, 90, 92-93, 97, 102, 104, 107-108, 113, 116, 120, 156, 168, 173, 187-193, 197-198.
tribes, 60-61, 64-65, 103, 178
Turco-Egyptian rule, 60-65, 150

ulama, 62, 101, 125-127
United States, 3, 23, 42, 76, 154, 159, 177-178, 185, 190
urban, 10, 106, 134, 160-161, 173, 188
usrah, 157, 171-174

vacuum, 6, 19, 38, 69, 196
vanguard, 78, 149
Voll, John, 21, 24, 44

Warburg, Gabriel, 38
women, 6-7, 9, 11, 20, 26, 34, 36, 49, 89, 96, 101-102, 107, 111, 112-113, 116, 133-149, 154, 168, 171, 173-174, 196-197
workers, 9, 49, 72, 89-90, 103, 121, 149, 169, 172, 174, 188-189, 190-193, 196

X

Y

Z